P9-AGU-725

TEACHING ENGLISH JAPAN

Jerry O'Sullivan

PASSPORT BOOKS
a division of *NTC Publishing Group*
Lincolnwood, Illinois USA

Published by Passport Books
a division of NTC Publishing Group
4255 West Touhy Avenue
Lincolnwood (Chicago), Illinois
60646-1975

ISBN 0-8442-0875-2
Library of Congress Catalog Card Number: 95-68430

First published by In Print Publishing Ltd.
9 Beaufort Terrace
Brighton BN2 2SU
UK

Typeset by MC Typeset
Printed in the U.K. by Bell & Bain

International House

International House (IH) began in 1953, when John and Brita Haycraft opened a language school in Cordoba, Spain. It has since developed into the largest independent British-based organization for teaching English, with over 100 000 students, 2 000 teachers, and some 90 schools around the world.

The home of the organization is International House in London, a non-profit-making eduational charity whose aim is to raise the standard of English teaching worldwide. Trustees include prominent academics, as well as representatives of the British Council, ARELS/FELCO and BBC English by Radio and Television.

International House in London, based at 106 Piccadilly, operates one of the principal schools of English in the UK, as well as International House Teacher Training. The latter offers a variety of courses leading to the UCLES/RSA Certificate and the UCLES/RSA Diploma, and courses for foreign teachers of English. It also offers specialized training courses – Teaching Business English, Development Course in Teacher Training, Director of Studies Training Course, etc. As well as being responsible for over half of the UCLES/RSA Certificate training in the world, International House Teacher Training is the sole body authorized to offer a Distance Training Programme leading to the UCLES/ RSA Diploma in TEFLA.

International House in London is also the home of the Central Department, headquarters of the IH World Organization. This is an association of independent language schools and teacher training institutes which are affiliated to, but not owned by, the International House Trust. The Central Department supplies the affiliated schools with materials and advice on a wide range of educational and administrative matters, organizes annual conferences, and monitors standards. Through its Teacher Selection Department, IH recruits teachers and senior staff for the affiliated schools and other approved institutes.

The opinions expressed in this book are not necessarily those of IH, and, while every care has been taken to ensure accuracy, IH cannot accept responsibility for any errors or omissions.

About the author

Jerry O'Sullivan has spent many years teaching English to Japanese people in Tokyo and London. In Tokyo he taught at a junior university for women, an oil company, a private language school, and privately. In London, he has been Director of Studies at Linguavox School, where he taught English to mainly monolingual Japanese classes, and a Teacher Trainer at International House.

In addition, he has trained and advised many teachers in the techniques of successfully dealing with Japanese students, and has written a series of English conversation textbooks specifically for use by Japanese students in monolingual classes.

The advice given in *Teaching English in Japan* derives essentially from first-hand experience.

Table of contents

About the author.. iv
Introduction xi

PART 1
TEACHING JOBS AND HOW TO FIND THEM

Chapter 1. Who goes to Japan? **3**

Chapter 2. Going to a prearranged job **5**
Finding work 5
    Starting points 5
    Interview tips.. 6
    JET Programme 8

Chapter 3. Arriving without a job **12**
Time and Money 12
    Blocking your time... 12
    Expenses and how much to take....................................... 13
Finding work 14
    Starting points 14
    Interviews... 15

Chapter 4. Where to teach English **16**
Conversation salons 16
Language schools 17
Universities and colleges 18
High schools.. 18
Companies... 19
Teaching privately 19
Japan Association of Language Teachers 20

Chapter 5. Visas **21**
Notes on resident status 22
Re-entry permit 25
Immigration offices 25
Alien Registration Card 26

PART 2
LIVING IN JAPAN

Chapter 6. How expensive is Japan? **29**
Living costs 29
    Eating and drinking.. 29
    Taxes 30
    Discos 30
    How far does the money go? 30

Chapter 7. Arriving and everyday living **32**
Before you go 32
    Travel preparations... 32
    Training and information gathering 33
    What to take.. 35
Arrival 36
    Immigration 36
    Urgent accommodation 36
    Urgent accommodation 36
    Transport from the airport 36
Accommodation.. 37
    Addresses 37
    Kinds of accommodation 38
Eating 45
    Chopsticks and etiquette 46
    Restaurants 47
    Eating out cheaply 48
    Japanese specialities... 52
    Confectionery and snacks 53
Drinking.. 53
    Cheap 54
    Medium-priced 54
    Expensive 55
    Drinking customs 55
    Drinking options 56
Transport... 57
    Trains 57
    Buses 59
    Taxis 60
    Bicycles 60
    Boat and ferry.. 60
    Driving... 61
    Hitching 62
    Air 63
Shopping 63
Facilities 65
    Public telephones 65

Baths 65
Libraries.. 65
Banks and financial matters 66
Health.. 66
Laundrettes.. 67
Media, culture and sport 68
Television and radio 68
Newspapers... 68
Music.. 68
Cinema and theatre.. 70
Sport 71
Cultural activities (traditional)...................................... 74
Other leisure activities 76
Festivals and public holidays 77
Local information – city by city 78
Help 80

Chapter 8. The country and the people **81**
The country.. 82
History... 82
Geography... 85
Climate 86
Politics, religion and beliefs 86
The people 89
The Japanese character... 90
Signs and gestures... 96
Typical lives 98
The environment 100

PART 3
TEACHING ENGLISH

Chapter 9. Setting the scene.................................... **105**
The nature of the task 105
The Japanese education system...................................... 105
The kind of language students need 107
Poor language learners 107
Reluctance to speak 108
Helping students relax – 20 tips 108

Chapter 10. The parts of a lesson **112**
Set the scene/arouse interest 112
Introduce the new language 112
Highlight form and explain meaning 113
Model and drill the new language 113
The first lesson.. 115

Chapter 11. Methods and ideas **117**
Methods and approaches.. 117
   Standard methods.. 117
   Non-standard methods 117
Helping students talk 119
   Begin a conversation gradually 120
   Closed pairs 121
Teacher-talk – when, how and how much? 125
Class management 127
   Seating system 127
   Writing on the board 128
   Nominating students 128
   Changing the focus and pace 129
   Large groups 129
   One-to-one 130
Communication – what language is for 130
   Information gaps 131
   Personalization 132
   Natural English 133
   Levels of politeness 133
   Communicating culture................................. 134
The four skills 135
   Listening 135
   Reading.. 138
   Writing... 138
Vocabulary 138
Correcting mistakes 140
Pronunciation 141
   Minimal pairs 142
   The weak sound – schwa 143
   Linking 144
   The letter 'n'... 145
   Consonant clusters...................................... 145
   Middle 'e' or 'i'.. 146
   Elision 147
   Other mispronunciations............................... 147
   Intonation... 147
Games 148
   Songs.. 149
Revision 150

Chapter 12. Specific Japanese problems **152**
What students don't use 153
What students overuse 155
What students confuse 157

Chapter 13. Teaching grammar and functions **163**
Grammar 163
  Tenses 164
  Articles 172
  Comparatives 172
  Questions 173
  Conditionals 174
  Modal auxiliary verbs 176
  Reported speech 178
Functions 179
  Greeting 180
  Introducing 181
  Inviting 181
  Offering 182
  Requesting 182
  Advising 183
  Suggestions 184
  Permission 184

Chapter 14. Planning **186**
Lesson Planning 186
  Lesson plan 1 – a beginner's lesson 186
  Lesson plan 2 – an early intermediate lesson 189
  Lesson plan 3 – a song 190
Using a textbook 192
  Designing a syllabus 193

Chapter 15. Business people and children **194**
Business people 194
Children 196

APPENDICES

Appendix 1. **Three case histories** 201
Appendix 2. **Some English schools** 204
Appendix 3. **Glossary of teaching terms** 206
Appendix 4. **English loan words** 208
Appendix 5. **Selective bibliography** 211
Appendix 6. **Classroom Japanese** 213
Appendix 7. **Japanese glossary** 215
Appendix 8. **Food and drink glossary** 219
Appendix 9. **Festivals and holidays** 222

Index 224

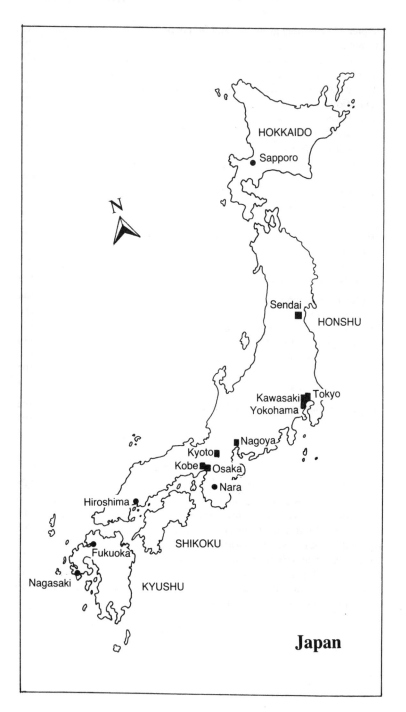

Introduction

My aim in writing *Teaching English in Japan* was to provide a much needed and easily accessible source of useful information on every aspect of going to Japan to teach English. This second edition was prompted both by the popularity of the first edition and by changes to the job environment for teachers in Japan.

Part 1 deals with finding a job in Japan, and gives details about the different places where you can teach English. **Part 2** covers preparing for your trip, and the practicalities of living in Japan, and gives some background on Japanese culture and society. **Part 3** provides a range of tried and tested ideas about teaching English to Japanese people.

I have made every effort to make the book user-friendly. In addition to laying out the information as clearly as possible, I have tried to make it easy to find a topic or a piece of information. There is an extensive Table of Contents, as well as an Index at the end. In addition, I have included eight **Appendices**, covering areas such as schools in Japan, Japanese food, classroom Japanese, recommended reading and a glossary of Japanese terms.

Many people go to Japan specifically to teach English. Many others go there for another purpose and find teaching English an easy and lucrative way to subsidize their stay. However, teaching Japanese to speak English is a notoriously tricky business. Although their students have mostly studied English for six years or more, many teachers find it frustratingly difficult to run classes in which students speak with any degree of fluency.

Teaching English in Japan helps you understand what makes Japanese students tick, and will be a source of ideas for 'unlocking' their capabilities. It contains, for example, 20 ways of helping Japanese students to relax – which is vital if there is to be any degree of fluency in the classroom. The book is full of practical ideas which you can put to immediate use in the classroom, whether you are already a practising teacher, or a complete novice to teaching.

Teaching English in Japan also deals with the practicalities of living in Japan. The needs of a medium- or long-term visitor are different from those of a traveller, and there is information on setting up an apartment and settling down, including many pointers and pieces of background information on day-to-day life in Japan to help you get the most from your stay. Everything from interpreting a Japanese address to making sure you don't make the wrong manual gestures is included.

Notes on the text

Native English speakers are referred to as 'Westerners'. This word includes people from such places as North America, and the Australian sub-continent.

In preference to the word 'foreigner', I have used the word *gaijin*. The word *gaijin*, which means literally 'outsider', is considered by some people, both Japanese and non-Japanese, to be pejorative. However, many foreigners in Japan feel comfortable using the word among themselves, and will use it in preference to 'foreigner' in most conversational situations. I have therefore used the word *gaijin* throughout the book.

I have done my best to ensure that details such as telephone numbers and prices were accurate at the time of going to press. Such information is, of course, subject to change.

Acknowledgments

I would like to thank the many people who provided assistance and encouragement in the writing of this book. In particular I would like to thank Bill Benfield for giving me the benefit of his long experience as a *gaijin* in Japan; Akiko Suzuki and Fumiko Tsuchihashi, for their help on the section on living in Japan; Heather Swabey for reading through the manuscript and making helpful suggestions; and Peter Duff, for interfacing himself between me and the often uncooperative computer on which I wrote this book. For help in preparing the second edition, thanks are due to the British Council in Tokyo, Michael Gibson, Richard Jenkinson, and Heather Swabey.

Jerry O'Sullivan

Part 1

TEACHING JOBS AND HOW TO FIND THEM

1 Who goes to Japan?

People who teach English in Japan fall into three main categories. First, there are those who go specifically to teach English. Second, there are those who go to Japan to study one of the many aspects of Japanese culture of interest in the West – for example, one of the martial arts. Finally, there are many people who are simply travelling, and find Japan an interesting place for an extended stay. People in the last two groups soon realize that they can earn a useful amount of money teaching English during their stay.

Undoubtedly one of the great attractions of staying in Japan is that so many of its inhabitants are keen to learn English. Although salaries have fallen somewhat in recent years in terms of yen per hour, there is still a healthy demand for English tuition. In addition, the spectacular rise of the yen – it has more than doubled in value since the mid-1980s – means that teaching salaries are still high, when converted back into dollars or pounds.

Teaching English in Japan is a different proposition to teaching English as a foreign language in most other countries. Japanese people have almost always studied English grammar for at least six years, and need to learn how to turn their grammatical learning into an ability to speak and understand the language. Thus, your feeling for English as a native speaker is probably more useful in the classroom than any academic knowledge.

On average, people who teach English in Japan are in their early twenties to mid-thirties, although there are many who are much older than that. Most people stay for one or two years, though some stay much longer, and some marry and settle down.

I first went to Japan at the age of 30. I had several reasons for going there. First, I was interested in a number of aspects of Japanese culture (mainly martial arts and zen). My experience of meeting Japanese people had made me curious about the country and society. Last but not least I had heard that it was relatively easy to find well-paid work teaching English (in fact I landed my first job offer less than 24 hours after touching down in Tokyo).

Despite having met and been friendly with a number of Japanese people before going to Japan, I was sometimes taken by surprise by Japanese customs and behaviour once living there. For example, one of my first jobs was teaching a group of businessmen in the conference room of their trading company. In the middle of a lesson, without warning, one man stood up and walked to the corner of the room, where he turned his back and discreetly pulled out a handkerchief and blew his nose before rejoining the class! I did not realize at the time that blowing your nose in public is considered extremely rude. Many instances of Japanese customs and behaviour are included in Chapter 8. An awareness of these will help smooth your entry into Japanese society. The more you learn, the more you will understand, and the richer and fuller your experiences will be.

Teaching English in Japan is an enormous challenge and an enormous opportunity. In this book I have tried to provide a comprehensive guide so that even the most inexperienced teacher will not feel completely alone on his or her first day in a Japanese classroom.

At the same time, I hope that teachers with some experience will find the sections aimed specifically at teaching Japanese students helpful. In the middle part of the book I have provided an outline of Japanese history, culture and lifestyle. I hope that this may both inspire waverers of the many advantages of spending a few years in Japan, and be useful to teachers during their first few months in the country.

Japan is a country thousands of miles away both in terms of distance and culture. The differences of culture, language and history, and the variety of experiences both in and out of the classroom mean that most teachers bring back much more than just a healthy bank balance.

2 | Going to a prearranged job

There are definite attractions in arranging a job before you go to Japan. This is the ideal way to do it and, legally, if you intend to work in Japan you should have a prearranged job and visa before entering the country. Besides, travelling a long distance to a country with such a different culture, you will undoubtedly feel more secure if you have guaranteed employment. You will be earning a salary from the time you arrive. Your visa will be arranged for you. And you will almost certainly have your flight paid, and have assistance in the administration and not inconsiderable expense of finding an apartment.

However, the fact is that it is often not easy to arrange work from outside Japan. Japanese employers are usually reluctant to hire at long distance, and non-Japanese employers typically have their own sources for recruitment and may not advertise abroad.

From your point of view also, the main drawback is that it will be much more difficult to check the complete details of employers when you are thousands of miles away (unless you go through an internationally recognized language school or organization). So it is important to be cautious, and to know what sort of questions to ask to make sure you will not be exploited once you arrive in Japan (see below, pp 6–7, for a list of key questions).

FINDING WORK

Starting points

Despite those reservations, it is certainly possible to arrange a job before you go. You can contact JET (see p 8), look out for advertisements in the press, or try to get yourself recruited on your own initiative. It is worth also bearing in mind the recruitment agencies which are operated, for example, by large language schools like the International Language Centre (ILC), Linguarama, or Berlitz.

In the USA, the United States Information Agency (USIA)

assists in placing teachers abroad. The Office of Academic Programs oversees the administration of thousands of grants each year to US citizens to study, teach, and conduct research overseas. The best known of these exchanges is the Fullbright programme. The Office of Cultural Centers and Resources provides policy directions and programme support to binational centres overseas. It also supports English-teaching programmes abroad. For information, contact either of these two offices at:

> **United States Information Agency**, 301 Fourth Street SW, Washington, DC 20547, USA. Tel 202-619-4700.

Newspaper ads. Look out for newspapers which carry ads for EFL (English as a foreign language) teachers. In the UK, these include *The Guardian* (Tuesdays for the Education Supplement) and *The Times Educational Supplement* (Fridays). There are also EFL ads in, for example, *The Independent*, and in the *EL Gazette* which can be obtained by subscription (Tel: 0171 938 1818). In the USA, there are the major metropolitan newspapers, such as the *New York Times* or the *Chicago Tribune*. For newspapers in Japan, see p 14.

Professional organizations. In the USA, TESOL (Teachers of English to Speakers of Other Languages) offers placement services and employment information. For a reasonable membership fee, you may list your name in a database for jobs in your area of interest. You will receive six bulletins per year announcing job openings around the world. At yearly TESOL conventions, you may visit the Employment Clearinghouse. Prospective employers will review your Curriculum Vitae and, if interested, follow up with an interview on the spot. For additional information, contact the Field Services Coordinator at

> **TESOL**, 1600 Cameron Street, Suite 300, Alexandria, VA 22314-2751. Tel 703-836-0774. Fax 703-836-7864.

Mailshot. In these days of personal computers, it is easy and cheap to prepare a Curriculum Vitae and a personalized covering letter which can be sent to the language schools listed in Appendix 2.

Interview tips

You may be interviewed by a Japanese person or a Westerner. Japanese are less likely or able to ask you probing questions on teaching methodology, and may be more interested in what you look like. Dress is important. The theme is conservative. A suit is preferable for men, and shirt and tie are essential. For schools and for company lessons, you will be expected to wear smart clothes. It is advisable for women to avoid trousers for work.

On personality, cheerful and lively is preferred (in the classroom if not in the interview itself), to thoughtful and serious.

Negotiating pay is best done with delicacy. The first time money is mentioned, if you do not think it is enough, do not respond with a counter-demand – simply look quietly unhappy. If there is any degree of flexibility, the interviewer will come back either immediately or, more probably, a little later in the interview with a higher offer.

After the interviewer has asked you questions to determine your suitability, there are a number of questions you should ask to ensure that you will have reasonable conditions of employment:

- *How many hours a week will I work?* (You want to be looking at a maximum of 25 hours per week teaching and a further 15 hours of administration and preparation, making a total of 40 hours.)
- *How will these be arranged?* (You want your work to be as well 'blocked' as possible, and not in a split shift, spread out over a long working day. In addition, it is preferable for the period each day to be similar, so that you are not teaching late into one evening and then early the next morning. What about weekends? Junior and senior high schools, universities and colleges have lessons on Saturday mornings. Language schools are open longer hours to accommodate their working students. Does the school run on a flexitime system (see pp 17–18)? If so, how does the system work?)
- *Where will I be teaching?* (If you have to work in different places, what will the travelling time be? It can be substantial. Will you receive travelling expenses? If so, will you be compensated for time spent travelling, or simply have your transportation costs covered?)
- *What is the salary?* (Is it guaranteed? Will you receive a fixed salary? If not, is there a guaranteed minimum, either in terms of hours or money? Is there a bonus – not uncommon in Japanese companies and schools? What happens in the event of a class being cancelled – will you be paid all or part of what you would have been paid for teaching?)
- *Do I receive any holidays?* (If so, are they paid? Are there any restrictions on when you can take them – either the dates or the maximum period you can take off at one time? If the position is part-time, will you be paid for public holidays?)
- *Who will I be teaching?* (What kind and size of classes will there be? How far apart are the levels which can be lumped together

to form a class if numbers are low? Will students be business people? Or children? If children, how young? Will you be teaching one-to-one?)

- *What is the academic set-up?* (What books/syllabus/tapes/other facilities are there? Who are the other teachers – Japanese or native speakers? Will you receive any back-up in terms of assistance in lesson preparation, etc, or by contrast, will you be obliged to use a certain teaching method or textbook, and if so, what will it be and will this be monitored? It is not unknown for the Principal to have *carte blanche* to come into your classroom mid-lesson, or even to have microphones in each classroom for monitoring classes!)

Of course, you must not fire out these questions as a list of demands. And you will have to balance unsatisfactory answers against other factors – how full your timetable is at that time; how much money you have in the bank; and, of course, how much they are offering.

Japan Exchange and Teaching Programme (JET)

One of the safest bets if you want to go to a prearranged job is to teach in junior or senior high schools in Japan under the well organized Japan Exchange and Teaching (JET) programme. JET also has a few places to teach in colleges and universities.

The JET programme is the largest recruiter of English teachers outside Japan. It has grown from small beginnings in 1978 to an intake of 2874 teachers in 1991, coming from all English-speaking countries. It also recruits in France and Germany now for French and German classes.

Of the jobs offered by JET, 95% are for Assistant English Teachers (AETs), 'team-teaching' English with the regular English teacher (a Japanese person) in high schools throughout Japan. In addition to teaching the students, an element of 'teaching the teachers' is expected – or at least exposing the Japanese teachers to some methods other than their normal, often almost fossilized, approach to teaching. The contracts are for one year (usually renewable), from 1 August to 31 July.

Applicants must be native English speakers with a degree and should be under 35. No experience or teaching qualifications are needed, and in fact the majority of JET teachers are new graduates.

Applicants are interviewed by a panel, and at least one Japanese national will be on it. So it is worth trying to express some sensitivity about the Japanese point of view, especially in terms of problems of international relations – eg the often troubled relationship with the USA. Bear in mind, also, that the aims of the JET programme are as much, if not more, about fostering international understanding, than just teaching English (see below).

The salary for 1994/95 for a 40 hour week was ¥ 3.6 million per year tax free for a one-year renewable contract. In addition, return airfare and onward transport to where you will be staying are paid (see Chapter 6, 'How expensive is Japan?').

Candidates receive the benefit of a comprehensive orientation programme to prepare them for living and teaching in Japan. There are pre-departure and post-arrival orientations, and a mid-programme training seminar. There is usually help with such things as finding accommodation. In addition, there is a support group (AJET) run by JET members which organizes social events, outings and meetings, publishes newsletters, and circulates teaching ideas. There is no obligation to get involved with this, and indeed many teachers feel they would rather spend their free time with things and people Japanese. It can nonetheless be reassuring to know that there is an available network of Westerners if alienation should set in.

The job itself entails going to a number of schools and helping the regular English teacher with the lesson. The frequency of visits varies: there is a range from schools you visit several times a week through to those that you go to just once in your whole year. The latter are called 'one-shots'. You will normally have a 'base school', where you teach most regularly, and go out to other schools on a regular or one-shot basis.

The main disadvantage of going to several schools is having to meet everybody and deal with each institution's slightly different methods and bureaucracy. However, one big advantage is that you tend to develop a small package of lessons which you find suit you, and you can often trundle these out at each school.

What you are actually expected or allowed to do in each class can vary quite widely, mainly depending on the whims, methods and friendliness and flexibility of the regular teacher. It can range from being given a free hand to simply acting as a mouthpiece for the regular teacher. It is important to establish as good a rapport as possible with the regular teacher to try to ensure that your lessons are enjoyable and successful. The students take a large part of their attitude from the regular teacher. If the teacher is clearly interested in the lesson, there is a much better chance that the kids will be too. If, on the other hand, he or she looks sulky or bored, you may have a job on your hands raising any enthusiasm from your students.

Bear in mind that Japanese teachers may well be very nervous both about having to communicate with you, as well as the possibility that you might show them up in your lessons. With this in mind, you might have to approach regular teachers carefully and diplomatically to get the best results from them.

Two frustrations are that you never have control of your class, and students are aware that English conversation is not normally part of their school-leaving exam, or the often even more important university entrance exams. These exams are almost totally made up of reading and writing grammar questions and translations and you will notice that the general English and idioms used are rather clumsy and antiquated. There are some indications that things are changing in this area. More and more universities, including Tokyo University, the most prestigious in Japan, now include a listening component and sometimes an oral section as part of their entrance exams.

The whole education system in Japan is moving gradually from the old grammar-translation method (*dokkai*) towards a more communicative approach. The aim is to produce students who have 'communicative competence'. Currently there is a wide range of types of teaching in high schools, from the traditional, usually older, teachers who do not want any change, to the more forward-thinking, and generally younger, teachers who are eager to promote and develop communication in the classroom. In reality, it is still probably true to say that what oral component exists usually consists of the whole class chanting in chorus. So, even if the students are willing to try communication or free speaking, it will be so far removed from their normal lessons that anything more than partial success is unlikely.

However, despite the drawbacks, most participants feel that they have accomplished something worthwhile just by being in the schools, helping to bridge the culture gap, and achieving some basic communication. It is perhaps worth noting in this respect that the teaching of English is just one of the aims of the JET programme. Along with teaching, it aims to foster good relations between Japan and the outside world and to overcome the '*gaijin* complex' – the fear of and difficulty in communicating with foreigners. Thus it aims to promote internationalization, improving Japan's reputation in the outside world.

In addition to AETs, 5% of JET recruitment is for the post of Co-ordinator for International Relations (CIR). This is a varied post which can cover lecturing civic groups, involvement in local exhibitions, proofreading/editing, etc, as well as some English teaching.

You can obtain information about JET from your Japanese Embassy or Consulate General, and applications should be made in the autumn before you wish to go. You should contact your Embassy (or, in London, the JET Programme Desk on 0171–224–

8896), in late September for an application form and have this completed and sent in by December. Interviews are in February and notification of selection is given in March. For successful candidates, there is a Japanese language orientation course in July for three days. Departure is at the end of July, and there is a further week of orientation in Tokyo before starting work. Addresses of Japanese embassies are:

Australia: 112 Empire Circuit, Yarralumla, Canberra, ACT 2600.

Canada: 255 Sussex Drive, Ottawa, Ontario K1N 9E6.

Ireland: 22 Ailesbury Road, Dublin 4.

New Zealand: 7th Floor, Norwich Insurance House, 3–11 Hunter Street, Wellington 1.

UK: 101/104 Piccadilly, London W1V 9FN.

USA: 2520 Massachusetts Avenue, NW, Washington, DC 20008–2869.

3 | Arriving without a job

Many people who have taught, and are teaching, English in Japan did not have a prearranged job to go to. However, although there is still teaching work available, it is a fact that (in these recessionary times) it is no longer as easy as it once was to find teaching work on the spot. Certainly, the number of advertisements for teaching jobs in *The Japan Times*, traditionally the main marketplace for teaching posts, is now rather less than a few years ago. In fact, with school closures and lay-offs, it may be the case that you are competing for job opportunities not only with other recent arrivals, but also with teachers who have been laid off from their job in Japan. It is probably therefore prudent, if possible, to arrange work before you arrive in Japan.

The main advantage of going to Japan without a prearranged job is that you will be able to check out each job before you sign a contract, and are much less likely to be exploited, especially if you have experience of other teaching jobs for comparison.

The main disadvantages are that you will have to get through Immigration alone (see pp 22 for information on entering Japan as a Temporary Visitor, and 36 for 'Immigration'), and you will probably need to bring a reasonable amount of money with you to Japan to see you through until you are on your feet financially (more on this in Chapter 6). One big financial item that you are much less likely to get help with is setting up your apartment – this can be a substantial amount (see Chapter 8). Another expense will be travelling out of Japan (possibly twice) for a working visa. Finally, of course, and as a stranger in a strange land, you have to get yourself a job.

TIME AND MONEY

Blocking your time

After a week or two, if they put some energy and initiative into the task, most people who turn up in Japan independently manage to obtain job offers of different kinds. Unfortunately, it is not always possible to find just one post which pays well enough on its own, and teachers therefore have to build up a number of part-time positions in order to earn a satisfactory amount of money. The first problem with this is that until you have built up a sufficient number of teaching hours, you will either be living on the breadline or partly supporting yourself from your savings.

The second difficulty that sometimes arises is that your time may not be satisfactorily 'blocked' – ie you have dribs and drabs of teaching from early morning to well into the evening. This is often coupled with a large amount of travelling, all making for a tiring and in many ways unsatisfactory lifestyle.

The good news is that situations develop and new prospects come up all the time, and it should not be too long before you have a timetable that is satisfactory in terms of scheduling as well as pay, as you shed the low-paid and awkward jobs. However, this does not happen overnight, and it can take anything up to a year before you have a 'perfect' timetable.

Money – Expenses and how much to take

The largest single financial outlay faced by most independents is setting up an apartment or home. With the current very high level of the yen, more and more teachers live for their first year or more in a '*gaijin* house', a cheap hostel for foreigners. If you want a place of your own, you will have to fork out from 3 to 6 months rent up front (around ¥400 000 to ¥600 000) before you even get through the door. It may be that one of your new employers is willing to lend you money to help you with setting up an apartment. Some of the front money will be returned to you at the end of your stay – usually it means a period of living rent-free after you have given in your notice – and many people find this a useful way to maximize their savings for going home.

The sum paid up front consists of 'key money' (*reikin*) and also a deposit (*shikikin*), usually two months' rent each, in addition to the first month's rent. Key money goes straight into the landlord's pocket, and is not refunded, and in fact many landlords take another month's key money after two years. Some estate agents who cater primarily for foreigners do not require key money. The deposit is placed with the landlord as security and is returned, less any expenses for repairs or damages, when you leave.

All in all, it is advisable to take as much money as you can to Japan if you have no job to go to, and you may be responsible for putting up all the expenses of setting yourself up. Some people arrive with very little, and manage to get organized, but a reasonable amount to minimize hardships is ¥500 000.

Certainly, although it is a potentially lucrative occupation, teaching in Japan is usually not the 'fast buck' some believe it to be. In fact, most people find that it is around a year before they have everything set up the way they want it – a pleasant apartment, all paid up, a satisfactory timetable and a proper visa.

FINDING WORK

The Japanese academic year begins in April. March and April are the times when most hiring takes place. There is another busy period in September. However, there are jobs available throughout the year.

Starting points

Job ads in the press. There are several English language newspapers in Japan. The biggest of these, and the best source of job ads, is *The Japan Times*. It is a daily paper, and the main day for job ads is Monday. Most of the jobs are in the Tokyo region, but there are a number of positions in other areas. Other papers include the *Mainichi Daily News*, the *Daily Yomiuri* and the *Asahi Evening News*. There are also a few national and regional magazines aimed at foreign visitors and residents which contain job ads and which can easily be obtained from any of the large bookshops in Japan. Examples are *Tokyo Journal* and *Kansai Time Out* (covering the Osaka/Kyoto/Kobe area).

Your chances of being employed will, of course, be increased if you do not insist on living and working in one specific area, and are willing to consider job offers in different parts of the country.

Contacting schools and companies on spec. The best way to find a list of language schools is through the *Yellow Pages* telephone directory, which is available in English (you can buy it in large bookshops or look at it in a local library). You can either phone round the schools or post an application. Many schools, even if they have no immediate openings, will hold your name and then contact you when they need a teacher. This may be for only a few hours a week initially, but as long as you keep your nose clean, as more hours become available they will normally be offered to teachers already on the staff before the job is advertised externally, so you will find that your hours at each school will soon increase.

You stand a much better chance of getting a job in a company if you have some kind of contact or personal introduction, so it is important to establish, maintain and develop all possible sources or leads.

Personal contacts. You can open a good many doors in Japan with a personal introduction. Often the fact that you are recommended for a job by someone the hirer knows, or knows of, means that you have as good as got it, and that any interviewing will be little more than a formality. It is possible that more teaching contracts are awarded through personal contacts than by formal open recruiting.

Through contacts you can find every kind of teaching work – in schools or companies, and also private work. The longer you stay in Japan, the wider your grapevine will extend, and the more job offers will come your way. This is true even if you put no effort into it whatsoever. However, in the beginning, it is important to get to know as many people as possible – both Japanese and Westerners.

You can meet Japanese people by striking up casual conversations, through your students, or at clubs and societies. One place to meet Japanese people in a relaxed and friendly environment is in a bar. If you go into a bar and sit by yourself, sooner or later you will be drawn into conversation by a group at a neighbouring table. It will not be long before they find out that you are an English teacher, and often they will ask if you would like to teach them. Usually the group is made up of a section from an office, and you will be asked to teach them either as a group or individually. Their alcohol-inspired enthusiasm for studying English regularly may not last beyond that evening and they may be unwilling to pay as much as they would be charged in a language school. However, even if you set up work with only a small percentage of such casual contacts, it does not take many groups to fill out your timetable. And although you may have to charge much less than a school, since you will have no overheads, 100% of the fees will come to you.

Interviews

All the points on interviews made in Chapter 2 (see p 6) are equally relevant here.

Generally, the fact that you have made your way to Japan shows a degree of commitment, which puts you ahead of any applications from outside the country. Negotiating is usually more of a possibility than when being interviewed outside Japan.

Turn up exactly on time, or a few minutes early. Bear in mind the difficulty of finding a building in Japan from an address, and allow plenty of time for getting lost. Plan to get there early, and then look around for a coffee shop (*kissaten*) if you have time to kill.

4 | Where to teach English

Places to teach vary from universities to tiny language schools run by a proprietor with hardly any English; and from massive international companies to your own living room.

Hourly rates are generally in the range ¥1500–3000. Depending on experience you may be able to push the rate up to ¥4000 or ¥5000 per hour.

You may be on the full-time staff of an institution, and receive many fringe benefits such as bonuses and a housing allowance in addition to a guaranteed income. Alternatively, you may opt for higher rates of hourly pay in a part-time position without benefits.

Students normally study once or twice a week. Motivation can vary. In many cases it is rather low. Children may resent English conversation tuition, not seeing its relevance in a life which is dictated by the hurdle of a university entrance exam. Adults may be studying English as a hobby, or for a kind of social *cachet*. Business people may be too pooped to pop after a long day at the office. On the other hand, more and more Japanese are beginning to realize the significance and relevance of being able to communicate in English, and such students are highly motivated, and a joy to teach.

The main places where you can teach English in Japan are listed below.

Conversation salons

There are a number of informal places, often known as 'conversation salons', where Japanese people can go and chat in English for a small fee, often not much more than the price of a coffee. The establishment provides English native speakers to sit and talk with the customers. Conversation is usually informal, with no lesson as such, nor any penetrating grammar questions or correction. The customers can usually be relied on to initiate and sustain conversations.

Pay for attending such establishments is low – around ¥1000 an hour, and the management may try to encourage foreigners to give their services free, saying that they, the foreigners, will have a good chance to meet Japanese people and find out about Japanese culture.

These places can be useful for finding private students, getting an initial feel for conversational teaching, or simply increasing your network. Certainly in the beginning, when you have nothing else to fill your time in the evenings, they can be useful places to get a handle on Japanese viewpoints and language problems painlessly and without pressure, and earn a little money in the process.

Language schools

Most *gaijin* English teachers in Japan work at a private language school. There may be early morning classes for the super-keen, who want to put in an hour's tuition before going to the office. During the day, classes are for housewives and others who are free in the daytime. In the late afternoon, children come to study English conversation after their regular schoolday. In the evening, most schools are busier than in the daytime, with classes for people who work, and students are predominantly business people. Most students come to school once or twice a week.

Since language schools are not accredited by the government, there are virtually no regulations stipulating curricula, or how the school should be run. Some specialize in one kind of student, such as children or business people. Some teach anyone and everyone. Some have been started by a Japanese entrepreneur with no academic background, while some are branches of international chains such as Berlitz or International House. There are also teaching jobs in the British Council and in the larger YMCAs and YWCAs.

Try to procure a commitment from the language school in terms of a guaranteed weekly minimum number of hours if the position is a part-time one.

In some private language schools a class consists of one (relatively unchanging) group of students who study together for a period of, say, ten weeks. However, many private language schools, especially in the Tokyo area, now run on a flexitime booking system. Students sign up for a block of, say, 80 lessons, to be used up in a specified period (perhaps six months). Schools vary widely in exactly how they run their flexitime systems. Better schools grade students according to their English ability, and have set class times for each level. Students have to call in at least an hour before their class is due to start if they want a lesson. If no-one calls in, the teacher is free to leave but is paid for the time the lesson would have taken. At the other extreme, students are not graded, can drop in at any time at no notice, and teachers have to remain on site for 40 hours a week ready to teach anybody and everybody.

One special kind of private school is a *juku*. These are 'cram' schools, to which children are sent from as young as five or six years old. *Juku* teach all the subjects which children study at their regular school. A *juku* can be a bit of a hot-house to work in, but, as a teacher of English conversation, you may be considered as outside the mainstream of teaching for exams, and may therefore have some freedom in running more relaxed classes. On the other hand, you may be chained to some tedious book and expected to crack the whip!

Universities and colleges

The two most important institutions in this category are universities (*daigaku*), and two-year junior colleges (*tandai*), often called *joshidai* (women's universities) when the students are all-female. There are also *senmongakkō*, which are technical colleges for studying practical subjects, such as computing or engineering.

You may have a full-time or part-time contract. The main advantage of a full-time contract is that you receive a salary during the vacations (which may total more than half the year). On the other hand, the academic environment can be difficult to operate in. Most of the professors have learned English by the grammar–translation method, and many are resistant to any changes to syllabus design or teaching methodology. If you work part-time, you will have more freedom to decide how much to participate in the life of the university outside the classroom. If you wish, you can merely turn up for classes and leave as soon as they are over.

Classes are usually fairly large – a minimum of 20 is common.

High schools

There is a wide variety of high schools. Schools are divided by age of student on the US system. Junior high school is for 12–15 year-olds, and senior high school is for 15–18 year-olds. Schools may be co-ed or single sex, and may be either state or privately run.

In general, students wear a constricting old-fashioned uniform which often reflects the kind of tuition they receive. Rote learning of facts is the norm and very large classes are to be expected (usually between 30 and 40 students per class – each lesson lasting 50 minutes). Teaching English conversation to students who are used to learning in this kind of atmosphere may mean slow progress adjusting students to your methods and improving their level of English. Some knowledge of Japanese can be an advantage in organizing the class, and giving explanations.

One way to obtain full-time employment is through the JET scheme (see p 8). Recruitment inside Japan for both full-time and part-time positions is very often by word-of-mouth.

A school may recruit a *gaijin* English teacher in order to enhance the school's prestige. If this is the case, the school may be prejudiced against non-Caucasian applicants, even if they are English native speakers and have educational qualifications, preferring instead someone it thinks looks the part.

Useful background reading for teaching in a high school is *Japan's High Schools* by T. Rohlen.

Companies

Some large companies have their own internal English teaching programme. They hire full-time instructors, who work a regular 40-hour week: around 25 hours are in the classroom, with the balance taken up by proofreading, writing business letters, etc.

One advantage of such a position is that you often receive many of the benefits available to the Japanese staff, such as bonuses, housing allowance and health benefits. The biggest disadvantage is that, as a regular employee, you are expected to fit in, and the life of a Japanese white-collar worker (*sararīman*) is not to everyone's taste. It may also be difficult to take on outside work (often lucrative), both because of scheduling difficulties, and because the company does not approve of your working elsewhere. Long holidays, too, may not be possible.

It may be more difficult for a woman to obtain a full-time teaching position in a company, since, as the word *sararīman* implies, women are still something of a rarity in the Japanese office, aside from clerks and secretaries.

Most companies cannot afford to hire full-time English instructors, and hire tutors by the hour, either privately or through a language school. Hiring privately is usually through recommendation, so keep your ears open.

Classes in companies are small, with typically half-a-dozen students. The great majority of the students are male.

Teaching privately

Often the highest hourly pay you achieve is teaching students you have found through your own efforts. Furthermore, they are usually keen and receptive, and show improvement. Teaching privately, however, does not entitle you to a working visa. Most people have at least a part-time contract (hopefully with guaranteed minimum hours) with a teaching institution as a regular flow of income, and then also teach privately.

One drawback to teaching privately is that your groups may be academically disparate. A group is often studying together because its members are friends or colleagues rather than because their English abilities or needs are similar. Perhaps more important from your point of view, another drawback is that private students are much more unreliable as a source of income – they are less likely than school students to study regularly. They tend to cancel a much higher percentage of their lessons, and often stop studying after a fairly short period, or have long breaks from studying. You can, of course, try to impose similar conditions on them to those made by schools, such as paying in advance for a term of a set of, say, ten lessons, but this is usually not feasible, and students often pay lesson-by-lesson, and are unwilling to pay for any except last-minute cancellations.

The Japan Association of Language Teachers (JALT)

The Japan Association of Language Teachers (JALT) is a network of foreign-language teachers in Japan. JALT publishes a monthly magazine (*The Language Teacher*) and a twice-yearly journal (*JALT Journal*). JALT has 37 local chapters throughout Japan, which hold monthly meetings and workshops. The high point of the year is its three-day annual conference in the autumn, where you can meet other teachers and discuss work and compare working conditions, and attend seminars and lectures on teaching English in Japan. Although JALT does not handle job placements, there is a Job Information Center at the conference, and you will also have many informal opportunities to make useful contacts and hear about job possibilities. The conference lasts for several days and is in a different location every year. Your school may pay transportation and expenses for you to attend it.

You can join JALT either inside Japan, or before you arrive. Membership details may be obtained from:

JALT, Glorious Tokyo #301, 2–32–10 Nishi Nippori, Arakawa-ku, Tokyo 116 (Tel 03–3802–7121; Fax 03–3802–7122).

5 | Visas

There is a range of visas, depending on purpose of visit and nationality. However, it can be difficult to obtain a clear and complete picture of the situation on visas, since it would appear that decisions are sometimes made by the Immigration Department on a case-by-case (a favourite Japanese term) basis. What happens to an application on a certain day in one office might not be the same as what happens to a similar application on a different day or in a different office.

A Guide to Alien Residence Procedures in Japan gives details on obtaining a visa and changing your visa status. It is available from:

The Japan Times, 5–4–5 Shibaura, Minato-Ku, Tokyo 108.

and costs ¥200 inside Japan and ¥300 outside Japan. Alternatively, there is *A Guide to Entry, Residence and Registration Procedures in Japan for Foreign Nationals*, published by Nippon Kojo Shuppan (¥1500).

Probably the most useful piece of general advice to someone trying to obtain a visa is to stay calm in the face of adversity. This is true in most countries, but is especially true in Japan. There is absolutely no improvement to be gained from losing your temper and/or shouting at Immigration Department officials. You will lose face, and it will, if anything, be counter-productive. If you are told that you need certain documents to back up your application, just go away and do it. If you hit a brick wall, ask what action or papers would be needed to advance your application, and go and take the necessary action.

A radical overhaul of the classification system in 1990 provided more specific categories, but did not give the hoped-for clarification. The new categories have names which reflect the area of employment, such as 'Engineer' or 'Entertainer', instead of numbers. If you apply for a work visa you will probably be eligible for the status of either 'Instructor' or 'Specialist in Humanities'. It seems to be rather arbitrary which category you are put under, but in practical terms it makes no difference.

The categories of visa which might be relevant to you are listed in Table 1.

21

Table 1. Relevant visa categories.

Visa category	Status of residence	Period of stay	Amount of work permitted
Temporary Visitor	Temporary Visitor	90 days	None
Employment or Working	Instructor	6 months or 1 year	Unlimited
Employment or Working	Specialist in Humanities /International Services	6 months or 1 year	Unlimited
Employment or Working	Professor	6 months, 1 year or 3 years	Unlimited
General	College Student	6 months or 1 year	Varies (about 17 hours/week) – check with Immigration
General	Cultural Activities	6 months or 1 year	Varies, depending on job offer
General	Working Holiday*	6 months	Enough to cover expenses
General	Dependant	3 months, 6 months, 1 year or 3 years	Check with Immigration 15–20 hours/week

*This status applies only to Australia, Canada, and New Zealand.

Notes on resident status

Temporary Visitor (Tourist). The entry permit (90 days maximum) can be obtained at the airport on arrival, if you have, among others, a Canadian, Irish, New Zealand, UK or US passport. For Irish and UK nationals, there is a possible 90-day extension if the visa is issued by Immigration. If you are Australian, you must obtain a visa before you leave. It is issued at the Embassy/ Consulate General. Some people now with Working visas entered the country initially with this status, left Japan when they found a sponsor, and returned with a Working visa obtained before re-entering Japan.

Working visa (Instructor or Specialist in Humanities). The only indispensable prerequisite for obtaining this status is a degree, which does not have to contain any English language or teaching training components, and a definite job offer in Japan. This visa can be obtained before you arrive, and getting a job and appropriate visa status before you leave for Japan is obviously recommended. Many people do, however, arrive on a Temporary Visitor status, find a job, and proceed as described above.

Very occasionally, people are allowed to upgrade their status in Japan, although this is impossible for US passport holders. However, in reality it is probably safe to assume that a trip outside Japan will be needed to obtain a Working visa. A typical pattern for this is: (1) enter Japan on a Tourist visa; (2) find an employer willing to sponsor you for a Working visa – the employer must obtain a work permit (Certificate of Eligibility) from Immigration for the potential employee which must then be submitted to a Japanese embassy or consulate; (3) leave Japan and apply for the new visa at the Japanese consulate of your own country or the country to which you have travelled. If everything is prepared in order, the application should be processed quite quickly, although processing times vary depending on the embassy or consulate concerned. You can then return to Japan with a Working visa.

You can travel back home or to other close locations to obtain your Working visa. The cheapest option is Korea. You can fly to Seoul for about ¥40 000. Apart from its proximity, Korea makes an interesting trip – the people and country are so like Japan and the Japanese in some ways, and yet in other ways so very different. Other possibilities are Manila (¥45 000 – take a bus to a lovely beach); Hong Kong (¥50 000 – catch all that freneticism before China takes control in 1997); and Taipei (¥50 000 – see the amazing treasure-trove of art brought to Taiwan from China by the bourgeois fleeing from Communism).

The documents you need for your application are:

- The school registration document.
- National tax certificate.
- Business tax certificate.
- The school brochure.
- Letter of invitation or contract to you from the school.
- Certificate of employment stating salary and work schedule.
- Witnessed and notarized contract between you and the school.
- Guarantee letter.
- List of the school's instructors.

Alternatively, it is easier to apply for a teaching visa with a Certificate of Eligibility obtained by the employer from Immigration in Japan. That is to say, the employer submits in Japan all the above documents and provides you with a Certificate of Eligibility which you take to your embassy or consulate to obtain your visa.

Professor. You will receive this status if you are employed from your own country by a Japanese university as a visiting professor.

College Student. This status is for people who have completed 12 years of education in their own country, and who wish to study at a place of higher education in Japan. This usually refers to somebody who is studying for a degree in Oriental Studies or Japanese (language), and is spending some time in Japan as part of the course.

Cultural Activities. This status applies to people who want to study the Japanese language or one of the aspects of Japanese culture, such as martial arts or tea ceremony. An 'Internship' visa has been introduced within the Cultural Activities status for 'scholars wishing to enter Japan to undertake advanced academic research or advanced cultural studies' (six months maximum, intended for university students – the reason for the visit has to be related to their course). You can apply for Cultural Activities status before you arrive in Japan, but you must have paid for a course in Japan, and submit proof of this with your application.

If you wish to find out about applying for this status before you go, contact a Japanese embassy or write to:

> **Association of International Education**, 4–5–29 Komaba, Meguro-ku, Tokyo 153 (Tel 03–3467–3521)

requesting a copy of their *Student Guide to Japan* and *ABC's of Study in Japan.*

The documents you will need to furnish when you apply for this status are:

- A letter of invitation from the school.
- Your CV.
- Your degree certificate.
- Details of the activities.
- Evidence of your ability to pursue the activities.
- Documents showing that you can pay for tuition and living expenses.

Working Holiday. This status is available to passport holders of Australia, New Zealand and Canada, aged between 18 and 30. It may be worth checking with your Japanese consulate if the scheme has been widened to include your country.

Application should be made before you leave, because this visa can be supplied only in your country. Obtain an application form and submit:

- Completed application form in duplicate, including a photo.
- Letter of guarantee.
- Documents showing the reason for wishing to go to Japan.
- School records or company documents, such as those detailed above for Working visa applications (but not necessarily all of these).

Dependant. If your husband or wife is working in Japan (but not in the diplomatic service), you may be allowed to work, but you must check at the Immigration Department in your city. This should not be done as soon as you arrive, but once you have settled in and registered.

Re-entry permit

If you are going out of Japan, with the intention of returning, you must obtain a Re-entry permit in order to preserve your status. This permit must be obtained from Immigration before leaving Japan. You can get a single-entry (¥3000) or multiple-entry visa (¥6000) – both are valid for up to one year or until the expiry of your status. If you are planning, or even thinking about more than one trip in a year, weigh up the extra cost of a multiple-entry against saving the hassle of going to and spending an hour or two at the Immigration Department.

Bear in mind that a Re-entry permit is not an automatic entry right (nor is a visa) – you may still have to satisfy Immigration at the point of entry when you arrive back.

Immigration offices

The regional Immigration Departments for the Tokyo and Osaka areas are:

> *Tokyo*: 3–1 Otemachi 1-chome, Chiyoda-ku, Tokyo 100 (Tel 03–3213–8111).
> *Osaka*: 1–17 Tani-machi 2-chome, Chuo-ku, Osaka 540 (Tel 06–941–0771).

The Otemachi office in Tokyo tends to be very crowded, with long waits. An alternative for re-entry visas is to go to the much quieter Immigration Office at the Tokyo City Air Terminal (TCAT, known colloquially as T-cat) at 42–1 Nihombashi Hakozakai-cho, Chuo-ku, Tokyo (Information Office, Tel 03–3665–7156). This is the quickest and easiest place to obtain re-entry visas. For anything more complicated, you have to go to Otemachi.

At the time of writing, the following costs apply:

- Re-entry (single) ¥3000
- Re-entry (multiple) ¥6000
- Extension ¥5000
- Change of status ¥4000

Alien Registration Card (ARC)

If you stay in Japan for more than 90 days (and even if you still have a Tourist visa), you must obtain an Alien Registration Card (commonly known as a *gaijin* card). Go to the Civil Registration Section of your local city (*shi*) or ward (*ku*) municipal office within 90 days of arrival. Take your passport and two recent passport-size photos, and complete an 'Application for Alien Registration' form, available at the municipal office. In about 10 days, you will be issued with a laminated card, which you should carry with you at all times. If you are stopped by the police without it you may be detained – in which case you will have to contact a friend to go to your home and fetch your card. If you apologize and look suitably crestfallen when you are stopped, you may be allowed to carry on.

The above details are true at time of writing, but may be subject to change – please check the process yourself before starting out.

Part 2

LIVING IN JAPAN

6 | How expensive is Japan?

Japan can be expensive in two ways. Fortunately, neither of these ways need apply to you.

It is expensive if you are a tourist, changing your currency into yen to spend in Japan. The yen has now become so strong that you can go through a lot of dollars or pounds very quickly. However, if you are working in Japan and being paid in yen, it will not seem so costly, and, of course, any money you save will convert healthily for your return.

Japan is also expensive if you insist on having a back-home lifestyle in every respect. The people who normally do this have been posted to Japan for a few years by their employer. Their salary and expenses permit them to live in a Western style and in a Western-size apartment, shop at the international supermarkets for unlimited imported goodies, and run a car.

LIVING COSTS

Most English teachers soon realize they can live very comfortably in an average-size Japanese apartment, which, while not perhaps as spacious as what they have back home, is larger than the exaggerated 'rabbit hutch' image which has been popularized in the West. Also, they quickly appreciate the excellence of Japanese public transport. This, coupled with the almost permanent jams on the roads, and the unavailability of free on-street parking, make owning a car an unnecessary and expensive luxury. However, if you live outside the big cities, and a parking place is not prohibitively expensive, you will find that a second-hand car, like second-hand anything in Japan, can be bought for a pleasantly small amount.

Eating and drinking

Eating and drinking are not expensive, if you do it the Japanese way. For home eating and drinking, restrict your trips to the foreign supermarkets to an occasional foray, and do most of your shopping at the local supermarket, where you will find 90% of your requirements, albeit sometimes in a slightly Japanified form. For eating and drinking out, there are plenty of ways to eat cheaply and well, as detailed in Chapter 7.

Taxes

There are two kinds of personal tax – national and local. Income tax is pleasantly low, averaging out to around 8%. Local tax is payable only after the first year's stay in Japan, and amounts to about the same again as income tax. In practice, however, it seems that the authorities start asking for money only after you have been resident for more than a year.

Discos

Aside from the unavoidable living expenses of accommodation, transportation, eating and drinking, and taxes, perhaps the biggest single social expense for many people is going to a club or disco. In your own country, you are probably resigned to a stiff entrance fee, then high-priced food and drink, as the management sting you because you are a captive audience and have no purchasing choice. In Japan, on the other hand, when you pay your not unreasonable entrance money (¥4000 for men and ¥3000 for women) you receive a drink token, and the more expensive places give you several tokens for food and drink.

How far does the money go?

A realistic full-time salary is between ¥200 000 and ¥250 000 per month. Most teachers do some additional private teaching, and this could take total monthly income as high as ¥300 000. Rent will probably be between ¥50 000 and ¥100 000. After tax and rent, you should be left with around ¥150 000 per month in your hand. This is enough to allow you a comfortable lifestyle without worrying over-much about being careful with your spending patterns. In addition, the current strength of the yen against other currencies means that when spending yen outside Japan, whether when taking or sending money home or going on a foreign vacation, a few yen go a long way.

On the other hand, you may choose to limit yourself to around ten hours of teaching per week – enough to cover your costs, and leave you plenty of free time. (Increasingly schools are hiring part-timers and paying them by the hour.) This lifestyle is preferred by some people on a cultural visa. The cultural classes are usually during the day, and teaching can be concentrated into the prime early evening time.

A comparison of living expenses in Tokyo with those in other major cities is given in Table 2.

Table 2. Comparative living expenses (yen).

	Tokyo	New York	London	Paris
Bread (1 kg)	413	301	107	502
Beef (100 g)	162	99	94	164
Milk (1 litre)	210	85	91	117
Sugar (1 kg)	284	135	115	135
Eggs (1 kg)	274	199	330	392
Onions (1 kg)	220	116	170	116
Shoes (one pair, men's)	11 670	7 608	5 507	9 903
Petrol (1 litre)	127	40	83	103
Laundry (man's suit)	1071	806	1126	1556
Electricity (250 kW/month)	6632	5153	4099	5000
Gas (550 000 kcal/month)	6616	3208	2082	3727

Figures are for November 1993. Taken from *Japan 1995 – An International Comparison*, Japan Institute for Social and Economic Affairs, Tokyo. *Original source:* Economic Planning Agency, Japan.

7 | Arriving and everyday living

This chapter deals with essential aspects of living in Japan. First, however, there are words of advice on preparing for your visit.

BEFORE YOU GO

Travel preparations

Maps and guides. Contact the nearest Japan National Tourist Office (JNTO). They have an excellent range of free maps, guides and information sheets on Japan.

Buy your ticket(s). For a long-haul flight, the biggest decision is whether you are willing to pay the high premium to travel on a major carrier like BA, TWA or JAL, or save your money by flying with a less well known airline. The seats may be a little tattier, but do you really want to pay out the equivalent of a month's rent for the prestige of a ticket with a major airline?

If you have the option, it is worth considering a China Airlines ticket. Since Taiwan is not recognized as a country by Japan, its national airline is not allowed to use Narita Airport. Instead, the planes land at the much more convenient domestic airport, Haneda, which is a short monorail line trip from central Tokyo.

If you are arriving at Tokyo Narita Airport, book a place on the Japan Railways Narita Express from Narita Airport to Tokyo Station when you buy your flight ticket. This service is the quickest and easiest way to get into Tokyo, and the tickets are usually booked up several days in advance.

Japan Rail Pass. As well as your airline ticket, think about buying a Japan Rail Pass. This pass, available only outside Japan, allows unlimited travel on all Japan Railways (JR) trains (including *Shinkansen*, the bullet train) for 7, 14, or 21 days. The cost of a 7-day pass (¥27 800) is less than a return Tokyo–Kyoto *Shinkansen* ticket, so it clearly offers considerable saving and an excellent opportunity to have a look around Japan before settling down. Buy an Exchange Order at an authorized travel agent before you leave, and exchange that for a Rail Pass within three months of your arrival in Japan.

Insurance. Take out a travel insurance policy which includes health-care cover.

Passport/visa. Make sure you have a valid passport. If you need to apply for a Tourist visa, do so. If you want to apply for any other kind of visa before you go, such as student or cultural, take the relevant action suggested in Chapter 5.

Vaccinations. No vaccinations are necessary for Japan if you are travelling from an area where there is no current epidemic. If you travel on to other Asian countries once you are there, it is easy and safe to obtain any necessary jabs in Japan.

Training and information gathering

Teaching course. Consider doing a short course on teaching English as a foreign language (TEFL). There is an excellent, widely available four-week course (RSA/UCLES Cert TEFLA). For details, contact International House in London (Tel 0171–491–2598), the Australian College of English in Sydney (Tel 612–389–0133) or English International Inc in San Francisco (Tel 415–749–5633).

Japanese language. Needless to say, any time you can spare for the study of the Japanese language (*Nihongo*) – in view of the generally limited ability among the Japanese people to communicate in English – will not be wasted.

As well as the basic grammar (in particular, the system of verb endings, which is easy to master but which foreigners consistently get wrong), you would be well advised to acquire knowledge of at least a few Chinese characters (*kanji*) which you will find useful to recognize: those for 'men's' and 'women's' toilets; 'entrance'; 'exit'; '1st/2nd/3rd Floor'; and perhaps the numbers.

In addition, you would also be well advised, if you have the time, to study the two Japanese scripts, which are used in conjunction with Chinese characters. One is *hiragana*, which, following and used in conjunction with Chinese characters, denotes the 'grammar' of the phrase or sentence. You would find a knowledge of *hiragana* useful in locating some restaurants and bars which have boards outside with the name of the establishment in *hiragana*.

The other Japanese script you need to master, if you have time, is *katakana*, which is used mainly for transcribing foreign words and names into Japanese. You will find *katakana* useful in locating all kinds of brand names (many of which mimic European languages), and, again, in finding restaurants and bars. When you are dying for something Western to eat, the labels attached to the plastic models in the windows of Western-style restaurants will be in *katakana*.

Books and bookshops. A list of recommended books is given in Appendix 5. Bookshops specializing in Japan are useful sources of information about the country, and of Japanese-language books and magazines. In the USA, the two largest are:

> **Kinokuniya**, 110 S Los Angeles St, Los Angeles, CA 90012.
> **Kinokuniya**, 10 W 49th St, New York, NY 10020.

In the UK, major specialists are:

> **Books Nippon**, 64 St Paul's Churchyard, London EC4M 8AA.
> **The Japan Centre**, 212 Piccadilly, London W1V 9LD.

Make contacts. Contact any Japanese people you know, or know of, in Japan or in your own country. It is never too early to start networking.

Mental preparation. Western influences are not absent in Japan, but many aspects of its culture, lifestyle, beliefs and philosophies are uniquely Japanese. You will find significant differences, to which you will need to acclimatize.

It is worth preparing yourself to deal with these differences. Bear in mind that your ways and values are not necessarily better or worse than those of the Japanese, and, whatever the case, it is not your brief to do anything about it. Being a cultural missionary should not be seen as your duty (or right). Nobody is paying you to change the Japanese people, and you risk causing yourself mental grief if you decide to try to do this. The advice of old Japanese hands is unanimous on this point – go with the flow, and merely observe the differences. In any event, you may find your views about what is 'right' or 'wrong' with Japan change during your stay, or even after you leave, when your experience has a chance to fall into perspective.

The fact that some Japanese people you meet may seem to want to embrace everything Western and reject everything Japanese should not alter your thinking in this area. Japan and its people will change in their own way and in their own time. When they feel ready to embrace a certain aspect of another culture, they do so, and with head-spinning rapidity.

What to take

The list of what you need to take for a stay in Japan gets shorter year by year, and Japan now offers most things you might want to buy. In addition to foreign goods being available, the large numbers of *gaijin* living in Japan nowadays has led to the opening of specialist shops, such as those selling 'outsize' clothes for long-legged foreigners. Although some of the younger generation in Japan are much taller than their parents, it is still true that *large clothes and shoes* are usually expensive and/or difficult to find, especially outside Tokyo, so pack a good supply if you are over size 38 and shoe size 10 (men), or size 7 and shoe size 7 (women). There are two possibilities if you find you need larger than available clothes. One is to have some of your own clothes sent to you by family or friends. Another is to take advantage of a visa trip to Korea to visit Seoul's Itaewon Market, where US clothes, and especially shoes, are available, due to the large US Forces presence in Korea.

One little parcel you should tuck in your case before you leave is the original, or lots of good copies of all your *official documents* – birth certificate, educational qualifications (certified copies are best), driving licence (international if possible), Youth Hostel Membership Card, etc. If you need passport-sized photos for job applications, etc, there are photo booths at many main railway stations.

A set of *conservative clothes* will be useful for Immigration, job interviews, and teaching.

Take your full *duty-free allowance* – three litres of spirits and 400 cigarettes. If you do not use them yourself, the items will be useful as gifts to Japanese friends and contacts.

A selection of *printed matter* from your country/home town will add interest and relevance to your teaching. The list could include maps and plans; menus; postcards and photos; timetables; and brochures.

Gifts are given on all sorts of occasions in Japan, so bring a selection of *souvenirs or memorabilia* from your country or area. Tea-towels are light and easy to carry, and are often printed with interesting local details. Small models of local buildings or tourist attractions make excellent presents.

Take as much *money* as you can manage. The more of this desirable stuff you take, the smoother will be your entry into Japanese society. While it is possible to make a start with almost nothing, a reasonable minimum would be ¥500 000, bearing in mind the high cost of setting up an apartment.

ARRIVAL

Immigration

Wear your set of conservative clothes. Even if you have already arranged your visa, you do not automatically have a right to enter Japan, so be properly deferential. If you do not have a non-tourist visa, the purpose of your visit is 'sightseeing'. Be prepared to show a ticket out, and funds or proof of funds.

Urgent accommodation

If you have no accommodation arranged, get change for the phone (¥100 coins) or buy a phonecard and buy a *Tokyo Journal* or *Japan Times*. Phone the *gaijin* houses and Youth Hostels listed on p 39 and in *Tokyo Journal*. If you cannot get a room with your own efforts, use the Hotel Reservation Counter at the Airport to book a room for that night (ask about *capsule* hotels). Make sure you find out the nearest station to the hostel or hotel, which line it is on, how to get to it, and directions from the station to the hostel or hotel. Accommodation is discussed in more detail later in this chapter.

Transport from the airport

Narita is a long way from Tokyo, and the best and quickest way into town is by train. Trains run to two large stations in Tokyo – JR Tokyo (Central) station and Keisei Ueno station.

Japan Railways (JR) to Tokyo (Central) station (¥2890). This is called the 'Narita Express'. All seats must be reserved, so it is necessary to book. If you did not book a ticket when you bought your airline ticket, ask when the next available train is, and if the next train or two are full, enquire at the Keisei Line desk. When you buy a Narita Express ticket, you will be able to buy a through ticket to your destination, and will be able to change at Tokyo station to another line.

Keisei Railways to Ueno (¥1780). This service, known as the 'Skyliner', is cheaper than the Narita Express, and there may be a shorter wait. However, the train terminates at Ueno, and to continue your journey you have to walk a few hundred yards to Ueno JR station and buy a fresh ticket to connect with JR trains or the subway system.

Limousine bus. The bus takes longer than the train, and the principal coach goes to JR Tokyo station. Other coaches go straight to the large hotels. You might consider taking one of these hotel coaches if your accommodation is very near a major hotel. You do not need to be a guest at the Hilton to use the service – just pay the fare (¥2900).

Taxi. Do not even consider taking a taxi into Tokyo. It will cost the earth. It will also take as long as the bus and much more time than the train. In the bad old days before the direct train service to Narita was introduced, and the taxi was the quickest means of transport, one teacher took a taxi out to Narita airport, and the fare (¥30 000) was more than the cost of his flight to Bangkok!

Haneda. If you come in by China Airlines and so land at Haneda Airport, simply buy a monorail ticket to Hammamatsucho, three stops south of Tokyo station, on the Yamanote Line. From there, it is easy to make JR and subway connections.

Other airports. The other airports which handle long-haul flights are Osaka and Fukuoka (Kyushu). These have good bus connections to the city.

Getting to your room. When you reach the nearest station to your hostel or hotel, look around for a police box (*kōban*) to confirm your directions, and to ensure that you start off in the right direction. If you cannot find one, just ask the ticket collector or railway official – they are usually delighted to assist.

ACCOMMODATION

Addresses

The address system in Japan is unusual in that it does not use street names. The country is divided into smaller and smaller divisions, the smallest being a building. This system is made more difficult by the fact that houses in a block are not numbered regularly. Building number two is the second building to be constructed in a block, and is not necessarily next to building number one. Finding an address is not easy even for the local Japanese themselves, and so near stations and at intersections there are often police boxes (*kōban*) whose main duty is to give directions. Do not be afraid to use *kōban*, even if you cannot speak Japanese. Just show the police the address, and they will show you directions on a large local map. In the absence of street names, directions are given by landmarks – 'Turn left at the *tōfu* shop, and then right at the *pachinko* parlour', 'get off the bus in front of the hospital', etc.

Typically, an address has two or three kinds of numbered areas:

5–1–24 Yoyogi
Shibuya-ku
Tokyo 155

In the above example, moving up from the bottom line by area size, there is Tokyo (the city); Shibuya-*ku* (the ward); Yoyogi (the area); 5 (the *chōme*, an area of a few blocks); 1 (the *ban*, a block), and finally house 24 (the building). The last two numbers are the most troublesome, and you will become expert at drawing mini-maps and giving and receiving directions.

Look out for area information on lampposts – a plate, usually green, with (in the above example) 5–1 Yoyogi. However, this will be written in Japanese.

The important point to remember when deciphering a Japanese address is to start with the first number. For an address with numbers 1–2–3, first find area 1, then, within that, block 2, and finally building 3.

Kinds of accommodation

The three main types of accommodation used by foreigners in Japan are: short-term accommodation on first arrival; long-term living accommodation; and holiday or travel accommodation.

Short-term accommodation on first arrival

Western international hotels exist, as do more reasonably priced smaller hotels and capsule hotels. However, they cater mainly for the needs of, respectively, the rich, Japanese business people, and people who have missed the last train home. They are not much used by independent travellers.

In the larger cities, the most convenient form of initial accommodation for you will probably be a hostel for foreigners (*gaijin* house). This is a cheap lodging house, with rooms rented by the day, week or month. Approximate rates are: ¥2000 per day; ¥22 000 per week; and ¥55 000 per month.

Gaijin houses are easy to find and cheap. An advantage of staying in one is that most of the other residents are in the same position as you – recently arrived in the country, and looking for work. You will get the latest low-down on visas, job prospects, cheap places to eat, etc.

Youth Hostels are another possibility for cheap accommodation.

A list of some *gaijin* houses and youth hostels in the larger cities is given below (*gaijin* houses are advertised in *Tokyo Journal* and *Kansai Time Out*):

TOKYO
(When calling from Narita, dial the number as given. From inside Tokyo, omit the first 03.)

Gaijin houses

Bilingual House, 03–3200–7082 (several houses on Seibu–Shinjuku and Keio lines)
Cosmopolitan House, 03–3825–0816 (Shinjuku station)
Fuji House, 03–3967–4046 (Shimura–sanchome station, Mita line)
Tokyo English Center, 03–3360–4781/1666 (Higashi Nakano station, JR Sobu line)

Youth hostels

Tokyo International Youth Hostel, 03–3235–1107 (Iidabashi station)
Yoyogi Youth Hostel, 03–3467–9163 (Shinjuku station, Odakyu line)

OSAKA

Gaijin houses

Adams House, 06–686–3866 (Kitagaya station, Yotsubashi line)
Osaka English House, 0720–41–0410 (25 mins from Osaka)

Youth hostels

Nagai Youth Hostel, 06–699–5631 (Nagai station, JR Hanwa line)
Hattori Ryoku-chi Youth Hostel, 06–862–0600 (Ryoku-chi-koen station, Midōsuji line)

KYOTO

Gaijin houses

Kyoto Green Peace, 075–791–9890
ISE Dorm, 075–771–0566

Youth hostels

Higashiyama, 075–761–8135 (Kyoto station)
Matsusan Youth Hostel, 075–221–5160 (Kyoto station)

FUKUOKA

Youth hostels

Daizaifu Youth Hostel, 092–922–8740 (Daizafu station)
Kita-Kyushu Youth Hostel, 093–681–8142 (Yahata station)

Long-term living accommodation

The first possibility for permanent accommodation is simply to stay in your *gaijin* house. The main financial benefit is that there is no 'key money' (see p 12) to pay.

Another way to avoid paying key money is to stay with a Japanese family. This is usually easiest to arrange through personal contacts. However, if you are working in a city, probably the only people with a spare room will live a long way out from the centre, so make sure you take your commuting times into consideration. In a homestay, you will, of course, have an excellent opportunity to observe and participate in ordinary Japanese home life, and your *Nihongo* will improve rapidly.

Most *gaijin* who stay in Japan for a year or more rent an apartment. For most rentals you will require a guarantor. This will usually be your employer. You can find a room or apartment from noticeboards in schools and *gaijin* supermarkets, or from ads in newspapers or English-language magazines, such as *Tokyo Journal* or *Kansai Time Out*. Estate agencies (*fudosanya*) are easily found clustered around stations (some agents specializing in *gaijin* advertise in the English-language magazines). These agents may not require key money. They will speak some English, and be used to *gaijin* ways. However, some of them specialize in very expensive rentals for expats on expense accounts, so make your budget clear.

In some areas, such as Kansai, it is possible to rent a local authority council house (*danchi*).

Buildings are either of traditional wood construction with one or two storeys (*mokuzō*) or more modern apartments in a block of up to ten storeys – usually referred to as a *mansion*.

If you go to a *fudosanya*, take a Japanese friend along if at all possible, or try to persuade your school to let you borrow someone from the office to go with you. This person will not only help you decipher the ads, and interpret for you in the *fudosanya*, but can also assure the agent that you will not destroy an apartment by walking on the straw mats (*tatami*) with your shoes on, or by soaping yourself in the bath (*ofuro*).

Layout. Apartments are described by a number plus the letters DK or LDK (eg 2LDK). 'L' stands for living room, 'D' for dining room, 'K' for kitchen, and '2' refers to the number of other rooms. The other rooms are usually *tatami*-covered general-purpose rooms, which function as living spaces during the day. At night, *futon* (rolled-up mattresses) are taken out and these rooms are used as bedrooms. Living in this way almost doubles the living area, maximizing use of floor space.

The size of rooms may be referred to in numbers of *tatami* mats (even if the floors are not actually covered in *tatami*), or in square metres. One mat, about 1.8 m by 0.9 m, is a *jō*, and the most common room sizes are 4.5 *jō* (*yojōhan*), which is medium, and 6 *jō* (*roku jō*), which is large. The other common sizes are 3 *jō*, 8 *jō* and 10 *jō*.

Just inside the front door will be a small entrance hall (*genkan*). Outdoor shoes are removed here, and slippers put on.

The apartment will also have a wc and a bathroom. The wc should have plastic slippers for which you exchange your usual slippers. The wc may be an Asian-style squat type. However, in a *mansion* it is usually the Western seat-type. To use the Asian type, squat facing the hood, and feel free to grip any available fixtures to aid your balance. You may be advised to empty trouser pockets or even remove trousers.

The bathroom will contain a bath (*ofuro*) and a means of washing yourself before getting into the bath. This will probably be a shower, but may simply be a tap on the wall, from which you fill a basin with hot water, and then use basins of water to wash and rinse yourself, with the wastewater running away through a drain in the bathroom floor. After you have washed and rinsed yourself, you can step into the bath and soak in hot water for as long as you like. The bathwater can be continuously circulated and reheated while you are in the bath. This means that not only can you stay in the bath as long as you wish, but other people can use the same bathwater after you, since it is still clean.

After use, the bath can be covered with a padded mat, which retains the heat, and means the water is not completely cold the next time it is used. Bathwater can be used up to half-a-dozen times before it starts becoming grimy. In Japanese homes, however, the *ofuro* is run, heated and used every night, and then it is emptied and cleaned when everyone has finished.

Electricity and gas. Your *apāto* will have piped gas. Electricity is 100 volts, 50 cycles in Tokyo and the north, and 60 cycles in Osaka and the south. North American appliances will work, albeit not at maximum strength. Appliances from Europe will, however, need a transformer.

Furnishing an apartment. Apartments are generally let unfurnished. Your minimum requirements will be:

- A *gas table* (or *konro*) – this is Japanese English for a two-ring gas stove.
- A refrigerator (*reizōko*).
- *Futon.* Since *futon* spend their time either on the floor with a body on them, or rolled up in a cupboard, they need to be aired

regularly. There is usually a bar outside one of the windows for hanging out your *futon* to air. A regular morning activity of Japanese housewives is beating the *futon* to plump it up.

- Some kind of heating. *Mokuzō* apartments are usually un-heated, and *mansion* apartments often have a unit which serves as a heater in winter and an air-conditioner in summer. Unfor-tunately, this is usually situated near the ceiling, and is not very efficient for heating the bottom part of the room. Fires are usually either paraffin heater (*tōyu*) or gas fire. A convenient Japanese appliance is a *kotatsu* – a low table with an electric heating element in the form of a large bulb underneath. The *kotatsu* is covered with a quilt: you tuck your hands and legs under the quilt, and keep your upper body covered with a sweater or Japanese cardigan. A *kotatsu* can serve as a dining and coffee table, and as a desk.
- Pots, pans, cutlery and crockery.

Furnishings can, of course, be bought new. However, especially in the larger cities, there are a number of cheaper alternatives for the wily *gaijin*.

The least costly is to obtain furnishings and appliances for nothing. Japanese domestic rubbish is separated into three types, and one day per week or per month, depending on the part of the country, bulky rubbish (*sodai gomi*) is put on the street. The particular day varies from area to area, so find out which day it is for yours. If you take a stroll round your neighbourhood the evening before, you will often see various kinds of nearly-new consumer durables waiting to be collected and there for the taking. Japanese people are both rich and very interested in keeping up with the Jones. It is infra-dig to buy second-hand merchandise, so there is not much of a market for used goods. As a result, last year's model of TV or hi-fi is often simply dumped.

To buy household goods in Tokyo for next to nothing, pay a visit to the regular Saturday Salvation Army jumble sale in Nakano. Just get to Nakano Fujimicho Station on the Marunouchi line west of Shinjuku around 9 am, and follow the stream of *gaijin*. Everything from *futon* to fridges is available at giveaway prices. If you don't see the style you like, go back the following week when much of the stock will have changed.

Another source of cheap household goods is departing *gaijin*. They advertise in magazines like *Tokyo Journal* and *Kansai Time Out*, and in the Sunday edition of the *Daily Yomiuri*. Noticeboards in language schools are another good bet for this, and you can put up your own notice, listing what you require. There are also noticeboards in international supermarkets. Notices are often headed '*Sayōnara* Sale'.

Finally, there are second-hand shops in most neighbourhoods of larger cities. There are general junk shops, selling everything under the sun, and also more specialized shops, often run by a person who repairs or reconditions electrical equipment.

Rubbish collection. Depending on where you live, household rubbish (*gomi*) may have to be sorted into three types. Burnable rubbish (*moeru gomi*), unburnable rubbish (*moenai gomi*) and bulky rubbish (*sodai gomi*) are collected by the local authorities on different days. You can find out the days from your *fudosan-ya*, a neighbour, or just by observation. In addition, paper may be collected privately by a person in a van, who will give you toilet paper in exchange. He will drive around the locality making announcements through a microphone against the noise of background music. You will hear his cry, '*Furuzasshi, furushimbun chirigami to kōkan itashimasu!*' ('Recycled tissue paper in exchange for your old magazines and newspapers!').

Private telephone. In order to obtain a private phone, you will need to pay a deposit to the phone company of about ¥75 000, some of which you will recoup through selling your phone back to the phone company, or to someone else. You can also buy one from someone who is moving or selling theirs. Your employer may be willing to lend the deposit to you, and you can return it at the end of your stay, when you relinquish your phone.

Below are some useful phrases for the telephone. You may find it helpful to take a copy of the panel and keep it by your phone.

Telephone phrases	
Hello?	*Moshi moshi?*
Can I speak to Mr/Mrs/Ms Saito?	*Saito-san irasshaimasu-ka?*
S/he's not here	*(Chotto) imasen*
I'll call back later/tomorrow	*Ato de/ashita denwa shimasu*
What time will s/he be back	*Nan-ji ni kaerimasu ka?*
I see (ordinary intonation)	*A so desu ka?*
Is that right? (questioning intonation)	*A so desu ka?*

In addition to the government-owned company, KDD, there are private companies which handle international calls. These companies, which are cheaper than KDD, advertise in the English-language magazines.

Cooking. Home cooking is limited by the fact that you generally have only a two-ring gas stove. Although you will have all the ingredients available to cook Japanese-style, most *gaijin* cook the food they are used to, and eat Japanese food when they eat out. Grilled fish, noodle dishes and rice dishes are, however, Japanese meals which are easy, cheap and quick to prepare at home.

Holiday or travel accommodation

When you take to the road, you can choose from several kinds of accommodation, each with its own character and advantages.

Minshuku. A *minshuku* is a traditional Japanese inn. For around ¥6000, you get dinner, breakfast, and a *futon* in a *tatami* room. These are delightful places to stay in. They are usually run by a family, as in the British bed and breakfast system. The proprietors usually have no English. Breakfast is often prepared the night before, and served cold, except for the rice and *miso* soup. Cold Japanese food may not seem surprising, but watch out for an egg fried in Western-style – but stone cold! It's also useful to know that if the egg is in its shell it will be raw, not boiled. Meals are either brought to your room or shared with the family and other guests. There will probably be a *yukata* (light cotton *kimono*) in your room. You should wear this to the bath and you can sleep in it. It is also sometimes worn by Japanese strolling around the village, especially at hot spring resorts.

Ryokan. A *ryokan* is an upmarket *minshuku*, too expensive to stay in regularly (around ¥10 000), but a great place to treat yourself occasionally.

Youth hostels. These are cheap (¥1800–2500, no meals). Accommodation is dormitory-style, either bunks or *tatami*. Tatami is more pleasant – however, the management may not put a limit on the number of bodies in your room, so it can get a mite crowded. If it is quiet, on the other hand, you have the room to yourself. Cooking facilities are usually available. There is often a noticeboard with local information, and the other residents tend to be independent travellers, and good sources of where to go and what to do. If you do not have an International YHA card, you can obtain one from the national headquarters in Tokyo. Details of the headquarters, and other youth hostels throughout the country are in the *Youth Hostel Map of Japan*, available from the Japan National Tourist Organization (JNTO) in Japan and its offices in other countries.

Temples. A certain number of Buddhist temples are open to travellers. Staying at these may involve participating in the routine (eg getting up at 5 am), so temples might be best for those who have an interest in experiencing the *zen* way of life. The food is unique – traditional Japanese vegetarian (*shōjin ryōri*).

Pensions. These are more modern cheap hotels in the countryside. They are often found in skiing areas. Prices are slightly higher than in *minshuku* – ¥7000–8000.

Breakfast. Often the best place to sample traditional Japanese food is in a *minshuku* or *ryokan*. A traditional breakfast includes rice, raw egg and lengths of crisp seaweed (*nori*), fish, *miso* soup, pickled vegetables and green tea. The method of picking up rice wrapped in *nori* is elegant, and not as difficult as it looks (or sounds):

- Crack the egg into the bowl provided, and whisk it up, using your chopsticks.
- Pour soy sauce (*shōyu*) into the egg and whisk again. Mix this with the rice, so that the egg cooks in the heat of the rice.
- Open the packet of *nori* and take one piece; dip it into the *shōyu* briefly to soften it slightly.
- Lay the *nori* on top of the rice.
- Holding your chopsticks in the normal way, put the chopsticks on the *nori*, close to (but not right at) the ends.
- Push down and in, forming a cylinder of *nori* filled with rice. Lift it up and eat it.

EATING

The greatest overall difference in the constituent parts of the Japanese and Western diets is that the Japanese traditionally obtain most of their protein from fish as opposed to meat, and their carbohydrate from rice and pasta as opposed to potatoes or bread. However, more and more meat, potatoes and bread are now entering the Japanese diet – which is possibly less healthy in consequence.

Presentation is extremely important with Japanese food, especially in formal situations. Vegetables are cut up artistically, and the food is carefully arranged on the plate.

There is a wide variety of Japanese cuisines available (see Appendix 8 for a glossary of food and drink names). Traditional ingredients are rice and various types of seafood and soya products. As well as fish (natural and processed in different ways) and shellfish, several kinds of seaweed are commonly eaten – *nori* is dried, *wakame* is in its natural state and *kombu* can be either. Squid and octopus are commonly eaten. From the soya bean comes not only soy sauce (*shōyu*), but also beancurd (*tōfu*); paste used for soup (*miso*); fermented soya beans (*nattō*), a little strong for some tastes; and fresh beans boiled in their pods (*eda mame*). Typical vegetables are *daikon* (a kind of radish) and *satsumaimo* (sweet potato).

The basic Japanese condiments are a sweet wine, somewhat like sherry (*mirin*), soy sauce, rice wine (*sake*), salt (*shio*) and sugar (*satō*).

Japanese food contains high quantities of salt, and this is often added during the cooking. Two ways to cut down are by reducing the amount of soy sauce you add to your food, and by cutting back on the pickles.

Chopsticks and etiquette

There are three kinds of chopsticks (*hashi*) in Japan. The most common are disposable chopsticks (*waribashi*). These come still joined together at the thick end, and must be broken apart. These chopsticks are light, small, and it is easy to grip food with them as they are made from rough, untreated wood. The other two kinds are less easy to use. Chinese restaurants have chopsticks with which you are probably more familiar – longer and made of plastic. Finally, expensive Japanese restaurants have small pointed lacquered chopsticks, which can be exquisitely frustrating to use.

Holding chopsticks

Place one chopstick down between your thumb and forefinger, and hold it firm against the first joint of your ring finger. This chopstick should not move. Hold the other one like a pen, opening and closing it against the lower one. It is a good idea to get in some practice with chopsticks before you leave for Japan. Practise while you watch TV, with a bowl of small food items, such as garden peas or nuts.

Etiquette

Use a chopstick rest if one is provided. Do not leave chopsticks stuck upright in a bowl of rice (this is what is done at a funeral). If taking food from a communal dish, you should use the other (thicker) end of your chopsticks (though in fact many Japanese do not do this). It is also considered bad manners to suck your chopsticks.

When you arrive at a bar or restaurant, you are given a wet towel (*oshibori*) to wipe your hands. Some people also wipe their face with it, but this is not really good manners. The *oshibori* is hot in winter and cold in summer.

Two important eating phrases are *itadakimasu* (bon appétit) which everyone says before meals, and *gochisōsama (deshita)* when you finish a meal and when you leave. These phrases are used whether eating in a restaurant or a private house. To remember which is which, focus on the first syllable of each: '*it'adakimasu* is when you eat, and '*go' chisōsama* is when you go.

There is not usually any special order to a Japanese meal in terms of courses. Just take bits of everything as you like.

Noodles, which are usually served in a soup, are eaten with appreciative slurps. (It can take a bit of practice to stop yourself breathing in noodles or soup.)

Restaurants – general information

One pleasant surprise to many newcomers to Japan is the wide variety of food and colossal number of restaurants. It has been said that Japan has more restaurants per head than any other country, and it is easy to believe this when you walk along any street. Restaurants tend to specialize in one particular type of cooking, and within a few hundred yards you can come across a dozen different restaurants, for *sushi, tempura, yakitori*, noodles, Chinese food, European-style food, as well as bars serving substantial snacks.

There is a high degree of standardization in the preparation of food. *Donburi* or *karē raisu* (curry rice) are prepared in almost identical fashion throughout the country. Wax replicas of meals which are available in a particular restaurant are often placed in the window. This means that you know exactly what you will receive, and also that if you have trouble communicating, you can as a last resort drag the waiter outside and point.

Almost all restaurants provide free water or Japanese tea (*chā*) with your meal. Refills are also free.

Coffee shops (*kissaten*) and modern or Western restaurants will have knives and forks. However, traditional restaurants and bars serving snacks (*aka chōchin*) may have only chopsticks.

Many small traditional restaurants and bars have a small curtain on a bamboo stick (*noren*), which is hung outside the establishment above the entrance to indicate that it is open.

Most Japanese workers take a strict 12–1 lunch hour, and long queues can develop in restaurants at this time. Have your lunch before 12 or after 1 if at all possible.

How to pay. Some cheap restaurants have a ticket system, and you buy a ticket as you enter. More usually, you pay when you have finished. You should ask for the bill (*okanjō*) and then pay the waiter or, more usually, at the cash desk. There is no need to tip.

Eating out cheaply

In a country with such a high cost of living, you can, with a little care, eat well for a very reasonable outlay.

At lunchtime, many restaurants serve the same high quality of food as in the evening, but at greatly reduced prices. These lunchtime specials are known as *teishoku* or *setto* (the Japanese pronunciation of 'set'). A standard meal consists of a bowl of rice, a bowl of miso soup, a main dish, and a few pickles. A more Western-style meal will serve rice on a separate plate at the same time as the main dish.

Often an easy way to find a restaurant which does *teishoku* is to look for a temporary board outside with the set meals on it, usually written by hand. You do not need to be able to read the writing, just look at the price – if it is between ¥500 and ¥1000, it's OK. Expensive restaurants in particular, such as *sushi* bars and authentic Western restaurants (eg real Italian, as opposed to a Japanified pizza and spaghetti place), offer very substantial lunchtime price-cuts. In some restaurants (such as those in department stores), *teishoku* may be available throughout the day.

There is a set breakfast in most coffee shops called a *morning set*. For the price of a cup of coffee (around ¥400), you get coffee, an egg, and a thick slice of toast with butter and jam.

Department stores

You will not be able to walk through the food floor of a department store (*depāto*) without being offered at least a few titbits. This is a handy way to keep the edge off your appetite until you have finished shopping. In addition to the free samples on the food floor, *depāto* have a floor or part of a floor given over to restaurants, usually in the basement or on the top floor, and these serve *teishoku* at reasonable prices all day. The food tends to be fairly standard Westernized, and may be a safer bet if you are not feeling adventurous. Many shopping centres and large office buildings have similar restaurant floors, and are open to the public.

Fast food

Many of the US chains you already know and love are now in Japan, and prices are much the same as in the West. Note that eating on the street is much less acceptable than in other countries, and that most customers who buy *takeout* food either take the food to their home or office to consume, or eat it right outside the restaurant, where bins are provided.

Cheap restaurants

Soba shops (soba ya). These are the cheapest and fastest places to fill up in Japan. For under ¥500, you can have *soba* (tasty wholemeal buckwheat noodles) in soup, with, for ¥100 or so more, a topping of your choice – *tempura* prawn, egg, etc. These places also serve various kinds of *donburi* – a bowl of rice topped with meat, fish or vegetables, and sometimes mixed with egg. Basic *donburi* is with an egg-based topping; *katsudon* is batter-fried pork with egg; *tendon* is with *tempura* prawn; and *oyakodon* is with chicken. The restaurant may have tables, but customers often eat standing or on stools at a counter.

Tonkatsu-ya. These specialize in a simple fried main dish, with rice and salad (chopped cabbage), and a sweet Worcester sauce and mayonnaise. The hot dish can be batter-fried pork cutlet (*tonkatsu*), potato croquet (*korokke*), or some other fried (*furai*) dish.

Chinese (Chūka ryōri). These are Japanese-run Chinese restaurants, mostly with a fairly restricted range of popular dishes, a variety of noodle (*rāmen*) dishes, which consist of *rāmen* in soup with toppings such as pork, meat dumplings (*gyōza*), or fried rice (*chā-han*). Prices are ¥800–¥1000.

Revolving sushi (kaitenzushi). These are the places to go if you want *sushi* in the evenings, and do not want to pay the earth. The chefs stand in the middle of the restaurant making *sushi* and putting it on a circular conveyor belt which goes round them. Customers sit at the belt, and take plates one by one until they have had enough. Each plate contains two pieces of sushi, and there is a two-tier price system, (usually ¥150 and ¥200), with *sushi* on the fancier plates being more expensive. You help yourself to free Japanese tea, or you can buy beer. When you have finished, you take your empty plates to the cash register by the door. You will probably have to be in Japan at least a year before your palate will be able truly to appreciate the difference between *sushi* in this kind of place and in a real *sushi-ya*, but you will certainly notice the difference in your pocket. The busier a place is the better, as the *sushi* on the plates will be fresher.

Okonomi-yaki restaurants. These are more common in west Japan, especially around Kyoto, but exist in other parts as well. *Okonomi-yaki* is a kind of filled savoury pancake which you make yourself on a hotplate on your table, using your own choice of ingredients which the waiter or waitress brings. It usually has a mixture of cabbage with a choice of different kinds of meat or fish. Once cooked, it is sprinkled with dried bonito flakes and dried seaweed as desired, and topped with a thick sweet or savoury sauce. It is usually eaten direct from the hotplate with a small metal shovel. This is good fun with a group of people, and costs ¥600–1000 per person.

Yakitori restaurants. *Yakitori* is a kind of small chicken kebab. *Yakitori* restaurants are usually small, and near stations. You can make a choice of plain chicken, chicken skin, liver, heart, etc, to have on your stick, which is often served with onion and dipped into soy sauce. Around ¥100 a stick.

Kissaten. These are coffee shops which do a range of Western-style food, such as fried rice (*pilafu*), rice with curry sauce (*karē raisu*), pork cutlet with curry sauce and rice (*katsu karē*), and omelette filled with rice and chicken (*omu raisu*), sandwiches (*sandoitchi*), hamburgers (*hambāgu*), and spaghetti (*supagetti*). All are around ¥600.

There is sometimes a diatribe in tourist books about the 'extortionately' high cost of a cup of coffee in a Japanese *kissaten*. While the price may be high (around ¥500), what must be taken into account is that you can spend as long as you wish in the very pleasant surroundings of a *kissaten*. Specifically, as an English teacher, you are free to take in a book or a newspaper if you have an hour or two to kill between classes. You can even arrange to teach private students there on a regular basis. If you are not a great coffee lover, you can order a marvellous ice-cream split or sundae for not much more than the price of a cup of coffee.

I had a conversation exchange lesson once a week – one hour's English followed by one hour's *Nihongo*. I lived on the other side of Tokyo from Kyoko, so we met at a station halfway, and had our conversation exchange in a *kissaten*, where we would sit for over two hours, having ordered one coffee each.

Patricia Hourigan (Australia)

Robata-yaki. These are lovely places, where you select the food which you want to eat, and it is grilled (traditionally over charcoal but more commonly on a gas-fired grill), and presented to you at the counter or brought to your table. *Robata-yaki* are more common in Kansai. The price is ¥300–¥500 per item.

Oden. If you are heading home late in the evening and are still feeling a little peckish, you can stop off at a late-night *oden* stall. *Oden* is a stew or filled soup, with vegetables and various kinds of vegetable and fish cake. It can be an acquired taste for foreigners, but after an evening's drinking your palate might not be too discerning, and it is very cheap – around ¥500.

Eating in bars. A great way to eat in the evening in a pleasant and relaxing environment is in a bar. However, the word *bar* is usually reserved for expensive establishments with hostesses. Ordinary bars are called *nomi-ya* (literally 'drinking place') and can often be recognized by red lanterns (*aka chōchin*) hanging outside. *Nomi-ya* usually do not have menus – the dishes available are written on strips of paper hanging down at the top of the walls – often as many as 30 or 40 in a bar. Small local *aka chōchin* may have only one barman who cooks all the dishes and serves all the drink at the same time, while keeping up a steady stream of banter with customers! In the absence of an English menu, perhaps the best approach is to have a basic repertoire of dishes, and to expand this by pointing when you see another customer who is eating something which looks appetizing. Most dishes are under ¥600, so even if you do not like something, you will not be too much out of pocket. Here is a short list to get you started:

Yakitori	Small chicken kebabs
Niku jyaga	Irish stew (If you say 'Mick Jagger' with a Japanese accent, your pronounciation will probably be close enough)
Potato furai	French fries
Eda mame	Fresh soya beans, which look like peas in a pod, boiled and salted, and eaten cold
Tori no karāge	Fried chicken
Udōfu	Boiled *tōfu*
Atsuage	Fried *tōfu*
Yaki nasu	Grilled aubergine
Yaki onigiri	Grilled rice balls
Yaki sakana	Grilled fish in season

All *aka chōchin* do a range of fish (*sakana*) dishes. These may include mackerel (*saba*); sardine (*iwashi*); herring (*nishin*); or whitebait (*shishamo*). Larger fish are often not boned, and can be tricky to manoeuvre with chopsticks.

The big bill

One worry which some people have about eating in Japan, where they can neither speak the language nor read the script, is that they will end up ordering a meal, only to be presented with a huge bill at the end of it. On the whole, this fear is baseless. The Japanese are so scrupulously honest that your chances of being ripped off are minimal (one exception is certain bars, more of which on p 55).

While there certainly are very traditional restaurants with prices far above those in day-to-day eating establishments, these are not places you might wander into accidentally. Such restaurants are usually not laid out like normal restaurants; there are usually no menus; the waitresses wear expensive *kimono*; and the places have the air of a private club or even a traditional upper-class house rather than a restaurant. The only time you are likely to enter this rarified atmosphere is if you are taken there as a treat by a Japanese friend, or for a celebration meal by your school or company. And in those situations you will not even get to see a menu or a bill, never mind worry about the prices. (Do not even discuss prices in such circumstances – it would offend your host.)

Other Japanese specialities

The following are some other kinds of Japanese food. For each, there are specialist restaurants.

Sushi is a small rectangle or circle of cold vinegared rice, a smear of *wasabi* (green horseradish) paste, topped with a variety of things, such as raw fish or omelette. (Fortunately, it tastes much better than it sounds.) Pick up a piece (many Japanese use their hands, although chopsticks are more usual), dip it in your little saucer of soy sauce (*shōyu*) and pop the whole piece into your mouth. When you have finished one piece, take a tiny piece of pink sliced pickled ginger (*gari*) to clear your palate, and start again. *Sushi* is surprisingly non-fishy in taste and smell, and has a taste which is so subtle you might wonder at first what the fuss is about. It takes most *gaijin* a while before they can begin to distinguish the tastes of various kinds of fish, but hang on in there, because once you have developed a palate for *sushi*, you will not be able to eat it often enough.

Sashimi is raw fish. It is served on a small wooden board or in a bowl on a bed of shredded white radish (*daikon*) with a green leaf and with a small portion of green horseradish paste (*wasabi*) at the side. Put some of the *wasabi* into your saucer of *shōyu* and mix it in with your chopsticks (it is very hot so be careful not to overdo it) and then dip the fish into this before eating it.

Sushi and *sashimi* are served in *sushi-ya* (sushi bars). You sit at a bar, with the fresh ingredients in a refrigerated glass case in front of you, and point to what you would like. You can order a mixture on one wooden board or, more normally, the same kind, when you will be given two pieces at a time. Japanese tea is served, or you can order alcohol.

Sukiyaki is beef fried at your table with a mixture of vegetables in a rich *shōyu* and *sake* sauce. The dish is well known abroad and in Japan is commonly eaten at home with the whole family. It is less common in restaurants and can be very expensive, due to the high cost of beef. *Shabu-shabu* is a similar dish to *sukiyaki*, but it is not as sweet and the beef and vegetables are cooked in boiling water.

Tempura. There are a few special *tempura* (fish or vegetables fried in batter) restaurants, but typically it is part of a meal in other kinds of restaurant. Dip the *tempura* in your bowl of sauce (*dashyiru*) before eating.

Confectionery and snacks

Most traditional Japanese confectionery uses *azuki* beans in the form of a sweet paste, or a jelly made from the vegetable *konnyaku*. Both can be rather an acquired taste (they are very sweet). Japanese people also tend to be very fond of Western confectionery – especially chocolate and cookies. French pastries and fresh cakes are popular.

Sembei are sweet or savoury varieties of rice crackers or rice snacks.

Dried fish is often provided as an accompaniment to drinks – there are numerous varieties of this.

DRINKING

There are three kinds of drinking establishments – ordinary bars, where you just pay for what you consume; hostess bars, where male customers pay a substantial amount for the attentions of a hostess, which may be only filling customers' glasses and lighting their cigarettes; and a variety of places, more or less Westernized, which are somewhere in between. You will probably normally go to ordinary bars, rather less often into places in the mid-price range, and male teachers may occasionally be taken as a guest to hostess bars.

The three types are easy to distinguish from the outside, and even more so once you enter, so the danger of being stuck with a huge bill for one drink and a plate of nuts is remote in the extreme. The golden rule is: if women are sitting with the customers, pouring their drinks and talking to them, it is an expensive place. This warning does not, of course, apply to establishments with waitresses who do what waitresses normally do – serve and leave. Terminology for drinking establishments is not exact – the words *snack*, *pub*, *bar* and *club* are each used to describe a variety of places, which may be very similar to each other.

Cheap

Ordinary bars are called *nomi-ya* ('drinking place'), *aka chōchin* ('red lantern'), or *izaka-ya* ('*sake* place'). These are cheap and cheerful places, loud and welcoming, and casual. They are often traditional and rural in style, and easily recognizable by the red lanterns and *noren* (small curtain over the doorway) outside. There is often a loud cry of *Irasshai (mase)!* ('Welcome!') as you walk through the door (usually a sliding door). There is rarely a hand-held menu – the names of dishes are written on strips of paper hanging down from the ceiling. The clientele is often mixed in age and social background, but is almost all male.

In summer, there are *beer gardens* on top of department stores and other buildings. These charge prices in the *aka chōchin* range.

Medium-priced

Establishments in the mid-price range tend to have brightly lit exteriors and signs. Both outside and in, they are more modern and Western-looking than *nomi-ya*. They usually do a much more restricted range of foods, and are a little (say 20%–30%) more expensive than *nomi-ya*.

There is a bewildering variety of places, such as rock-bars or café-bars, which come into this middle category, and more appear every year. In general, they cater mainly to younger clientele. Japanese women are much more likely to go to these kinds of places than to somewhere at the top or bottom of the price range.

One of the more traditional kinds of bar in this middle area is a *snack*, which often has a lady owner (*mama-san*) who pours the drinks and chats to the clients. These places are not nearly as expensive as hostess bars, and the atmosphere is usually more relaxed and appealing to the average *gaijin*. However, smaller places like this (and even very small *aka chōchin*) have a small and regular clientele, and usually new customers are introduced by regulars. In addition, as noted above, terminology is not exact, and some *snacks* are expensive.

Expensive

Hostess bars do not usually try to look welcoming from the outside. They have a quieter, almost subdued atmosphere, and cater mainly to regular clients, almost all businessmen (*sararī-man*), and have hostesses to pour drinks, light cigarettes, flatter the clients, and make, or respond to, mildly suggestive remarks. Bills seem excessive to Westerners, since you are paying for the hostesses' time. As a rule, the atmosphere in these places does not appeal enough to foreigners for them to want to pay the steepish prices. Male teachers will probably be taken to them often enough by their students, and in that case there is usually no question of having to pay. In practice, most hostess bars will not welcome a strange *gaijin*.

The other expensive places to avoid are those with a sharply dressed caller outside. Such places will welcome any mug off the street, and will happily try to take you to the cleaners (exactly as would happen in equivalent establishments in other countries). The general name for this kind of place is a *kyabarē* ('cabaret'), and a *kyabarē* is usually some variety of strip joint where you can drop a lot of money in a very short time.,

Drinking customs

It is impolite to allow someone to fill their own glass. Wait to have yours filled by someone in the company, and take the bottle from them in order to fill their glass. He or she may try to prevent you from doing this, but in the end will probably relent gratefully. Toast for the first drink, even on informal occasions. Wait until everybody has a full glass, and say *kampai* ('cheers') and touch glasses.

Many Japanese people need less alcohol to become drunk than Westerners (something to do with their enzymes, apparently). After a small glass of beer, they may become red of eye and face. One advantage of this is that a *sararīman* can be rip-roaring drunk at midnight, and be sitting soberly, and apparently hangoverless, on the next morning's train at 7.30 am. If you want to talk about your hangover, the word is *futsuka-yoi* ('second-day drunk').

Being drunk is a licence for many kinds of antisocial behaviour. Almost all social excesses, and on occasion some crimes, can be excused by saying 'I was drunk at the time'. Japanese people may pretend to be drunker than they are in order to take advantage of the licence, for example to criticize their employer.

Bar bills are settled when leaving. The word for splitting a bill among members of a group is *warikan*.

'*Ikki!*' is shouted to encourage someone to drink a glass down in one. It is commonly heard among students, and even spirits such as *shōchū* are tossed back in this fashion, causing alcohol poisoning and the occasional fatality.

There is a great deal of social pressure to drink alcohol. If you do not like drinking alcohol, it may be easier to refuse if you use an excuse, such as religious or medical grounds.

Drinking options

The four principal forms of alcohol drunk in Japan are beer (*biru*), whisky (*uiskī*), *shōchū* and *sake*, with much more consumed of the first two than the last two.

Beer. The beer is almost all lager. The main brands, *Kirin*, *Asahi*, *Sapporo*, and *Suntory*, are all much of a muchness as regards taste. *Yebisu* is less common, better than the others, and a bit of a cult beer with some *gaijin*. In large cities, a few bars, mostly imitation *bier kellars*, sell *Black Beer*, a kind of stout, as well as lager.

Beer is usually sold in bottles. One bottle is *ippon*, two is *nihon*. If it is on draft, a large glass is a *dai jockey*, and a medium is a *chū jockey*.

Whisky. Not much whisky is drunk in ordinary bars. However, if you are taken to a more upmarket bar, such as a *snack*, by a *sararīman*, you will find most of the clients drinking whisky with ice and a lot of water (*mizu warē*). *Suntory* is the most popular brand of domestic whisky, but imported whisky – bourbon and scotch – is becoming more common as import duties have fallen, and carries more prestige. The system of purchase is usually *bottle keep*, where you pay for a bottle and, if you do not finish it, it is kept behind the bar for your next visit. Next time you just pay for the ice and any snacks you consume, and, of course, the hostesses' time.

Shōchū. This is a clear vodka-like spirit, distilled from anything distillable. It is not very palatable neat, but is now fashionably and commonly drunk in large glasses diluted with fruit juice and ice. The most popular concoction is a highball with lemon juice (*chū hai*). *Shōchū* is most popular with students, though in the hot summer almost everybody will have some.

Sake. This is much less popular now than it was twenty or thirty years ago. *Sake* (rice wine) has rather a dated image – and in the main you will see it drunk by older people, and away from the cities. Usually drunk warm, it is most enjoyable in winter, to warm you up on a cold night. It is served in small china vessels, and poured into tiny cups, all in traditional Japanese pottery. It is occasionally drunk cold, especially in summer, from small cedar-wood boxes – drink out of one corner of the box.

TRANSPORT

Public transport in Japan is efficient and clean. Using it in cities is usually faster than going by car, because roads are crowded and parking difficult. All public transport can get very crowded, and if at all possible, avoid the morning rush hour from 7 am to 9 am. The evening traffic is more staggered, since so many Japanese work late, or go drinking after work. The peak is from 5 pm to 7 pm. The last trains can also be very crowded, full of people going home after an evening's drinking, but drunken brawls, or un-pleasantness of any kind (apart from the occasional regurgitation of excess alcohol) is extremely rare. People wait in orderly lines on station platforms which are usually marked to show where the doors will open. In the rush hour, station staff wearing white gloves give protruding bodies a push so that the doors can close.

Trains

Trains (*densha*) are fast, regular, and always on time. Trains and subways (*chikatetsu*) can be either public or private.

Private lines are more common on popular routes in well populated areas. As such, they tend to run for short, often commuter distances, although they sometimes extend to resort areas. They are also common linking the large cities in Kansai. They are cheaper than public lines. Many private lines are owned by companies who also own the principal department stores, and the lines run into the city and terminate in the basement of the *depāto*. One-stop shopping with a vengeance!

The national rail network is Japan Railways (JR). Several years ago JR was divided into a number of smaller, regional companies. However, as a traveller this will not affect you, because you can buy one ticket through several regions.

The various kinds of train, going from fastest to slowest, are:

- *Shinkansen* (bullet train)
- *Tokkyū* (super express)

- *Kyūkō* (ordinary express)
- *Shinkaisoku* (extra rapid)
- *Kaisoku* (rapid)
- *Futsū ressha* (ordinary stopping train)

For the first three trains listed above, a supplement is charged, depending on the type of train, distance travelled, and class.

Tickets

For local travel, whether by public or private networks, almost all ticketing matters are handled by machines. Change is given, tickets sold, and even discrepancies at the other end are handled by machines. Prices start at ¥140. You may be able to use one ticket to travel between networks, or you may have to buy a separate ticket when you change (*norikaerimasu*) to a different company's line.

When you buy a ticket from a machine, you will see a large area railway map above it with a price displayed by each station. You will soon get to know the shape of your local map, and even with the station names displayed only in *kanji*, you should be able to locate the station you require and so find the price. If you cannot work out the correct fare, just buy the minimum ticket and pay the balance at the other end.

There are two kinds of tickets you can buy for your regular routes:

- *Teikiken.* This is a season ticket, which can be for one month, three months or six months. It offers savings even if used only twice a day for commuting, and of course it can be used as often as you like in addition to that. If you travel outside your *teiki* route, pay the difference at the other end.
- *Kaisūken.* This is a strip of eleven tickets for the price of ten. It is useful for places you visit on less than a daily basis. One ticket is valid for a fixed-length journey from any station on a line owned by that railway company.

For longer-distance journeys, carriages are divided into two classes: first (*greensha* – signified by a *green car*) and ordinary. These are found only on the *shinkansen* and on most of the *tokkyū* and *kyūkō* trains. When you travel by *greensha* you must buy a special ticket. If you travel by express train, you also have to pay an additional charge. Limited express tickets for specific trains, seat reservations and berth tickets for overnight trains are sold from about one month before departure and can be bought from the station or a travel agent.

All tickets must be kept until you have reached your destination.

Information

Each station's name is clearly displayed on the platform, together with names of the previous and next station. The names are usually in *kanji, hiragana* and romanized script (*romaji*). Many of the larger railway stations in Japan have English signs (such as 'exit').

You will have plenty of opportunities to practise listening to *Nihongo* when you travel by train. Announcements will be made telling you 'The next train will be . . . '; 'Stand back'; 'The doors are about to close'; 'The next station is . . . '; 'Don't leave anything behind'.

For information on distance travel, consult the master railway timetable (*Jikokuhyō*) at any JR station. It is entirely in Japanese characters, but all routes are numbered, and it is easy enough to use even if you cannot read any Japanese. From the Japan National Tourist Office (JNTO) you can obtain the Japan Travel Bureau's mini timetable and *The Tourist's Handbook*, both of which are useful.

When you leave a station, make a note of the exit for your return journey. There may be a dozen or more exits in one station. There is often a map of the area at the exit. Japanese often do not stick to the convention of north being at the top of the map, which can take a little getting used to.

There is an annual spring rail strike. It is pretty much a formality, short-lived, and causes little disruption. Many Japanese regard it as one or two days off work.

Trains stop running around midnight, or a little later in the major cities.

Buses

In cities, with traffic so heavy, buses (*basu*) are most useful for short trips, such as getting to and from stations. Only away from heavily built-up areas can buses travel any distance in a reasonable time. Pay as you enter on buses boarded at the front. On buses boarded at the back, collect a ticket as you board, and pay as you get off according to the display at the front. *Kaisūken* and *teikiken* are available, as for trains, and obtainable at the bus ticket office at the terminus or main stops. Announcements (taped) on buses include not only the name of each stop, but also advertising for local shops. Bus fares are similar to those for trains, starting at around ¥150.

Long-distance buses are a cheap, though not very comfortable way to travel distances. They are the cheapest way to get to skiing areas.

Taxis

All taxis have automatic doors, which are opened and closed by the driver. Minimum charge is ¥650, although this differs slightly from city to city and with the size of the car. From 11 pm to 5 am, there is a 30% surcharge. If you miss the last train, you could share the cost of a taxi by travelling with someone who lives on your route.

> I got into a taxi, and the driver turned round with his thumb in his mouth, glaring at me. I had closed my door, not realizing it was controlled by the driver, and the mechanism had jarred his thumb.
>
> *Carol Lemar, Australia*

Taxis have a sign with their company name on the roof, which is lit when the taxi is free. Taxis can be waved down on the street, or, at busy times, you may have to wait at a taxi stand.

Taxi drivers have the same difficulties with the idiosyncratic address system as everyone else. If you cannot give precise instructions, the driver may stop at a police box (*kōban*) for directions.

Bicycles

These, like buses, are useful mainly for getting to and from stations. All stations in Japan have a bicycle (*jitensha*) parking area. Bicycles are ridden on the pavement, and both as pedestrian and cyclist you will have to learn to take care, although cyclists constantly use their bells in warning.

Boat and ferry

Travelling by ferry can make a change from the train. Ferries are often less crowded, and you get to see a horizon, which can be a rare sight in hilly and crowded Japan. However, they can be slow, and unless you use them overnight you may not have the time to spare. The cheapest tickets are *tatami* class, where you sleep in a large room with Japanese families spread out all over the *tatami*. This is a marvellous way to be with Japanese people relaxing. One bonus of travelling by ferry is that the heating in the bath is switched on at the beginning of the journey, and you can have the whole bath to yourself as the temperature goes from *gaijin* tepid to *nihonjin* thermidor. It can be quite exciting, because as the boat rocks and rolls waves are created in the bath.

The following are some recommended inter-island ferry journeys, which are more pleasant and less taxing than their overland equivalents:

- from Maizuru north of Kyoto to Otaru in Hokkaido;
- from Tokyo to Tokushima in Shikoku;
- from Higashi-Kobe to Kokura in Kyushu.

Tokyo has a number of local ferries which run along the Sumida River and across Tokyo Bay. It is possible, for example to board at Asakusa in the north of the city, and travel the length of the city, trying to recognize the bridges, down to the beautiful Hama Rikyu Gardens, one of Tokyo's loveliest and most spacious parks.

Driving

For you, driving in Japan will probably be in a rented car, unless you live away from the cities or in Hokkaido. It is very slow travelling around town by car, and parking is prohibitively expensive – there is effectively no free parking in Japan, and you must produce a receipt for a permanent parking place before you are permitted to buy a car in built-up areas.

Even outside cities, roads are usually narrow and crowded, and overtaking is difficult. People tend to drive defensively – for example, if somebody pulls out of a side road, drivers on the main road are expected to give way. Some Japanese drivers habitually drive in a higher gear than appropriate for the speed, which can be irritating if you are a passenger.

If you do live in an area where it is worth having a car, you will be able to buy a used car cheaply. It is not uncommon to be offered a car at a giveaway price by somebody who is buying a new one, or when the *shaken* is due. Every two years, cars are liable to pay *shaken*, a combination of registration, road tax, vehicle roadworthiness inspection and insurance, which can be expensive.

Motorways (*kōsoku-dōro*) are toll-roads. There are automatic flash cameras to catch speeders located strategically and visibly along the roads. The speed limit is typically 100 km/hr, but it can be lower.

It is quite rare to find roundabouts in Japan, but traffic lights are everywhere. Green traffic lights are referred to as *aoi* (blue), although they look green to *gaijin*.

Driving is on the left.

Car rental

It is very easy to rent a car in Japan. Companies such as Nippon Rentacar and Hertz are usually situated near railway stations.

Although office staff will probably have no English, they should have pictures of the types of cars available and tables of rates, so communication is no great problem. As in other countries, they will need a deposit and a copy of your driving licence. They may require a Japanese driving licence, but an international one is normally acceptable. Special rates are often available at weekends.

Driving licence

If you are in Japan for a year or less, your international driving licence (*unten menkyo*) should suffice. However, it is relatively easy to obtain a Japanese driving licence. First, your licence must be officially translated into Japanese, which will cost ¥2000, and is obtained by taking your passport, alien registration card, and licence to the nearest office of the Japan Automobile Association (JAF). After that, you need to take the same documents, plus the translation and at least two colour photos of yourself (2.4 cm × 3 cm) to your local licensing centre (*shiken-jo*). They will check your licence and give you an eyesight test, for which you may need the following words:

- *migi* (right)
- *hidari* (left)
- *ue* (above)
- *shita* (below).

The need for these four words will be immediately apparent when you see the special symbols used on the eyesight charts. They look like the letter 'c' in different inversions, and your task is to name the location of the gap.

You should be prepared to spend most of the day at the licensing centre, but each centre does vary slightly in the length of time it takes to issue licences.

Hitching

Hitching is not nearly as common in Japan as in some other countries, and many drivers will not understand the meaning of a raised thumb. However, hitching is by no means impossible, and I have hitch-hiked extensively all over Japan's four main islands.

One difference about hitching in Japan is that not many cars travel long distances. This is mainly because highway tolls are prohibitively expensive. This means that if you want to go any distance in a reasonably short time, you will almost certainly have to use lorries.

Most lorry drivers have very little English and often speak

Japanese with a strong local accent. Coupled with this is the fact that there is often loud engine noise, and communication is all but impossible. On the plus side, lorry drivers are very friendly, and will often go out of their way to get you a connecting lift, perhaps walking from table to table in a truckstop to find someone going your way.

Your chances of getting a long lift in a private car are greater if you are on the road during a public holiday period, such as August. Many city dwellers have country roots, and spend vacations with their relatives in the part of the country where they were born.

Air

Domestic air travel is expensive. Frequent flights connect the major cities, and you can make reservations at the travel agents located throughout the country up to one month before departure. Given the expense, you will probably prefer to use other methods of transport most of the time, but you may, for example, decide to fly to the resort island of Okinawa – the economy return fare would be around ¥68 000 from Tokyo.

For international air travel, travel agents selling discounted tickets advertise in newspapers and magazines. At time of writing, some approximate return air fares are: Hong Kong – ¥66 000; Seoul – ¥44 000; Bangkok – ¥71 000; Singapore – ¥82 000; US West Coast – ¥110 000; Sydney – ¥165 000; and Europe – ¥192 000.

SHOPPING

The Japanese word for a shop is the product sold plus *ya*. So, meat is *niku*, and a butcher's shop is *niku-ya*. *San* is added for the proprietor, so a butcher is *niku-ya-san*.

Department stores (*depāto*) usually open at 10 am and close at 7 pm, and close for one day a week. These are sophisticated and luxurious establishments. As well as all the shopping facilities, they have a floor of restaurants and often a private art gallery and ticket agencies.

Local shops stay open fairly late, till around 8 pm or 9 pm, and, like depāto, are open on Sunday, which is perhaps the busiest shopping day of the week. Some small neighbourhood shopping streets are closed to traffic on Sunday and a Sunday stroll can be an enjoyable affair – displays from local shops spill out onto the streets, and small stalls sell snacks.

Here are some shops which you will probably find in your neighbourhood:

- *All-night store.* There is an all-night store in most neighbourhoods of large cities.
- *Tōfu-ya.* There will be a *tōfu* shop in your area, with *tōfu* made on the premises and sold at giveaway prices.
- *Kusuri-ya or yakkyoku.* A chemist, selling medicines.
- *Kome-ya.* Rice shop – this is the place to buy brown rice (*genmai*), which is otherwise extremely rare, as well as many varieties of white rice (*o-kome*).
- *Yao-ya.* Greengrocer's.
- *Pan-ya.* For bread, cakes, milk, cheese, etc.
- *Niku-ya.* In your local butcher's, chicken and pork will be cheaper than beef.
- *Saka-ya.* Off-licence. Domestic spirits are very cheap. For example, a bottle of gin costs ¥1200.
- *Sakana-ya.* Your local fish shop will stock a wide variety of fish, both for cooking and for eating raw. Japanese fish is so fresh, and the shops are cleaned so well, that fish shops do not have a fishy smell. It is, of course, much cheaper to prepare your own *sushi* or *sashimi* then to buy it in a restaurant. Many Japanese people are in awe of the *sushi* chef's art, but amateurs can make it. *Sushi* rice is just ordinary boiled rice, with a piece of *kombu* seaweed and a dash of vinegar added to water at the start. You can buy powdered *wasabi* (mix it with water like mustard) and *nori* seaweed at your local supermarket. You can imitate the action of your favourite *sushi* chef, and make all the kinds of *sushi*. One tip – keep a bowl of water by you to moisten your hands regularly to prevent the rice sticking to them. This is a great way to spend a Sunday afternoon with friends.
- *Kanamono-ya.* For hardware, soap powder, etc.
- *Hon-ya.* There may be a small shop selling books and magazines in your area, but it is unlikely to stock any English books. Two bookshop chains which sell English books are Maruzen and Kinokuniya. There is also Jena in Tokyo. In addition to general-interest books and books on Japan in English, they have a wide range of up-to-date books for teaching English. Bookshops are larger, more numerous, and have more customers than in the West. It is quite acceptable to browse for as long as you wish in a bookstore.

One further piece of advice on books. English books are fairly expensive, and bookshops do not, of course, have the range of a bookshop in your own country. As a result, there is a small but thriving trade in second-hand English books. Most cities with a sizeable *gaijin* population now have at least one used-book store. Here are some:

    The Bookworm, 550–8 Kaitori, Tama-shi, Tokyo 206 (Tel 0423–71–2141).

Juso Academy, 2–6–8 Juso-higashi, Yodogawa-ku, Osaka (Tel 06–303–3538).

Wantage Books, 1–13 Ikuta-cho 1 chome, Chuo-ku, Kobe 651 (Tel 078–232–4517).

Vending machines. Japan has more street vending machines than any other country in the world. You can buy a vast range of items, from beer and food to *manga* (adult comics).

FACILITIES

Public telephones

There is a confusingly wide range of public phones of different colours, all with slightly different facilities. Those not in a booth generally take ¥10 or ¥100 coins only. Phones in booths take a wider range of coins. Phones in green booths take cards, which are available at prices from ¥500 upwards.

Baths

Japanese have enjoyed bathing for hundreds of years. All areas will have a public bath (*sentō*). As well as *sentō*, there are hundreds of natural hot springs (*onsen*) dotted around the country. The routine is the same for *sentō–* and *onsen*:

- Pay at the entrance (around ¥400).
- Remove your clothes, and put them in a basket or locker.
- Hold the mini-towel provided over your private parts, as you make your way into the bathing area.
- Sit on a low stool. Soap, wash, rinse your body – either by pouring basins of water over yourself, or, less commonly, showering.
- Get into the large public bath slowly. The water will be very hot, and the less you disturb it the less it will sting.
- When you cannot bear the heat any more, get out and wash yourself a bit more, or wash a bit you have not washed yet. If you like, wash your hair, or have a shave.
- Repeat soaking and washing as often as you want.
- Get dressed and leave.

A *sentō* is a pleasant place to kill a few hours if you are between classes.

Libraries

There will be a local library in your area, but it is unlikely to have many English books. There are British Council and US libraries in Tokyo and Kyoto (see p 78).

In Tokyo, there is an excellent magazine gallery with an extensive range of magazines from many countries, most of which are unavailable in bookshops. It is situated two blocks behind the *Kabuki-za* theatre in Ginza:

> **World Magazine Gallery**, 3–13–10 Ginza, Chuo Ku (Tel 3545–7227).

Banks and financial matters

There are coins of ¥1, ¥5, ¥10, ¥50, ¥100, and ¥500, and notes of ¥500, ¥1000, ¥5000 and ¥10 000.

Banks are open from 9 am–3 pm, Monday–Friday. Cash-withdrawal machines stay open 8.45 am to 7 pm, but are closed at night and are open from 9 am to 5 pm at weekends – this can be inconvenient in a society which relies mainly on cash. Most financial transactions are in cash. Cheques are rarely used. Credit cards are used in department stores and for large purchases.

Your employer may want to pay your salary in cash, handing you a white envelope each month, or may pay it directly into a bank account. Opening an account is a simple matter. If you have to do business in a bank, you will receive a token once you have stated your business. Sit and read until your transaction is completed and your name is called.

Envelopes are available in banks. If you have to give money over, other than in a shop, put it in an envelope. (For example, your private students will normally hand you their tuition fee in an envelope.)

The traditional way of endorsing a document is with a personal stamp (*hanko*). As a *gaijin*, it is acceptable to sign (*sain*) in the space provided, but as a *hanko* is very small there is usually only room for your initials. If you want your own *hanko*, it can be made up quite quickly.

You can arrange to have your utility bills – gas, electricity, water and telephone – paid directly from your bank account.

Health

Japan has excellent medical facilities. Most doctors will speak some English, and although they may have an extensive English medical vocabulary they may prefer you to write down details of your symptoms, as they will probably have been exposed to English mostly through reading medical journals.

There are several international hospitals in Tokyo with English-speaking personnel, and an outpatient service. Two of them are:

St Luke's International Hospital, *Sei Roka Byoin*, 10–1 Akashi-cho, Chuo-ku, Tokyo (Tel 3541–5151).
International Catholic Hospital, *Seibo Byoin*, 2–5–1 Naka-Ochiai, Shinjuku-ku, Tokyo (Tel 3951–1111).

I strongly advise you to arrive with travel insurance which includes coverage for health expenses. If this runs out before you finalize your employment position, you can always take out more to tide you over. Then it is usually a question finding out whether your employer belongs to a health insurance scheme which you can join at a subsidized cost, or whether you will have to make your own arrangements.

There are three types of health insurance schemes in Japan:

- *Shakai Hoken* (national insurance). This is expensive, as it includes (compulsory) pension contributions. These are not always transferable to a scheme in your own country – they are transferable for US citizens, but are not for UK citizens. *Gaijin* tend to join this scheme only if their company uses it, and is paying their contributions.
- *Kokumin Kenkō Hoken* (health insurance organized through the ward, ie district, not hospital ward, office). This is the most common scheme for *gaijin*. It is less expensive than the state scheme, especially in the first year, since contributions are based on your previous year's income in Japan. However, it could become much more expensive once your earnings are taken into account, and could work out at something like ¥10 000–¥20 000 per month. Generally, you have to cover the first 30% of any costs for treatment out of your own pocket, although the proportion decreases in relation to the seriousness of the illness. A word of warning to anyone thinking of taking this out for a year and then going private: officially, once you are in, you cannot get out. However, it has been done (by failing to re-register for the scheme when changing address).
- *Private*. There are private schemes, some of which are cheaper in the long run than the ward-organized scheme. It is very rare for a private scheme to cover dental costs.

The first two schemes have the advantage of covering all dependants at no extra cost, although obviously a spouse's income would be taken into account when assessing the level of contribution. You are under no obligation to belong to either scheme.

Launderettes

Launderettes are widely available. They are known as *koin rendori* ('coin laundry').

MEDIA, CULTURE AND SPORT

Television and radio

There are two television (*terebi*) channels run by the government broadcasting corporation (NHK), and several independent channels, the number depending on the area. Channel 1 (NHK1) and Channel 3 (NHK2) are the government-run ones. NHK is very similar to the BBC in the UK, in that it is supported by public money, and has no commercials. Specifically, the two channels are similar to BBC1 and BBC2. NHK1 is more popular entertainment, and NHK2 is more cultural. The commercial channels are all fairly similar to each other – a large number of game shows, with a small group of popular personalities who ring the changes as guests and presenters.

Samurai drama are period pieces similar to Westerns with their imposed moral codes and differences from reality. *Family drama* are soap operas, which offer interesting insights into everyday living. Foreign programmes are usually dubbed, but can be undubbed with the help of a bilingual converter. As well as movies, programmes in English tend to be popular US shows made five or more years previously, so you can catch your favourite re-runs of *Starsky and Hutch* and *Hill Street Blues*. News broadcasts in English include CNN and CBS.

Music on the radio (*rajio*) is a mix of Japanese and Western popular and classical. There is one English station – the Far East Network (FEN), broadcast by the US troops.

Newspapers

The Japan Times is the largest English-language newspaper in terms of both number of pages and circulation. This is the only independent newspaper. It has the most extensive classified section – Monday's issue has teaching jobs. Thursday's issue has ads for accommodation, mostly in the high price-bracket.

The other three English-language newspapers are subsidiaries of Japanese-language newspapers. Domestic news consists of translations of stories in the parent papers. Foreign news is often syndicated. *The Mainichi Daily News* is the other main morning paper – much foreign news is syndicated and similar to that in *The Japan Times*. *The Asahi Evening News* is the only evening daily. It is fairly thin. *The Daily Yomiuri* is even more so.

Music

Japan is on the world concert tour itinerary, and most performers – popular and classical – visit the country. Tickets are

¥5000–¥10 000 and sell out quickly. Most department stores have a ticket-agency booth, such as Playguide, Ticket PIA, or Ticket Saison. If you cannot get a ticket in advance, you can obtain one from the touts outside the concert hall. Japanese audiences need little encouragement to start (and keep) clapping along. Fans are dedicated – don't be surprised if the person beside you does not understand the simplest English conversation, but has no difficulty singing along faultlessly to every song in the show.

Discos. For one payment of around ¥4000 for men, ¥3000 for women, you not only get in to boogie, you usually get something to eat and drink. Sometimes there is a buffet, sometimes you are given food coupons and order from a menu, sometimes snacks are just brought to your table. The food is generally Western (pizza, sausages, etc), and usually at no extra cost. The most common system for drinks is that you are given two coupons at the door for cocktails – or sometimes cocktails are free and you need to pay only for beer. The management can afford to do this because domestic spirits are often extremely cheap – volume for volume the cheapest brands of spirits are only a little more expensive than beer.

In the Roppongi area of Tokyo, there are buildings with a disco on each floor. Just get into the elevator, and press any button.

A bar with live music is called a *live house*. Entry is from ¥1000. All standard kinds of modern music (pop, jazz, country, etc) are catered for. Two *live houses* in Tokyo are:

> **Hot Corocket**, (Reggae), Dai-ni Daisho Building, B1F 5–18–2 Roppongi, Minato-ku (Tel 3583–9409). Station – Roppongi.
>
> **Crocodile**, New Sekiguchi Building B1F, 6–18–8 Jingu Mae, Shibuya-ku (Tel 3499–5205). Station – Shibuya.

Japanese music

The best known traditional instruments are:

- *Koto.* A horizontal harp, plucked from a kneeling position.
- *Shamisen.* A banjo-like instrument with three strings, used to accompany popular ballads and in traditional Japanese theatre.
- *Shakuhachi.* A type of wooden flute, rather like a recorder.
- *Biwa.* A kind of lute, shaped like a mandolin.
- Various drums – from normal size to enormous. Examples are *da-daiko*, covered with hide for court ceremonies; *tsuri-daiko*, a hanging drum covered with leather; and *ninai-daiko*, a portable drum which is carried and beaten on a pole.

Traditional Japanese theatre (see below), which normally has a musical accompaniment, is one of the best settings in which to listen to traditional Japanese music.

Cinema and theatre

Cinema

All blockbusters are screened, but there is rather less interest in movies without big stars or mass appeal. Foreign movies are subtitled rather than dubbed. Admission is around ¥1800, but this does not guarantee a seat. To be sure of a seat, you have to pay a supplement for one of the white reserved seats in the middle of the cinema. Every seat for weekend screenings is usually taken, and there is a rush for seats at the end of each performance. Before a performance, most people wait in the foyer. However, to be sure of a seat, some go into the cinema and sit through the end of the movie, or stand at the side to grab a seat as soon as one becomes vacant. If you want to do this, but do not want to know the end of the movie, take your walkman and don't look at the screen. To avoid the rush, go to midweek matinees.

Theatre

There are few large modern theatres in Japan. Cultural institutes such as the British Council put on small productions, and some small modern theatre groups advertise in *gaijin* magazines such as *Tokyo Journal*.

The various forms of traditional Japanese theatre are:

- *Kabuki.* Probably the most accessible, but still a very stylized form of theatre. All parts are played by men (as in Elizabethan England). Actors wear elaborate costumes and make-up. Performances can last for a long time, and it is quite acceptable to wander out for a snack if you get bored or hungry, and then eat it in the theatre. The Kabuki-za Theatre in Tokyo (4–3 Ginza-Higashi, Chuo-ku, Tel 541-3131) provides headsets for tourists with excellent English translation and explanation. It is possible to buy a ticket for only one act (*tachi-mi-seki*), and although this means a seat at the back of the theatre, the view is quite adequate. Kabuki can also be seen at the National Theatre (Kokoritsu Gekijo, 13 Haya busacho, Chiyoda-ku, Tel 255–7411).
- *Noh.* This is one of the world's most stylized and subtle theatre forms. It is static, symbolic and solemn and yet is uniquely graceful and elegant to watch. Movement is very slow and tiny motions transmit emotion and carry immense symbolism.

● *Bunraku.* This is puppet theatre. The distinctive feature of *bunraku* is that the puppeteers manipulating the two-thirds life size puppets are on the stage. They may be dressed in black, and so be symbolically invisible. Bunraku can be seen at the National Theatre in Tokyo (address above), Kyoto Gion Corner (Yasaka-Kaikan, Higashiyama-ku, Kyoto, Tel 561 1115) and Asahi-za Theatre (1–1, Higashi-Yugaracho, Minami-ku, Osaka (Tel 211 6431).

Sport

Martial arts

In Tokyo, the Budokan Hall is often used for martial arts displays and practice sessions on Sunday afternoon, and it is usually open for anybody to wander in and watch. It is easy to join a club to study each of the martial arts (except *sumo*). The system of instruction is usually strict and traditional, mainly watching the master (*sensei*) and repeating actions over and over until they become internalized. Explanations are rare.

The Japan Martial Arts Society, run by *gaijin*, produces a newsletter, and can advise on schools. To join and receive the newsletter, send US$35.00 or ¥5000 to:

Japan Martial Arts Society, CPO Box 270, Tokyo 100.

The main forms of Japanese martial arts are:

● *Jūdō.* A system of throws and holds. It has its origins in the days when only *samurai* were permitted to carry weapons.
● *Karate.* A system of punches and kicks. Feet and hands are used instead of weapons (*karate* means 'empty hand').
● *Kendō.* Originally fencing with swords, now the only weapons are bamboo sticks. *Kendō* is very popular in high schools. *Naginatā* is a form of *kendō* and is often practised by girls in high schools.
● *Aikidō.* A system of locks and throws (a defensive art).
● *Kyudō.* A system of archery which has almost as much to do with *zen* as it has to do with archery as we know it.

Sumō. In addition to the above, there is *sumō.* More and more foreigners are becoming aware of this sport through television, and thanks to tours by the wrestlers to the USA, the UK and France in recent years. This ancient form of wrestling is beginning to be appreciated by *gaijin* as much more than just two fat men heaving at each other. Their skill, speed, dexterity and seemingly endless variety of techniques, coupled with the colourful rituals, make *sumō* a fascinating spectacle.

There are six tournaments (*basho*) a year – three in Tokyo alternating with one a year in Nagoya, Osaka and Fukuoka. Each *basho* runs for 15 days, and works on a league basis, the wrestler (*rikishi*) with the most wins receiving the Emperor's cup and numerous other trophies.

Tickets for 'boxes', tiny squares of *tatami* holding four at a pinch, are prohibitively expensive and very difficult to obtain, but seats in the gallery are much cheaper and can usually be bought on the day. Do not be put off by what you hear or read about the difficulty or expense of obtaining tickets. There is a commonly held idea about this – often based on hearsay, or on trying to obtain tickets for a box. You should be able to buy tickets at the door if you turn up at around 11 am on the second and third Sunday of a tournament (the most popular days), and before 4 pm on other days. The cheapest seat (confusingly called 'stand', although you have an allocated seat), gives a good enough view to identify your favourite *rikishi*, and costs under ¥1000 – one of Japan's bargains.

Each day of a tournament begins before noon and ends at 6 pm, but the quality fighting gets underway some time after 4 pm. Each bout is preceded by seemingly interminable rounds of salt throwing and glaring, but you will know the action is about to start when the referee holds his fan (*gumbai uchiwa*) directly at the two fighters.

It is possible to visit a stable (*heya*) where the fighters live, to watch them training.

A useful bimonthly magazine, written in English and called *Sumo World* is available at large bookshops in Japan. It gives background and up-to-date information on the sport and popular *rikishi*. It is also available on subscription from:

> **Sumo World**, c/o Foreign Press Club, 1–7–1 Yurakucho, Chiyoda-ku, Tokyo 100.

Modern sports

Baseball. This is by far the most popular spectator sport in the country, and probably the most popular participant sport. The game is not played at the same level of ability as in North America. The grounds are smaller, making home runs easier. The number of *gaijin* imported players is therefore strictly limited. There are two leagues, East and West.

Most professional teams are sponsored by a national or local company – the Tokyo Giants, for example, by the Yomiuri newspaper group, the Tigers in Osaka by the Hanshin Railroad (and called the 'Yomiuri Giants' and the 'Hanshin Tigers' respectively).

The game is played enthusiastically at all levels. All high schools have teams: the High School Final is televized and attracts a great deal of interest. Many companies have a baseball ground for their employees.

Tennis. This is a very popular participant sport, especially among young women, with more than 3000 clubs throughout the country. Many schools and colleges have courts. Other courts in cities can be expensive and difficult to book, and many people travel out of the cities to play.

Golf. Many Japanese men are keen on playing golf to the point of fanaticism. Unfortunately, land prices mean that green fees are so high that membership of clubs is mostly restricted to companies and millionaires. As a result, if a student tells you on Monday that he has been playing golf over the weekend, you can be fairly certain he has been standing on a driving range with a bucket of balls.

Skiing. Many of Japan's mountains have skiing facilities. Runs and lifts tend to be short, and popular resorts can get very crowded. If you are ever able to go during the week, it will be well worth it, especially if you are used to skiing in Europe, the USA, or New Zealand. You will find the slopes quite empty, no lift queues, and really wonderful mountains and scenery. Many ski resorts have natural hot springs, and all types of accommodation have large communal baths. Arriving back from a day's skiing cold and tired and sinking into a hot Japanese bath is a superbly sybaritic experience.

The best skiing is in Hokkaido, but unless you are living there, it is feasible only if you are going for a week or more. Nowadays there are plenty of skiing packages to Hokkaido, including flight and accommodation, at quite reasonable prices. Furamo and Niseko are the most popular places.

Fortunately, there is also plenty of skiing in Honshu, especially in the Jyoetsu and Shinshu areas, with runs which are easily accessible for a weekend's skiing.

The most popular and fashionable resort to be seen at (and to have a patch on your jacket from) is the Shiga National Park (*Shiga Kogen*), including places like Echigo, Yuzawa, and Myoko. Another trendy resort is Naeba, which becomes extremely crowded and is best avoided. One of the best resorts, with powder snow and not too many people, is Zao. This is a bleak but stunningly attractive mountain with beautiful snow-covered trees.

It is not so popular because some say it is too wild, inhospitable, and not at all sophisticated. Real enthusiasts, however, love it. As well as being less crowded, Zao is also easier to get to – it is the only resort in the area and there is less likelihood of traffic jams.

If you live in Kyoto, skiing is available on nearby Mt Hiei, just 30 minutes from the city.

It is quite possible to get away for a weekend's skiing. There is plenty of cheap accommodation (*pensions*). Equipment can be hired at the resorts (although it is quite expensive). There are several ways of reaching a *gerende* (many Japanese skiing terms are derived from the German – in this case *galände*):

- Car. This is the most flexible way – if one resort is too crowded, you can move on to the next. However, it can be extremely slow and tiring. Roads can be very crowded, and jams are common, especially coming home on Sunday evening.
- Train. The fastest way to reach the slopes. There are cheap *shinkansen* returns available (still fairly expensive, however), and you can be on the slopes for some floodlit Friday evening skiing.
- Coach. The cheapest way to go. Coaches travel overnight, so unless you sleep well on a seat, you may be tired when you start your skiing, and close to death for work on Monday morning. However, you have only one night's accommodation to pay for. In Tokyo, coaches leave from outside Tokyo and Shinjuku stations.

Japanese people wear all the latest fashions on the slopes, both clothes and equipment – in fact, often the easiest way to spot a fellow *gaijin* is to look out for a less fashionably dressed skier. Equipment can be hired at resorts. You can buy used clothing and equipment at *sayōnara* sales (see p 42).

Professional wrestling. Professional wrestling (*puroresu*) of the knockabout variety is extremely popular with many men. Many senior businessmen enjoy it, and appear to take it seriously.

Horse racing and *cycling*. In Japan, these are mainly of interest only for betting. They are both considered low-class activities, and have none of the mass appeal of the Derby or the Tour de France.

Cultural activities (traditional)

Ikebana

Flower arranging (*ikebana*) is a traditional 'finishing' skill for a young lady. The angles of stems, and their length, shape and position all have vital significance. The end result is often asymmetrical but very beautiful.

Tea ceremony

The tea ceremony (*cha-no-yu*) must be carried out quietly, gracefully and precisely. The tea is made, frothed up with a bamboo instrument rather like a shaving brush, and each person turns the cup three times before taking three sips. Like *ikebana*, *cha-no-yu* is studied seriously, and at no small expense, perhaps for years, mainly by women, although many of the 'masters' are male.

Bonsai

This is the cultivation of dwarf trees. As well as pruning the roots, *bonsai* are fashioned by means of wire to give a 'natural' weatherbeaten appearance. Cultivating *bonsai* is a hobby much like gardening, in a country where gardens are rare. *Bonsai* can be bought at reasonable prices, and make a lovely addition to your apartment.

Zazen

This is purely meditation. The word *zen* has a wider meaning than *zazen*, and includes the consideration of 'one hand clapping' riddles. Both *zen* and *zazen* are almost as esoteric to the average Japanese person as to the average Westerner, and it may be easier to find out information from a *gaijin* if you are interested.

There are two main schools of *zen*: *Soto* and *Rinzai*. *Rinzai* uses more riddles, and instruction is usually in Japanese only. There are *Soto zen* sessions in English available in the Tokyo area, in various kinds of facilities ranging from universities to temples. Classes can be for under an hour or may take an evening, or an entire weekend spent in a temple, involved with the monks' activities – work, eating and meditation. Classes are advertised in *Tokyo Journal*. Try to find out before you go if it is one of the stricter sects, in which the priest strikes you forcibly on the shoulder with a wooden stick if your posture is incorrect – this might not be conducive to peaceful contemplation!

Go and shōgi

These are two traditional Japanese board games. *Go* is a territorial game in which you try to surround your player with your own pieces. *Shōgi* is a board game very similar to chess, played on a

64-square board, with 16 pieces each, 8 powerful pieces fronted by 8 'pawns'. Unfortunately, the pieces are differentiated not by shape, as in chess, but by having different writing. When playing, the most significant difference is that you can use a captured piece again as your own.

Other leisure activities

Three popular activities among Japanese, aside from sports, are *karaoke, pachinko* and *mah jong*.

Karaoke

Literally 'empty orchestra', *karaoke* is a means whereby you can imitate your favourite singer. The backing track of a record is played, and you sing along on top of this, with the words in a lyric book in front of you, or, more commonly nowadays, on a video screen.

Karaoke is definitely popular in the sense that almost everybody does it. However, many Japanese claim privately that they get up and perform only out of social pressure. Whether this is true or not, *karaoke* is strongly linked to drinking, and most performers are strengthened by more than a little Dutch courage.

There are special *karaoke* bars, where you can listen to the customers perform and, for a small payment, a hostess will cue the song of your choosing, and she will often help out with the female part in duets. The most popular songs are *enka* (which recount the passions of everyday life) and Japanese pop songs. Most bars have a number of English songs, and you may find yourself unable to resist having a go at *My Way, Yesterday*, or an Elvis number.

If you are invited to be part of a group going to a *karaoke* evening, it is probably better to beg off rather than go along and refuse to sing, because however much you insist you will be pressurized into singing anyway. If you decide to perform, you will be sure of an appreciative and uncritical audience, however bad you are!

Pachinko

Pachinko is a kind of machine which was popular in amusement arcades perhaps fifty years ago in the West. It is a sort of vertical pinball. A ball-bearing is propelled in ever-decreasing circles around a vertical board, disappearing into a winning or losing hole in the middle.

Pachinko is generally not popular with foreigners in Japan. A *pachinko* parlour is crowded, smoky and ferociously noisy – the metallic sound of hundreds of machines competing with music blaring at disco-level. The game seems boring and pointless. Many exponents find what they consider to be a good position for the starting handle, jam a coin into the handle to hold it there, and sit for hours smoking and watching the balls go round. Until recently a male activity, *pachinko* has become popular with bored housewives who have more spare cash in these affluent times.

Part of the attraction of *pachinko* is undoubtedly the fact that off-course or off-track betting is illegal in Japan, and this is the easiest way to gamble. Winning balls can be exchanged for items such as cigarette lighters or toys. However, there is usually a local spot, such as a bar, where these can be exchanged for cash.

Mah Jong

Mah Jong (*Mōjan*) is another pastime whose popularity is partly due to restrictions on legal gambling. It is a game similar to playing cards, and it enjoyed a limited popularity in the West in the 1920s and 1930s. Each player receives a number of tiles, and by a process of picking up and discarding, tries to make matching sets. The game, as its name suggests, came originally from China.

Mah Jong is mostly played by older businessmen in semi-private clubs. You are unlikely to end up in a parlour unless you ask a Japanese student or friend who plays the game to take you along. Mah Jong is not too difficult to understand. What makes it impossible for a non-enthusiast to follow is the amazing speed at which it is played. If you get together with some *gaijin* friends one Sunday afternoon, you will be able to work out the rules and have a game. However, tiles will probably be discarded at the rate of about one every minute or two, compared to the Japanese speed of every second or two.

Games are played between friends, with much informal side-betting, which can be for substantial amounts.

Festivals and public holidays

Japan has a comparatively large number of public holidays throughout the year. Several of these involve traditional activities, such as New Year. In addition there are a number of days, roughly equivalent to our Halloween, when throughout the country people carry out the same traditional activity or ritual. Finally, there are hundreds of local festivals (*matsuri*), mostly in summer. Many of these involve dancing (*odori*) and the carrying of a portable shrine (*mikoshi*) through the streets. In the summer, also, there are a great number of firework (*hanabi*) displays.

Dates of national public holidays, other national occasions, and major local festivals are given in Appendix 9.

Local information – city by city

In this section, you will find places where you can meet other *gaijin* and learn more about a particular area.

Tokyo

For books, magazines, newspapers and videos, there are the *British Council* and the *American Center*:

> **British Council**, 2 Kagurazaka 1-chome, Shinjuku-ku, Tokyo 162. Tel 3235–8031.
>
> **American Center**, ABC Building, 2–6–3 Shibakoen, Minato-ku, Tokyo 106, Tel 3436–0904.

You have so many opportunities to meet other *gaijin* in Tokyo that no specific bars or clubs are mentioned here. Likely areas, however, are:

- Shinjuku. Bright lights and lots of night life, but be careful about going into establishments with callers outside who look as though they may be in the *yakuza* (the Japanese version of the Mafia).
- Ginza. Shopping area – all the big department stores are here. Nightlife tends towards the expensive (Japanese businessmen) clubs.
- Shibuya. Lots of cheap bars and restaurants filled with noisy students.
- Roppongi. International district. Discos and Western-style clubs and restaurants.
- Harajuku. Teenyboppers' heaven. Go on Sunday for the famous street dancing.

Kyoto

There are so many *gaijin* living in Kyoto that they have developed a fairly sophisticated infrastructure of societies and organizations in addition to the usual *gaijin* houses, bars and restaurants.

The New International Community House is one of these. It presents a range of cultural shows, exhibitions and demonstrations, not only about Japan, but also about the cultures of the many *gaijin* in Kyoto. It produces a quarterly magazine containing forthcoming events at the Community House and elsewhere in Kyoto.

For books, magazines, newspapers and videos, there are the British Council and the American Center:

> **British Council**, 77 Nishi-machi, Kita-shirakawa, Sakyo-ku, Kyoto 606 (Tel 075–791–7151).

American Center, Chiyoda Seimei, Kyoto Oike Building 9F, Nakagyo-ku, Kyoto 604 (Tel 075–241–1211).

One *gaijin* bar is:

Pig & Whistle, Shobi Bldg 2F, 115 Ohashi-cho dori, Sanjo Dori (Tel 075–761–6022). Opposite Keihon station.

Osaka

Osaka has a good many *gaijin* haunts. Among them are:

Pig & Whistle, IS Bldg 2F, 43 Tatamiya-machi, Minami-ku, Osaka (Tel 06–213–6911).

Goodies, Daikyo Shinsaibashi Bldg 1F, Chuo-ku, Osaka 542 (Tel 06–245–0596).

Country Life (vegetarian buffet), 2–13 Kitahama Higashi, Chuo-ku, Osaka (Tel 06–943–9597).

Uncle Steven's, Opus-1 Bldg 2F, America-mura, Chuo-ku, Osaka (Tel 06–212–1741).

Kobe

The area alongside the tracks between Sannomiya and Motomachi stations is packed with bars and restaurants. Two *gaijin* bars in this area are Rub-a-Dub and Escape Magic. On Yamamoto Dori street there are two other *gaijin* bars, The Attic and the spin-off Attic Junior.

Just off Flower Road is the American Church, which usually has a foreign resident in attendance to help *gaijin* with queries, both spiritual and non-spiritual.

In the Kitano area, the Kobe Club caters mostly to well heeled expats, but has activities such as aerobics which might be of interest and within the budget of English teachers.

The YMCA, to the west of Flower Road, offers a number of sports, classes in *Nihongo*, and also runs English classes which pay quite well.

Cultural exchange societies

In most areas there is some kind of organization or club involved with welcoming or helping foreigners to the area. The society may be government-run, or, more usually, set up by local residents with an interest in cultural exchange. It will organize such things as home visits or home-stays, give advice and local information for visitors, and provide information on studying the Japanese language or aspects of its culture, such as *ikebana*.

The following list is not comprehensive, and if there is not an organization very near you, the nearest one may be able to put you in touch with a society closer to hand:

Japan Hot Line 03–3586–0110
Aomori 0172–32–3912
Chiba 0472–23–2251
Fukuoka 092–733–2220
Hiroshima 082–247–8077
Hokkaido 0138–22–0070
Ibaragi 0289–518–204
Kanagawa 045–671–7070
Kanazawa 0762–31–3291
Kobe 078–241–2588
Kyoto 075–8958
Nagoya 052–581–5678
Okayama 0864–24–3593
Osaka 06–923–2691
Shikoku 0899–48–6242
Shizuoka 0534–52–1111
Tokyo 03–3320–7744
Toyama 0764–45–4591

Help

In an emergency, dial 110 for police, and 119 to report a fire or to call an ambulance. (Police boxes – *kōban* – are located at major street junctions).

There are various telephone information services:

Tourist Information Center 03–3502–1461 (or dial 106 and say 'Collect call TIC')
Daily Information 045–671–7209
Foreign Residents Advisory Center 03–3211–4433
Telephone Directory Enquiries (English) 03–3201–1010
Railway Information (English) 03–3423–0111

If you start feeling unstuck, two numbers to call are:

Japan Helpline 0120–46–1997 (24-hour toll-free information and counselling)
TELL (Tokyo English Life Line) 03–3264–4347 (counselling and help)

8 | The country and the people

There is no doubt that Japan is a fascinating country to visit. It is easy to catch glimpses of its past preserved in, for example, festivals (*matsuri*) and the tea ceremony (*cha-no-yu*). In addition, there is the chance to see modern Japanese society at close quarters, and to try to learn what makes it tick. How could such a small and resourceless country, damaged and defeated in the second world war, now produce the best in the world in so many fields?

Japan has undergone huge changes in the last century or so. As recently as 40 years ago, more than 50% of the Japanese population were farmers or fishermen. This figure is now less than 10%. The businessman (*sararīman*) has replaced the farmer as Mr Average.

Most Japanese people today live lives modelled to a large extent on the West, but the resemblance is superficial. Theirs is a life of extreme conformity, of knowing one's place and behaving in the manner expected. To a remarkable degree, it still reflects the feudal world of the *shōgun*.

Japan's rich and varied traditional cultural aspects are well known to the outside world. However, do not go there expecting to see them on display. You won't see many *kimono*, and if you want information about going to a *sumō* tournament, or studying *karate* or *zazen*, you will often find it easier to get answers from another foreigner than from a Japanese person. In Japan, as in many other countries, it is not fashionable to be very interested in things traditional. In my experience, most Japanese sleep in a bed, while most foreigners are eager to sleep in a *futon* on a *tatami* floor during their stay. This is not to say that Japanese do not practise their culture, but they do not do so in such numbers or as publicly as people in the West may be led to believe.

Two books which will give you some feeling for Japan and the Japanese are *The Japanese Mind* by Robert Christopher, and *The Insider's Guide to Japan* by Peter Popham.

THE COUNTRY

History

The history of Japan can be divided into periods, often corresponding to rulers or dynasties.

Pre-history

The earliest evidence of habitation would seem to have been by migrants from China, Korea, South-east Asia, and Polynesia. The national myth has it that the grandson of the sun goddess was sent to rule the country. He landed on Mt Takachicho in Kyushu, and became the first emperor. His descendants have reigned ever since.

A stone-age people, the Jomon, were superseded by the Yayoi around 300 BC, who moved up from Kyushu. The original people in central and northern Japan, the Ainu, were gradually pushed up to the northern island of Hokkaido.

Nara era 600–784

Nara, which was in fact the capital for only 70-odd years, was laid out in 710. The various Chinese and Korean influences were unified into what could be termed the first Japanese state under the then Prince Regent. His successors sent envoys to China. Buddhism became the state religion, and many temples were built in Nara.

Heian period 794–1192

The capital then moved to Heian-kyo (modern Kyoto) to the north. Both Nara and Heian-kyo were built on a grid layout, based on the Chinese capital Ch'ang-an. Heian remained the capital, at least in name, from 794 until 1868.

The Heian court was peaceful and artistic. The younger sons of the aristocracy developed into warriors, defending the capital against armed Buddhist monks. Two of these families, the Genji and the Heike, began to compete and in the end the leader of the Genji, Minamoto Yorimoto, seized power and transferred the capital to Kamakura, an obscure but easily defended fishing village south of Tokyo.

Kamakura era 1192–1333

Although Kamakura became the seat of power, Kyoto remained

the capital. Zen Buddhism developed in Japan at the beginning of this era, and formed the basis for the *samurai* philosophy.

Muromachi and Azuchi–Momoyama periods 1336–1598

During the Muromachi period (1336–1573), central authority having largely broken down, the country was divided into a patchwork of fiefdoms, each under the control of a feudal lord (*daimyō*). The first Europeans, Portuguese, arrived and introduced, as well as tobacco and spectacles, guns. The introduction of guns escalated the fighting between *daimyō*, and a large number of stone castles were built. The fighting was finally resolved, and the country was unified under three generals. The first two of these, Nobunaga Oda and Hideyoshi Toyotomi, ruled in total from 1568 to 1598 (the Azuchi–Momoyama period).

Edo or Tokugawa Era 1603–1867

The third general, Ieyasu Tokugawa, as *shōgun*, skilfully arranged for power to remain with his family for 250 years. One strategy to achieve this was to insist on all *daimyō* spending alternate years in Edo (Tokyo), and keeping their wives and children there as virtual hostages. During this period the country was closed off from the rest of the world. Christianity was suppressed (30 000 Christians were massacred), and Europeans were banned from the country, and permitted only to trade in the port of Nagasaki in the south of Kyushu. Any Japanese who left the country and returned were executed to prevent the introduction of new ideas. To ensure political stability, society was stratified and rigidly controlled.

There were four layers of society (*samurai*, farming peasants, artisans, and merchants, in that order). Families had to post details of their status on their door. Every aspect of people's lives was dictated according to their status – occupation, dress, movement and even hairstyle. The punishment for even looking unhappy at receiving the order of a *samurai* was death. During the long peace, workmanship reached a very high standard, and education improved to the extent that 35% of the population was literate by the 19th century.

In 1853, the self-imposed isolation was ended when Commodore Perry led the Black Ships of the US Navy into Tokyo Bay and demanded that Japan open its doors to trade.

Meiji Era 1868–1912

In the ensuing upheaval, Emperor Meiji managed to supplant the *shōgun*, and during the 'Meiji Restoration' Japan went from being an isolated feudal state to one of the most powerful military forces in the world, defeating China, occupying Korea and Formosa (Taiwan), and defeating Russia. A railway network and industrial base were established, and many aspects of Western culture were embraced, such as clothes, music and dancing.[1]

Taisho era 1912–1926

The Emperor Taisho is rumoured to have been mentally unstable, and not much is known about him. The most significant event of this period was the recognition of Japan as one of the Big Five nations of the world, after it had agreed to side with the Allies during the first world war. This enabled it to seize German colonies in the Far East.

Showa era 1926–1989

Under Emperor Hirohito, Japan continued to grow industrially and militarily. The need for raw materials, and the desire for empire, led to the invasion of China, subsequently to Pearl Harbour, and finally to the nuclear devastation of Hiroshima and Nagasaki. Russia opportunistically joined in the war against Japan as soon as the nuclear attacks started, and claimed four islands north of Hokkaido which are still a source of resentment among Japanese. It seems possible that in the present economic climate they will be returned to Japan for economic favours.

After the war, the Emperor renounced his divinity, and the country remained under US occupation until 1952. During the 1950s, the spectacular economic recovery started aided in part by the involvement of Japanese industry in the Korean War effort.[2] A

---

[1]Japan has twice taken a short cut to modernization by enthusiastically embracing what the current leading countries had to offer. The first time was in the 7th and 8th centuries, when envoys were sent to China to study, gain experience, and bring back ideas to develop art, religion, political structure and literature. The second time was after Japan opened up in the 19th century, and the country embraced Western ideas on industry and transport to move from the Middle Ages to the industrial age in just two generations. This may go some way towards explaining why Japanese people do not view copying in a negative way.

[2]It could be said that Japan has benefited from all the major wars this century. The destruction of the country's industrial base in the second world war had the positive effect of forcing it to renew and revitalize its industrial infrastructure. However, other wars this century also affected Japan. The first world war meant that the Western powers began to

watershed year in Japan's progress occurred in 1964, when Japan hosted the Olympic Games, joined the OECD, and inaugurated the bullet train (*shinkansen*). Its subsequent rise to industrial and financial eminence is well documented.

Heisei Era (1989–   )

Emperor Hirohito died in 1989 after reigning for 63 years, and was succeeded by his son who became Emperor Akihito. Japanese people tend to refer to him simply by his title, *Tennō* (Emperor), and may not know his name.

Geography

Japan is an archipelago made up of hundreds of islands. By far the majority of the population live on the four main islands and most live on one of these – Honshu. The islands are mountainous, with narrow coastal strips onto which cities are crammed.

Honshu is the largest, and contains most of the largest cities – Tokyo, Osaka, Yokohama, Kobe, Kyoto, Nagoya, and Hiroshima. The islands of Kyushu and Shikoku lie to the south. Hokkaido is the northernmost of the main islands. It is the most recently populated by the Japanese people from further south, displacing the Ainu, the original inhabitants. It is the least densely populated of the main islands, especially in its northern part.

Of the other islands, the largest and most important is probably Okinawa, to the south of Kyushu, which is a tropical resort. There are also a number of islands between Honshu and Shikoku, to the south of Tokyo, and around Kyushu.

Japan is on the 'ring of fire', and has a number of active volcanoes. These can lie dormant for hundreds of years before erupting. A volcano on Kyushu, Mt Unsen, erupted in 1991 after it had been inactive for 250 years, claiming 12 lives. Earthquakes are a regular feature of life in Japan, especially in the Tokyo area, but these are almost all mild and do no damage. The disastrous earthquake in Kobe in 1995 was of course a tragic exception. Before that, the last great earthquake was in Tokyo, in 1923. Although thousands of lives were lost, only two deaths are known to have been directly caused by the earthquake itself – the vast majority were caused by fire.

---

neglect trade with the Far East, and Japan was able to gain entry into these markets with no resistance. Later, in both the Korean War and the Vietnam War, the USA used Japan as a repairs depot and supply base. The Korean War in particular was instrumental in boosting industrial growth.

Climate

The climate can vary from the long harsh winters in Hokkaido and northern Honshu, to the semi-tropical climate of Kyushu and Okinawa in the south.

The country may be considered as falling into three climatic zones: very cold winters and moderate summers in the north; moderate winters and hot, humid summers in central and south Honshu; and semi-tropical in the south. In general, however, there are four distinct seasons.

Spring and autumn are ideal both climatically and in terms of nature. Spring is the season of the famous cherry blossoms (*sakura*). These are very transient, lasting a week or two at the most. Autumn has gorgeous colours on display as the leaves change colour.

Summer is hot, humid and oppressive. August is the month when everybody tries to get out of the city and into the mountains. Summer is preceded by the *tsuyu*, or rainy season. This is more violent in the south. In Honshu, it takes the form of persistent, but not permanent rain, rather than storms of any intensity.

Winter is cold and dry. Snow is common in the north, and in the mountains, and many villages are snowed in for the winter, with the menfolk leaving in autumn to spend the winter working in the city. From Tokyo south, however, snow is a rarity at sea level. The days are pleasant, with blue skies. However, temperatures drop suddenly at nightfall.

I lived in a large-windowed apartment in Tokyo. During the winter the sun kept the flat pleasantly warm during the day. I had *shiatsu* once a week in the early afternoon, and even in the depths of winter, the sunlight was warm enough that I was able to lie on my *tatami* in shorts and a T-shirt with no heating on, while the *sensei* thumbed me for an hour.

Alan Baldock (USA)

Politics, religion and beliefs

Politics

The present constitution in Japan is a parliamentary democracy. There are two Houses of Parliament, an Upper and a Lower. The Upper House has only an advisory capacity.

The Liberal Democratic Party (LDP), despite many scandals and resignations, held on to power for 38 years, until it was finally toppled in July 1993. It was replaced by a short-lived coalition, and in June 1994 the LDP, New Party Sakigake (a splinter party from the LDP), and the Social Democratic Party of Japan (SDPJ) formed another coalition government.

In December 1994, the old coalition parties not in the current governing coalition were integrated into the New Frontier Party. These included the Democratic Socialists Party, the Japan Renewal Party, and Komeito (the Clean Government Party). At the time of writing, the Communist Party alone (apart from independents) remains outside both the coalition government and the New Frontier Party in the Lower House.

There tends to be an inherent conservatism and less public interest or debate about politics in Japan than in many other countries – this has been attributed to the considerable peace and prosperity the country has enjoyed since 1945.

Religion and philosophy

Japanese people generally are not deeply religious. As in the West, religion is important mostly for ceremonies, such as weddings or funerals. However, in most houses there is a family shrine to remind members of the family of their ancestors.

Japanese people have been influenced by, and follow, to a greater or lesser extent, three religions or philosophies.

- *Shintō*. The indigenous collection of beliefs is *Shintō* – the way of the gods. This is an unsophisticated animist cult, with gods of nature, such as the sun and rivers. The concept of the Emperor as a deity comes from Shinto, and it has strong connections with nationalist or militaristic elements of society.
- *Buddhism*. Buddhists believe that in reincarnation you carry over your *karma* (the results of your good and bad deeds in previous life) into your next birth. If your karma is good, you move up through higher spheres to achieve *nirvana* (bliss). Buddhism was founded in India around 500 BC. It travelled to China by two different routes, developing into two different schools. These two schools came to Japan in the 7th century AD. Both schools, together with elements of *Shintō*, were united in the 8th century by the priest Saicho into an eclectic Japanese form of Buddhism. Later, numerous sects appeared, each emphasizing a different Buddhist idea, such as ordinary *zen* (meditation), *zen* on riddles (What is the sound of one hand clapping?), studying holy texts, or chanting sutras.

- *Confucianism.* A moral code, or philosophy, rather than a religion, Confucianism was another import from China. Although few Japanese would admit it, and still less recognize the Western name Confucius, the influence of Confucius has probably been more influential than any religion or philosophy. The concepts of the importance of the family, and of hierarchies in their various forms, come from Confucianism.

There are around 1 500 000 Christians in Japan at present, representing about 2% of the population. There are also many new religions, some of which have evolved out of *Shintō*, Buddhism and Christianity.

Beliefs and superstitions

Almost all Japanese know their astrological sign, and will give it to one of the fortune tellers who set up shop on the pavement at night in entertainment districts. The animal for the year of your birth is considered important in determining personal characteristics. In addition, people all know their blood type, as this is regarded as an important indicator of a person's character. It is particularly important in male–female relationships, as certain combinations are regarded as compatible or incompatible. Most people, of course, take superstitions with a pinch of salt, rather like the Western attitude to horoscopes.

In a class I was teaching, the subject of blood types came up, and I was amazed that everybody in the class knew their blood type. They seemed surprised when I could not name mine. A few days later, another teacher approached me and said that she had been asked by the class to apologize to me because they had embarrassed me. When I asked how, she said that they felt bad forcing me to claim that I did not know my blood type. Since this claim was obviously false (after all, *everybody* knows their blood type), it must have been because I was ashamed of my blood type!

Debbie King (Canada)

Two kinds of lucky doll can commonly be seen, especially in bars and restaurants. A *maneki neko* is a cat with one paw raised in welcome. It is often seen in shops. A *daruma* is a face with only one eyeball coloured in. The doll is bought with both eyeballs uncoloured. One eyeball is coloured in while a wish is made, and the other is coloured in if the wish is granted. The dolls are often associated with politicians wishing to be elected.

The numbers 3, 5 and 7 are considered *lucky numbers*. The number 4 is thought to be particularly unlucky, as one of the pronunciations of it (*shi*) is identical to the word for death. The only baseball players you will see with a 4 on their backs will be *gaijin* imports. When counting, another word, *yon*, is often substituted for *shi*. The number 9 is also unlucky, sounding like agony (*ku*).

I took over a flat from another teacher when she left Japan. The flat was easily the nicest one in the apartment block – it was the sunniest, and had a marvellous view. I asked the teacher how she had managed to get the apartment. She told me that no Japanese wanted it, because it was number 42, which sounds like 'dead man' in Japanese.

David McCance (Canada)

THE PEOPLE

Japanese people like to consider themselves a unique race. This is clearly not true. Even among the inhabitants of Honshu, different varieties of facial features can be noted. Most notably, in Hokkaido around 20 000 Ainu remain. These were the original inhabitants of Japan from Tokyo to the north before being displaced by the Yamoto. The Ainu are said to be the most hirsute race on earth. To the south, the people of Okinawa are also from a different ethnic group.

There is one group of people who, while not distinct racially from mainstream Japanese, are considered as a separate group. They have been compared to the untouchable caste in India. The reason for their social banishment is not entirely clear, but it seems likely that they were engaged in handling dead animals, for example as butchers or tanners, at a time when Buddhism held sway and meat eating was forbidden. Their original name was *eta*, but they are now known more euphemistically as *burakumin* (village people). They live in separate communities, and mainstream families will sometimes investigate the background of a proposed bride or groom to ensure that there is no taint of *eta* blood. *Eta* are a taboo subject in Japanese conversation.

The only sizeable addition to the Japanese population since the 9th century has been the 600 000 Koreans who were brought over before and during the second world war as slave labour. Although most of the Koreans are now third generation, they are still considered foreign, and must carry an Alien Registration Card (as you will have to do). They pay taxes and social security, but are not entitled to a state pension. They are also not permitted to hold a state job, such as teaching.

Although not unique or single racially, Japanese are one of the most homogenous peoples on earth. Not only have they not had any addition genetically for more than a thousand years, but for a period of around 250 years there was virtually no contact with the outside world, and homecoming travellers were put to death to prevent their ideas contaminating the purity of Japan (see p 83).

Many of the younger generation in Japan are noticeably taller than their predecessors. The main difference seems to be their longer legs. There are also a number of youngsters who are overweight – a condition almost unknown among the older generation. Many young people have difficulty in sitting on the floor cross-legged for any length of time. Older people also complain about young people's inability to use chopsticks properly – many are more at home with a spoon and a fork.

The Japanese character

Many attempts have been made to explain the general character of the Japanese people. Rather than try to explain it comprehensively, I will look at what I consider to be some important points about Japanese society and the way people behave.

Quiet, reserved and polite

Japanese people tend to be quiet and reserved (until they have a drink or two, when they can become fairly raucous). They are reluctant to show emotion, and it can be difficult to get to know their true feelings. They are very polite on the surface, and are very keen to keep harmony (*wa*). They will go to great lengths, even to the extent of bending the truth out of recognition, to preserve *wa*.

Stratification, or knowing your place

An important factor in binding people together is the rigid and stratified society – a holdover from the Tokugawa era, when detailed and strict rules kept everyone firmly in their place. The Japanese language is rich in ways of addressing people of different ranks. This stratification is still present today. One reason for the prevalence of name cards (*meishi*) among businessmen is that until you know somebody's company and their position in the company, it is impossible to know how to address them.

Despite this stratification, 87% of Japanese consider themselves middle class. It is also, perhaps, surprising that most neighbourhoods have a wide mix of houses of different value. Your ¥50 000 a month apartment may face a house with ten times the value.

The importance of groups

'The nail which sticks up must be hammered down' (Japanese proverb). If I had to name one point about Japanese culture which most differentiates it from other cultures, I would probably pick the importance of groups, and the fact that, in order to fit into the various groups, Japanese people often have to suppress their personal wishes, desires and emotions. The significance of groups has repercussions through many aspects of the society. Japanese people spend much of their time in groups; voluntarily obey the rules of the group (and punish those who break the rules by using peer pressure); subliminate their personal feelings for the well-being of the group; and tell what we would call lies to enable harmony to reign.

The fact that the Japanese think, work, play and relax in groups is in large part responsible for their phenomenal economic success. On a personal level, spending so much of their time in controlled groups perhaps goes some way to explaining people's apparent awkwardness and difficulty in relaxing. They seem to be slightly on edge lest they break a group rule.

The importance of groups in the culture cannot be over-stressed – groups and their repercussions permeate many elements of Japanese life. Japanese people feel at home when part of a group – be it a family, a school, a club, a company, or the country. As strong as the wish to belong to a group is the pressure they feel to conform to its rules. Individualism has negative rather than positive connotations, as implied by the proverb above.

Several reasons have been put forward as to why Japanese are willing to sacrifice individualism and work in groups. It may have its roots in the fact that Japan has been more subject to catastrophes than many other countries – earthquakes; volcanoes; tidal waves; typhoons; and even nuclear attack. Under those circumstances, the best way to survive was 'All for one and one for all'.

Additionally, given the high population density, the best way for everyone to get along is to suppress personal desires and feelings to a large extent, sublimating their own feelings for the good of the group. Historically, suppressing personal feelings was necessary for survival in another way: in the Tokugawa era, it was an offence punishable by death to show emotion when given an order.

So, in the normal course of events, there is little open emotion shown, especially of a negative kind. When a person shows negative emotion, it is usually in an extremely tentative way. Occasionally, however, it all gets too much and someone blows their top in a fairly spectacular fashion. There is usually no warning of this explosion before it occurs (none that a *gaijin* can pick up, anyway). Such events are an unusual occurrence, but they do happen and can, for example, be observed in *family drama* programmes on television.

The Japanese have no absolute moral code equivalent to Christianity, and the correct way to behave is that dictated by the group – in essence, this strengthens the group and helps ensure its survival.

The fact that the only sin is to break a group rule means that personal conflict can be avoided by the use of white lies. The person being lied to may well know that the truth is being bent (and not worry about it). The lie is accepted in the knowledge that the motive is not selfish, but to preserve harmony (*wa*). In other ways, of course, Japanese are scrupulously honest.

> When I encountered the Japanese 'white lie' my reaction was to class the Japanese as dishonest. When I went back to New Zealand on holiday, I was struck by the number of times people said things which were unnecessarily negative or confrontational. I went back to Japan thinking that perhaps the occasional bending of the truth was an acceptable price to pay for keeping a smooth atmosphere between people, and for making others feel good.
>
> *Dave Rowe (New Zealand)*

Within a group, there is continual striving for consensus. It is often difficult to ask a Japanese person what he or she wants to do. The answer will be preceded by 'I should', 'We usually'. Any proposed changes to the group will be preceded by *nemawashi*, informal individual consultations to ensure that all the group members are content with the change. This means that although the Japanese are conservative in many ways, when a new idea is formally proposed, since it has already been privately approved by everybody, radical change can come about with unparalleled swiftness.

Both personally and as a nation, the Japanese benefit from working in groups. On a personal level, many needs are met by the group without the individual having to voice them. As long as you obey the rules of the group, you will be rewarded with everything the group can offer you. In terms of the nation, the group ethic has clearly contributed to Japan's economic success.

You can recognize members of many Japanese groups by their clothes and behaviour. Below are a few to get you started.

Sararīman. Businessmen wear blue polyester suits, black shoes, and sport a *shichi/san* (seven/three) haircut, with the parting three-tenths of the way up the left side. Sober and quiet in the morning, you can marvel at the way they are able to fold, unfold and refold a newspaper and read it on the most crowded of trains. In the evening, they undergo a sea-change, and after a night's carousing, can be seen staggering from lamppost to lamppost.

Golf is an obsession with a *sararīman*, but scarcity of land makes it unlikely that he will actually play on a golf course more than once a year. This does not deter him, and if a *sararīman* has a spare moment, while waiting for a train or an elevator, for example, he will practise his golf swing – with or without his umbrella.

Schoolboys. They wear Prussian soldiers' uniforms, with stiff collars which look extremely uncomfortable. If a schoolboy has a spare moment, and he does not attend a very strict school which insists on close-cropped hair, he will whip out a comb, find the nearest mirror, and re-do his James Dean mop.

High school girls. Dressed in their imitation 19th Century German Navy uniform, they carry their schoolbooks in cute bags with Japanese English writing on them. They giggle a lot, and say 'Bye Bye' when they part from each other. Out of uniform they become *burikko*, dressed in 1950s-style fashion, like extras in an Elvis movie.

Primary school children. Recognizable by their yellow hats, they walk to and from school in groups. They carry huge satchels on their backs, and wield umbrellas obliviously when it rains, giving no quarter.

Jikatabi. Crew-cut labourers, building a house which seems to go up in a matter of days, wear *jikatabi* – a special kind of soft boot which separates at the front between the big toe and the other toes. They also wear trousers which look like jodhpurs, a white T-shirt, and a sweatband.

White gloves. A large number of people doing some kind of public service, usually connected with travelling, wear white gloves: taxi drivers; elevator girls; railway guards who push people onto trains so that the doors can close; and elevator operators. They are also sometimes worn by politicians, and even the Prime Minister can occasionally be seen wearing white gloves when making an important speech.

Yakuza. These are the Japanese version of the Mafia. They are much more open than gangsters in other countries, and, for example, a gang will have a celebration dinner which is openly reported in the press. They often have permed hair, and many have tattoos, both of which are virtual trademarks, since they are so unusual in male society generally. Another trademark in the past, less often seen nowadays, was a missing finger joint – a self-amputation to atone for a bungled job.

Yakuza originated in Kobe, and are more common in Kansai, although they can be found all over the country. They are involved with money lending, gambling and prostitution. Two areas in Tokyo where you might see them are Ikebukuro and the Kabukicho entertainment district in Shinjuku. Top *yakuza* often have large imported cars, US or German being the most popular – and there is something a little ludicrous about a huge Cadillac trying to squeeze its way along narrow Japanese side streets. Young punks are called *chimpira* – they are very sharp dressers who run around for their *yakuza* bosses.

I was in a bar in Ikebukuro, and got talking to a Japanese man. After a while, he asked if I would like to go upstairs for a while with his girlfriend. Thinking this an unusual offer, I asked him his job. In answer, he pulled out the collar of his shirt to reveal a back covered with an extensive tattoo!

David Yenches (USA)

Cuteness

Cuteness is an important and widespread feature of modern Japanese society. Enjoyment and admiration of things cute (*kawaii*), seems much more widespread than in the West. Serious engineering instruction manuals are illustrated by cutesy figures, many people in their 30s or 40s continue to wear cute sweaters in cute colours with cute (and nonsensical) English slogans. The abiding symbol of cuteness, and the figure most commonly plastered on clothes and accessories is Mickey Mouse. You will see more evidence in Japan than in the rest of the world put together that Mickey Mouse is alive and well, in the form of clothes, bags, accessories, stationery and every other conceivable item.

The idea of cuteness applies strongly, of course, to little children. And there's no doubt that Japanese kids *are* cute, like little dolls.

However, little children are not the only section of the population who are expected to dress and act cutely. Girls are under severe cultural pressure to slow down their development shortly after puberty and remain relatively naive and unsophisticated until they either marry and start a family or pass marriageable age. Women in their twenties often display behaviour which would not be out of place in a girl in her early teens.

The behaviour of many young Japanese women could be said to resemble that of Jane Austen's more demure characters, or the archetypal Victorian maiden – shy and unassuming. The apotheosis for many Japanese women is the character played by Audrey Hepburn in the 1950s movie, *Roman Holiday*. If you ask a Japanese woman what her favourite Audrey Hepburn movie is, she will probably name this film before, say, the more internationally recognized *My Fair Lady*. In *Roman Holiday*, Hepburn plays the part of a princess who goes AWOL from her formal life and has a holiday romance, which apparently captures all the ideals of Japanese young womanhood.

Gambatte! (Go for it!)

A quality encouraged from an early age is endurance (*gaman*). It is considered important to keep trying even when it appears that you will fail. This is especially important for boys. On Boys' Day (5 May), boys fly carp streamers, because this fish is supposed to show great endurance in fighting its way upstream against the current, as a salmon does. New *sararīman* recruits sometimes have to stand outside a station and shout or sing their company's praises at the top of their voice; or make rounds of 'cold calls' on new clients with no hope of making a sale – both extremely embarrassing for the normally reserved Japanese. On TV endurance shows, young people are pushed right to their physical and mental limits. One of the prizes in a *sumō* tournament is for Fighting Spirit, which is awarded regardless of the fighter's success in terms of winning bouts.

The cry '*Gambatte!*' is often heard, and an interesting contrast is that in many situations where we would say 'Good luck', Japanese say 'Go for it'.

Apologizing and peer approval

Japanese people apologize at every turn. At times the Japanese you hear may seem to be an endless litany of '*sumimasen*' ('excuse me') and *'gomen nasai'* ('I'm sorry'). Politicians appear on TV apologizing for mistakes and misdeeds. If a company is involved in wrongdoing or a scandal, the head of the company will make a public apology and resign (only to be immediately reinstated in a slightly less senior capacity.)

Apologies are important in a group-oriented society because, having offended against the group, an apology restores harmony and means that the offender can be readmitted. An apology can take the place of punishment or retribution. Apologizing in court and showing contrition can markedly reduce the sentence.

Being excluded from a group is a severe punishment in Japan, and many of the controls which bind Japanese society together so tightly are self-imposed at grass-roots level, with offenders being 'sent to Coventry' unless or until they make retribution by apologizing. Peer approval is thus very important to a Japanese person.

Copying

Copying does not have strong negative connotations as it often does elsewhere. Education is based on rote learning, with little encouragement of imagination or inventiveness. Traditional arts are taught by observing the teacher (*sensei*) and repeating the *sensei*'s actions over and over. If you ask students to draw a dog, they may be unable to start, but if you give them a picture of a dog to copy, they will probably produce startling likenesses.

Laughing

Laughter is often used to cover embarrassment, and in such cases has absolutely no humorous content whatsoever.

A *sararīman* student, the most senior Rolls-Royce salesman in Japan, approached me at the end of a lesson giggling uncontrollably. Through his laughter, he apologized in advance for being unable to attend the next lesson, as he was going to visit his mother, who was terminally ill, and was expected to die at any time.

Simon Hollington (Canada)

Signs and gestures

As well as having signs and gestures for many of the functions for which we use them, the Japanese have a number of additional signs. For common situations, their gestures are often different from our own. You may have difficulty in imagining these gestures from a verbal description, but when you are in Japan you will soon start recognizing these movements around you. By the way, Japanese people sometimes assume that all signs are international and will use them in communicating with you, thinking they will be more easily understood by *gaijin* if they use gestures rather than their own attempts at English.

Not all gestures are considered proper for use in formal situations, and may be thought of as vulgar or childish. Nonetheless, you will see the following being used by all sorts of people in all sorts of situations.

Messages which have different signs (and signs which convey different messages)

Come here. Beckoning is done with the hand turned palm down, and the four fingers moved to and fro.

Money. An imaginary coin is made by touching the tips of the thumb and forefinger to form a circle.

Eat. The first two fingers of the right hand (chopsticks) are dipped into the cupped left hand (bowl) to scoop up food.

Counting. This is done in the opposite way to the method with which you are probably familiar. All ten fingers are extended for zero. One thumb is turned in for one, the forefinger for two, and so on. Six can either be the thumb of the second hand, or bringing out the little finger that has just been turned in.

No. The right hand is held up in front of the face, with the thumb nearest, and the hand is fanned from side to side.

Me. The right forefinger touches the nose.

Joining little fingers. To seal a promise, two people interlink the little fingers of their right hands, rather as we would 'shake on it'.

Banzai! Both arms are held up three times, shouting '*Banzai!*' ('Ten thousand years!') each time. This is roughly equivalent to 'Three cheers!' It is used at the high point of a celebration of any kind, and has no specific military connotation (but it can nonetheless be a little startling the first time you hear it).

Jan Ken Pon. The scissors, paper and stone game (scissors cut paper which wraps stone which blunts scissors) is widely used to select a volunteer or a winner, rather as we toss a coin. Raise your right fist in preparation as you say '*Jan Ken*' and bring your hand down in your chosen gesture as you say '*Pon*'.

Pulling down the lower eyelid with a forefinger. This means roughly 'I don't like you', rather than 'I don't believe you.'

Gestures which have no equivalent

Excuse me. A kind of karate chop, coupled with a bow of the head, with which you make your way between two people you don't want to disturb, or through a crowd.

Yes and no. A circle (*maru*) means 'yes' and a cross (*batsu*) means 'no'. These two signs can be made with fingers, hands or arms. One person might go to the other side of a crowded bar, and signal back to his friends whether there are enough places. It is worth remembering these signs when marking students' work – a tick will totally confuse them.

'V'. The victory (or peace) sign is used generally as a positive or happy sign. It is *de rigueur* among young people when being photographed. A 'V' with each hand, opening and closing, signifies a crab.

Men and women. The little finger going up from a fist signifies 'woman' and a thumb held out from a fist signifies 'man'. One of these two gestures (depending on your sex) may be used, together with an enquiring expression, to mean 'Are you married?'

Writing on the palm. Japanese have a very limited sound system, with many words having ten or more meanings, but written with different *kanji*. Often the only way to communicate meaning, in the absence of pen and paper, is to 'write' on your palm with your forefinger.

Stirring. Turning a fist in a small circle, as though using a mortar and pestle, means that someone in the company is currying favour. This contrasts with the English meaning of the phrase 'stirring it', which is almost the opposite.

Turning the head sideways. This gesture, usually accompanied by a sharp hissing intake of breath, means that there is a problem, and the Japanese person is too polite or reserved to say so directly.

Kubi. Cutting your throat with your hand has the specific meaning of being fired from your job, and not the more general idea of death.

Kashiwade. This describes clapping hands at a shrine to awaken the gods. After the clapping, Japanese people join their hands in a gesture we can recognize as that of prayer, except that the thumbs are not crossed.

Typical lives

The following descriptions are of typical white-collar families. Less traditional Japanese people claim that many of the distinctive features noted here, such as the sharp division of responsibilities of husband and wife in marriage, are changing as the society modernizes and becomes more international.

Japanese babies learn early on the security of the family – their first group. Physical contact with parents (*skinship*) is high – young children sleep with their parents, are carried on their mothers' backs, and bathe with their parents. There is no concept of Original Sin in the culture, and children are considered pure, and almost up to school age, are not thought accountable for their actions. As such, they are rarely censured, to the extent that *gaijin* often consider them hopelessly spoilt.

School is the start of the treadmill. After school, it is off to the cram school (*juku*) for hours, then back home for homework. The aim is to pass the entrance exam at a prestigious university such as Tokyo University (Todai) or Kyoto University (Kyodai), which will effectively set them up for life. There is little time for dating, which means that many of them will rely on an arranged marriage.

University is usually a time of relaxing. The main hurdle, gaining university entrance, has been achieved. Students know that the fact that they have managed to pass the very stiff university entrance exam is a major factor in employers' minds when it comes to recruiting graduates. So university students can have a fairly relaxed time, knowing that the quality of their degree is more a matter of icing on the cake than a vital deciding factor in the kind of job they get. In fact, many university students spend at least as much time and effort working on their tennis and skiing as on academic subjects.

After university, it's back on the treadmill again, for men at least, as businessmen (*sararīman*). If a woman takes an office job, it is likely to be as an *office lady*, or *OL*, with low status or decorative duties such as filing or making tea, and looking pretty.

Finding a partner for life can be done through an *omiai* (arranged meeting or marriage). In practice, this can be as informal as a couple who are already going out with each other each bringing a friend to make a double date. It can, however, be done formally, with both sets of parents and the couple meeting, after a suitable amount of background vetting has been undertaken on each side. Dating as we know it is not common, although things are changing fast in this area, especially among university students. Aside from *omiai*, a common place to find a partner for life is in the office.

Once married, the roles divide, with the father having breakfast with the family – one of the few times he may see his children – before leaving for the long commute to the office. After work, there is often obligatory socializing with his section at work, and so he usually arrives home, rather the worse for wear, after the children have gone to bed. On his only free day, Sunday, he may be so tired that he spends most of the day catching up on lost sleep.

The mother has total control over the household, the family

budget, and caring for the children – of which there are probably two, and unlikely to be more than three. She develops a close relationship with her children, which is sometimes considered unhealthy in Western eyes, and is certainly unbalanced, since there is so little contribution from the father.

Marriage tends to be seen more as a duty than an enjoyable and loving experience. As such, there are perhaps lower expectations on each side, which may account for the rather lower divorce rates. The most difficult time for Japanese marriages is reputedly after retirement, when two people who have led largely separate lives are thrown together 24 hours a day, only to find how little they have in common.

In the past, old people lived with younger generations, but the extended family has largely broken down, at least in the cities, and this, together with the longest life expectancy in the world, means that the care of the elderly is a pressing and increasing social problem.

THE ENVIRONMENT

Crowds, organization and noise

One aspect of life in Japan you have to get used to is crowds. Space is very limited, and in the cities whatever you want to do, or wherever you want to go, there will likely be several or more other people with the same idea. However, every situation is very organized, and one can only marvel at the efficiency which enables so many to do so much in so little time.

One of the methods of organization is by public loudspeakers. There are loudspeakers everywhere – in trains, in parks, at pedestrian crossings, and in many other places. Japanese people show no signs of being disturbed either by the large number or by the volume of loudspeakers. To get an idea of the noise levels which they find tolerable, it is only necessary to step inside a *pachinko* parlour (and then step briskly out again before you are deafened).

Efficient, clean and safe

One of the pleasures of living in Japan is that everything works. Machines are rarely out of order. Roads are repaired during the night with incredible swiftness. If you order something, you will receive exactly what you ordered at the correct time. Everybody does their job, no matter how menial, to the best of their ability. One particular pleasure is to walk into a rough and ready *yakitori-ya* (a small bar selling grilled chicken) under the railway tracks, and be given the kind of jump-to-it service you might imagine being afforded a millionaire at his favourite table at the Ritz.

Japanese people are, as a rule, punctual, and it is important not to be late for an appointment. The saying about never having a second chance to make a first impression is very relevant when you are meeting a Japanese person for the first time. The Japanese person may have preconceptions (true and untrue) about foreigners, and you will do well not to reinforce the commonly held idea of *gaijin* as rather less concerned with attention to detail than the Japanese themselves.

Litter is less evident than in other countries, and vandalism is not the problem it is elsewhere. Most people pay great attention to dress, general appearance, and cleanliness.

There is very little street crime or burglary. You will feel safe walking home alone at any time of night. Mugging is virtually unheard of. In contrast to the not uncommon and unwelcome attention by gropers (*chikan*) on crowded public transport, serious sexual assault on foreign women is almost unknown. Unfortunately, however, the sarin gas episodes in Tokyo in 1995 were a reminder that Japan is not immune to terrorism.

Of course the *yakuza* have their interests and empires. However, they do not directly affect the life of ordinary citizens unless they become involved with money-lending (*sarakin*), drugs or prostitution.

Part 3

TEACHING ENGLISH

9 | Setting the scene

It is compulsory for all children to attend school from six to fifteen years of age. Many start earlier than this, attending kindergarten at the age of three or four. Almost all children stay on at school until they are eighteen, and one-third go on to some form of higher education after the age of eighteen.

The school year runs from April to March. In addition to eighteen public holidays there are six weeks of school holiday in the summer, two weeks at New Year and two weeks in spring. The school week runs from Monday to Friday, but most schools have classes on Saturday morning as well. The school day usually lasts from 8.30 am to 3.00 pm, with many students staying on until 5 or 6 pm to participate in sports or other organized activities. After this, many attend cram schools (*juku*).

THE NATURE OF THE TASK

The Japanese education system

There are five basic stages in the education system:

- Kindergarten (*Hoikuen* or *Yochien*), 3–6 years old
- Primary school (*Shō gakkō*), 6–12 years old
- Junior High school (*Chū gakkō*), 12–15 years old
- Senior high school (*Kōkō*), 15–18 years old
- University (*Daigaku*), Junior College (*Tandai*), or Technical College (*Senmongakkō*)

The Japanese education system has been described as the best in the world. It produces probably the most highly skilled and motivated workforce in the world. However, it is a narrow and restricted system which fails to develop important areas of pupils' characters, especially during the crucial years of adolescence, producing school leavers who are excellent at learning rules but seriously deficient in such skills as thinking for themselves. Tasker and Woranoff vividly outline the successes and deficiencies of the education system.

'The extraordinary achievement of Japanese education speaks for itself. High school students are two years ahead of their Western counterparts in mathematics and physics. Most young Japanese people can read music, know calculus, and have a fair grasp of statistical analysis. There are more universities in Japan than in the whole of Western Europe, and they produce double the number of engineers per head of population than the United States. In a sense the system fails nobody. It produces no long lines of alienated, unemployable youngsters; no crack-snorting behind the bike sheds.' (P. Tasker, *Inside Japan: Wealth, Work and Power in the Japanese Empire*)

'The children may have any number of facts and figures in their brain, but they are in some ways poorly adapted and integrated, and uncomfortable in many situations that would not concern children in most other countries. They are robbed of their spontaneity when young and, more seriously, the crunch comes at the age of about sixteen or seventeen, when the late maturing Japanese also have the growing pains of adolescence and young adulthood. This is the time when they would like to live and breathe, discover what life is about and perhaps enjoy it to some extent, show natural signs of rebellion and form a personality. Instead, they are locked up at school, drummed into further study at home, and sent off to cram school (*juku*) during evenings, weekends and vacations in order to pass the major hurdle of a university entrance examination.' (J. Woranoff, *Japan: The Coming Social Crisis*)

Pupils study English for six years. However, this is with a teacher who gives students facts and rules about English, with no discussion or opinion from the students. Even the asking of questions to clarify is generally frowned on in Japanese schools. The language taught is almost totally grammar-based, using reading, writing, and lots of exercises on paper. And oral work usually takes the form of the whole class repeating phrases in unison.

Much of the English taught in Japan is still formal, stilted and dated. Some books still teach sentences like 'If tomorrow be fine, we shall go on a picnic'. What they need from you as a native speaker is practice of natural English through speaking and listening, developing from and building on their present knowledge. Faced with weak oral skills, the teacher has to go right back to very simple English dialogues, and slowly build up from there.

The kind of language students need

Language can be broken up in several ways for the purposes of teaching. The two most common in modern English teaching books are *structure*, ie grammar, and *functions*, ie the uses we put the language to.

STRUCTURES		FUNCTIONS	
Present simple	**I go**	Suggesting	**Why don't you . . . ?**
Present perfect	**I have been**	Inviting	**Would you like . . . ?**
Nouns	**chair, Tokyo**	Requesting	**Could you . . . ?**

In the main, Japanese students need functions rather than structures, which they learn so relentlessly, and often out of context, at school. You may not always be permitted to concentrate your efforts on anything other than structures, but the fact remains that a functional approach which is more directly applicable in real situations will probably be more useful in helping students 'unlock' and release their potential when and if they ever want to speak English outside the classroom.

So, although it will be useful for you also to have some degree of familiarity with structures, especially for fielding learned (often useless) questions, students will generally have learned more than enough about grammar. Often, however, you might not have the final say in deciding the syllabus. If you find yourself with a heavily structural textbook or course, try to find ways of practising the grammar in a functional and communicative way, rather than just working your way through exercises and drills – adapt your material accordingly.

Poor language learners

Teaching English in Japan can be very enjoyable, but it can also be a frustrating business. The profile of a typical Japanese student is in many ways that of a poor language learner – shy, afraid of making mistakes, and unwilling to offer opinions, disagree with others, or show or talk about feelings and emotions.

On the other hand, Japanese students also have very positive qualities – they are usually hard-working, diligent, eager to learn, well behaved, polite, and loyal. Adults will have been learning English for at least six years, but in a way which will have led them to regard it not so much as a vehicle of communication as an academic subject with a body of rules and information. They will hope that you, the teacher, will be able to fill them with 'English', and somehow transform the grammar and rules in their minds into a facility for verbal communication. This process is much harder and slower than is often anticipated, and requires patience, time, and effort on both parts, especially since the students are living in Japan, and cannot be immersed in the language and cultural background of the countries whose language they are learning. As the teacher, your key task is to use and encourage their strengths to improve on their weaknesses.

Reluctance to speak

The greatest overall problem is that students find it hard to verbalize their ideas. This is related to a number of factors:

- The non-communicative way in which English has traditionally been taught in high schools. Many Japanese are not trained to think of English as a means of communication.
- Japan has been isolated from the West for large chapters in its history and is still in the early stages of 'internationalization'. You may even be the first foreigner your students have spoken to – especially if you are teaching away from the major cities.
- Silence, or at least a fair degree of reticence, is often more admired and desirable in Japan than volubility.
- Japanese people are on the whole rather more reserved with strangers than their Western counterparts. They are in general less used to speaking to people outside their normal circles, which are mainly family and work/school. As a result, even when speaking in Japanese they can be less than forthcoming with strangers. In fact, even when Japanese people are with people they know well, they may be content to sit in silence, rather than keep up what to their minds would be an artificial stream of conversation.
- Japanese are reluctant to disagree with a person or opinion so it is hard to achieve what we would term a healthy discussion and debating is extremely difficult. They prefer to try to find a general compromise solution to which the whole group can agree, rather than voice their own opinion.

HELPING STUDENTS RELAX – 20 TIPS

Japanese people spend a high proportion of their lives, some might say all of it, looking over their shoulder for the approval or disapproval of a superior or a group. The superior at different stages of their lives might be their mother, a teacher, a more senior student, or a boss. The group might be the family, their class in school or university, or Japan Inc. The rules of different groups are usually clearly defined, and Japanese people are trained from an early age to learn them, and to obey them without question.

One result of this is a high degree, to Western eyes, of nervousness, and a seeming inability to relax. These feelings are usually exacerbated by the potentially threatening environment of an English class, where every utterance is a possible mistake, and therefore a transgression of the rules. It is important, therefore, if you want to maximize your students' potential, to think of ways of using your position as group leader to make it clear, both explicitly and implicitly, that your group has few rules, and that you are not too concerned and will not punish students for transgressions. In general, aim to make your class as non-threatening as possible, and encourage students' self-confidence and ability to take control of their own learning. The twenty suggestions that follow will help you achieve this.

(1)   Sit down for all or part of the lesson. Except for specific activities, like writing on the board, it is quite feasible to run all but the very largest of classes from a seated position.

(2)   Do not talk too loudly. Of course you must be heard, but do not be domineering or threatening, either in volume or manner.

(3)   Put students into pairs or small groups which can be re-arranged from time to time to improve class harmony and mixing. Surprisingly, perhaps, students are often at least as embarrassed about performing and making mistakes in front of a large number of their peers as they are nervous of you. So reduce the size of their audience to a manageable number as often as possible. As well as being more relaxed about speaking in small groups, students will be more confident about repeating or reporting back to the whole class later.

(4)   Have brief pauses between sections of the lesson to allow students' minds to settle. These may only be a matter of 20 seconds or so – you can use the excuse of cleaning the board, or setting up the tape recorder, or sorting out your papers.

(5)   Correct as gently as possible – try to avoid the word 'No'. Try expressions such as 'Well . . .', 'Maybe', or 'Anybody else?'. Use self and peer correction (see p 140–141).

(6)   Explain that making mistakes is part of the learning process, everybody does it, and there is no punishment for this. Rather, attempts at fluency, or trying out new ways of expressing yourself, are to be admired. Here, if you are learning Japanese, you can point out that you understand their difficulty and make howlers yourself – but you learn by making mistakes.

(7)   Be positive and congratulate your students as often as possible. Make your comment on a successful attempt at something reflect in the way that you say 'Yes' or 'Good'. If a student makes a real effort and produces a difficult (for that student) sentence, show that you are pleased. Try, in a way that feels natural to you, to let your pleasure be clear in your voice and face. This will give great encouragement and sense of achievement to the student.

(8)   Encourage autonomy, and praise any student who shows the slightest sign of any.

(9)   Give students chances to take control occasionally. For example, let a more confident student run a game. Try to think of ways to let them set the agenda. (However, bear in mind that a teacher is a figure both of authority and respect, so try to make it clear that you have made a thought-out decision to hand over control, and that you are not abdicating it, and allowing your class to go to pieces. In other words, make it clear that what you are doing is part of the lesson and has a purpose.)

(10)   Never ridicule students or belittle their efforts at English, or abuse your power in any other way. This is very rude and destructive, and can have grave repercussions on future lessons with the class.

(11)   Set clearly achievable tasks. They do not have to be childishly easy, but students may be unwilling to go out on a limb with a speculative answer. Try not to allow your students to 'fail' or to lose face. The ideas of keeping and losing face are still remarkably strong in Japan. This is especially important in front of classmates who are younger or socially inferior (in the Japanese sense).

(12)   Do not always 'win', or insist on having the last word. Remember your special advantages in this unbalanced situation – you are the native speaker, you have set the agenda for the class, you come from the 'louder' society, and, indeed, you are not always right.

(13)   Be wary of joining in class laughter, if it is at the expense of a student. As long as laughter is not obviously malicious, there is no need to be authoritarian and put a stop to it. However, be aware that laughing yourself can give a strong seal of approval.

(14)   Be sensitive and restrained about bringing up any negative aspects of Japanese culture, such as *yakuza* (p 94) or, especially, *burakumin* (p 89), and of making negative comparisons with other countries. Many Japanese feel embarrassed or even threatened by criticism of their society, especially when it is brought up by a foreigner.

(15) Japan is very much a group-oriented society, so take every opportunity to strengthen the bonds of the class. Often, the easiest way to do this is to spend some time together as a group in a coffee shop or a bar, perhaps after the lesson. Drinking alcohol, under the influence of which Japanese can begin to let down barriers, is a widely recognized way of improving relationships, especially in business. However, daytime drinking is extremely uncommon, so go to a bar with students only after an evening class.

(16) Do not touch students. Japanese do not show their emotions in public. Farewells at airports seem very restrained to us, with very little bodily contact and no hugging or kissing. Touching a Japanese student can cause alarm or stiffness. This is especially true for male teachers and female students.

(17) Do not worry if there are periods of silence in your class. It is virtually impossible to keep a group of Japanese students going at full pace throughout a lesson. If you show impatience when they are not as responsive as you would like, this can have a negative effect of increasing tension. This is not to say that you should not step in and pick up the conversational ball if it becomes clear that nobody else is prepared to. But it is important to realize that silences often might not concern or worry your students as much as you, so try not to rush them into doing anything.

(18) Introduce new ideas, concepts and methods slowly and gradually. The Japanese education system is extremely conservative, and forcing students into new methods too quickly can often be counterproductive.

(19) Give them room to move, mentally as well as physically. Do not stand too close; give them time to gather their thoughts; and do not jump on every mistake. Approach students slowly, do not stand too close or tower over them, and perhaps crouch or kneel to have level eye contact.

(20) Finally, never show students that you are angry with them, either individually or as a group, unless it is a matter of discipline with children.

10 | The parts of a lesson

The outline of many lessons is similar. However, this outline is fairly flexible, and even staying within the basic format, there are many variations. The basic shape looks like this:

(1) Set the scene/arouse interest.
(2) Introduce the new language.
(3) Highlight form and meaning.
(4) Model and drill the new language.
(5) Allow students to practise the new language.

Set the scene/arouse interest

In some way, either use the item of language to be taught, or show a situation in which it would be natural to use it. This can be done in various ways – for example,

- Tell a story.
- Show pictures.
- Ask questions.
- Relate the new item to a story in the news/pop star/something of popular interest.
- Have the students listen to a tape.
- Have the students read a passage.

Introduce the new language

If the new language item has been used in the introduction, ask students to find or repeat it.

Alternatively, you can deliberately *not* use the new language item in the introduction. You can then ask the students to supply suitable language for the situation. This is a good idea for two reasons. It should give you an idea of how well the students know something. If they do not know it at all, the method should ensure that they start off with a fairly clear idea of its meaning, as you have given them a natural context for the new language.

Highlight form and explain meaning

The next step is to highlight the new item, for example by writing a sentence containing it on the board, and underlining it. Students now need to learn two things about the item. In the first place, they need to learn its *form* or physical make-up. For example, to form a regular past tense we add 'ed', and 'walk' becomes 'walked'. There are three basic sentence forms in which students should be able to use the new language item:

- Affirmative – **He walked.**
- Interrogative – **Did he walk?**
- Negative – **He didn't walk.**

Secondly, they need to learn the *meaning*. For example, we say 'How do you do' when we meet someone for the first time in a formal situation.

Model and drill the new language

Give the students a model of the new language – demonstrate it by saying it to them. Then drill it – ask them to repeat it in various ways until you feel they can say it sufficiently well (not necessarily perfectly).

Drilling is an area of teaching which has been much maligned. It has often been (and in places still is) carried out in a dreary and boring fashion, and some teachers are now wary of their lessons or themselves being labelled boring or old-fashioned. It is true that unless it is done with care, drilling can easily become very stodgy and lifeless.

The two important points to remember about drilling are:

- *Drill selectively.* Do not drill unless you are sure there is a need for it – in other words, do not drill for the sake of it. And as soon as students demonstrate competence, stop.
- *Keep the lesson moving along.* Do not spend too long on one drill or kind of drill, or with one individual.

Below are some, although by no means all, of the main kinds of drills.

Choral drill. This is where the whole class repeats together. This should be well orchestrated (literally start it off as though you are a conductor) and must not go on too long – once or twice is usually enough. This is the kind of drilling which got drilling its bad name through flagrant overuse, so beware. It is certainly overused in many high schools in Japan.

Individual drill. Students repeat one-by-one. The easiest way to run this drill, from the teacher's point of view, is to move regularly round the class, from one student to his or her immediate neighbour and so on. However, this tends to create a small, steadily moving pool of interested and involved students. This group is made up of the next few students in line to be asked to speak. Those who have spoken, and those who will not be called for a while, switch off, or worse, if they are children, energetically put into practice the saying 'The devil makes work for idle hands'. If, by contrast, you dot round the class at random, this helps to keep interest up. Do not worry too much about trying to remember exactly who you have asked. Asking someone twice will keep the class on its toes. You will find, in fact, that with a bit of practice, you can conduct this exercise with ease.

Mumble drill. This is sometimes useful if students still cannot get their tongues round the new language. Ask them to repeat the phrase or sentence a few times (say, five) to themselves quietly.

Substitution drill. One student says a sentence – for example, 'I like skiing'. The teacher says a word to another student, eg 'swimming', and the second student must substitute that word into the sentence, and says 'I like swimming'. The grammar, as well as the vocabulary, can be substituted and the teacher might give a cue of 'quite like' for the response 'I quite like swimming'.

There is sometimes a feeling among teachers that this form of substitution must be done with a large number of substitutions, both of vocabulary and grammar, and should go on for at least five or ten minutes. However, this can put an unnecessary strain on teacher and students alike. In any lesson, you should not normally have more than two grammar forms, and three or four vocabulary substitutions is plenty. In general, the drill should not last more than three or four minutes. The substitutions can be in your head, in your notes, or written on the board. For the lesson demonstrated above, your list might be:

like	**skiing**
quite like	**swimming**
don't like	**jogging**

Practice

Once students have repeated the new language in drills sufficiently, they can move on to practising it in a wider context. If possible, try to make practice purposeful – give students a reason to use the language, other than the fact that you are standing over them.

Practice can be communicative, for example an information gap (see p 131), a questionnaire or personalization (see p 132).

Games can provide painless and enjoyable practice. The students' involvement in a game is often intense enough for them to forget that they are actually learning through it. Some specific ideas are given later (see p 148).

THE FIRST LESSON

The first lesson with any student or group of students can be a little nerve-wracking. You may not know their level, or range of levels, their motivation or their previous learning experience. Then there is always the big question 'Will they like me?'.

First lessons always contain an element of introduction, and this can be usefully exploited in several ways. While this is going on, you can be getting a picture of the students to help you plan for future lessons.

The first unit of many textbooks has material on introductions, and you can use the allocated textbook, if there is one, or borrow from one at an appropriate level. Some specific ideas on introductions are given below.

You can, for example, use self-introductions – 'My name's Hiroshi. I come from Saitama. I'm 19. I'm a salesman'. Note that I have used a first name in the example. With in-company classes, it may be too much to expect businessmen, who may not even know each others' first names, to use anything but surnames. The embarrassment, especially between people of different ranks, would upset class feelings.

If the students are all adults, you may wish to allow them to give their age as '21' if they want.

You can do some drilling on typical mistakes:

- **My name is Suzuki.** (No contraction, inappropriate use of surname.)
- **I came from Saitama**. (Wrong tense – 'come'.)
- **I am 19 years old.** (No contraction, do not need 'years old'.)
- **My job is salesman.** (Unnatural sentence, no article – 'I'm a . . .'.)

The question forms can be practised, with the following typical errors:

- **What is your name?** (No contraction, intonation going up instead of down.)
- **Where did you come from?** (Wrong tense – 'Where do you come from?')
- **What is your job?** (Unnatural – 'What do you do?')

After practising the questions and answers with the whole class, students can copy a cued questionnaire into their notebooks (see below), and mingle with other students. You can either organize the seating, changing the seating until everyone has asked everyone else, or let them organize it, either moving from seat to seat or with everyone standing up and mingling.

Name? From? Age? Job?	1	2	3	4

At the end, have a feedback stage, with each student introducing another student:

This is Hiroshi. He . . .

Another useful technique for the first lesson may be the *information gap grid*. Students can complete a personalized grid with different answers, and then explain their grid to their neighbour.

For example, prepare sheets of paper with a triangle, a square, a rectangle and a circle. Hand out sheets to 'A' and 'B' alternately round the class.

A	B
In the triangle, write how many brothers you have.	In the triangle, write how many sisters you have.
In the square, write the name of your best friend.	In the square, write your mother's first name.
In the circle, write something you like.	In the circle, write something you hate.

'A' students and 'B' students can be grouped together when they are writing their own answers, and then they can be paired 'A' with 'B' to explain their grids.

11 Methods and ideas

This chapter contains a collection of ideas and methods looking at different aspects of teaching as they relate to Japanese learners.

METHODS AND APPROACHES

Nobody knows definitively how people learn languages. Despite this (or perhaps because of it) theories abound. There has been in the past a kind of pendulum effect, with successive styles, each a reaction to the extremes of the method which preceded it.

Standard methods

Language teaching remained largely unchanged throughout history until around a hundred years ago, using the Grammar–Translation method, which produced students who knew a lot about the language, but could not use it. The first reaction against this was the Direct method, which emphasized use of the target language only, with little or no consideration of grammatical rules. The Audiolingual approach was based on Behaviourism (with the idea that language learning is a habit) and had (often mindless) repetition and transformation in oral drills. The extreme disregard of rules of grammar in the Direct and Audiolingual methods was counteracted in the Cognitive Code method, which viewed language learning as rule acquisition rather than habit formation. The Humanistic approach added human and social elements, emphasizing communication and respect for the learner as an individual. Finally, the Functional approach focused on teaching relevant language, giving students useful and useable practice from the first lesson.

Most modern language teaching is based on the core concept of the Direct method, that the lessons are carried out in the target language, and also takes elements from the succeeding methods.

The traditional way of teaching languages, Grammar–

Translation, is still very much the norm in Japanese high schools. However, the relevance of other methods, in particular the importance of communication, is beginning to be realized.

Non-standard methods

As well as the above standard ones, there are a number of other methods of teaching languages which deserve mention. One or other of these 'non-standard' approaches are popular in a number of schools in Japan.

Total Physical Response

Total Physical Response (TPR) is an approach in which students act out the language. The concept can most easily be seen with imperatives. The teacher says 'Walk to the board' and the students get up from their seats and walk to the board.

Proponents of TPR say that the language learned is meaningful and memorable. Critics complain that its use is limited to very simple utterances such as imperatives. For example, it is difficult to act out tenses, or make clear the meaning of words such as 'so' or 'since', or show distinctions between different grammar forms, such as 'happy' and 'happiness'.

Many teachers use TPR when teaching young children, who can become restless if they sit inactive for long. The kind of concrete language which they need is ideally suited to TPR, and the method can be very successful in this context. Planned and properly prepared, it can also be effective at other levels, especially in large high school classes.

Community Language Learning

In Community Language Learning (CLL), the students sit in a circle and have a conversation. If a student cannot formulate an idea in English, he or she says it quietly to the teacher, who is standing outside the group. The teacher translates it, and the student repeats the translation to the group.

This method had its roots in clinical psychology and counselling, and is claimed to be a calm and non-threatening way to learn and practise language. It does, of course, require the teacher to have a certain level of competence in Japanese. It also depends on the atmosphere and level of the class. If students are too shy, self-conscious, unwilling to talk, or have insufficient vocabulary, it should be avoided.

Suggestopedia

In a Suggestopedia lesson, students are put into a very relaxed, almost hypnotic state. It is claimed that when one's mind is extremely relaxed, it is also very receptive to language input, and that very large amounts of language can be learned in a single lesson. This would seem to be a very attractive approach for teaching Japanese people, since so many of them have great difficulty relaxing in class.

A number of teachers, while not wishing to go all the way down the road of Suggestopedia, have introduced relaxing music and simple relaxation tapes into their classes in Japan, to try to remove students' tension and nervousness. Much New Age music is designed for relaxation. However, if you think your students would be suspicious of this kind of music being introduced into a classroom, baroque music may be more appropriate. Many of the slow movements of baroque music have a beat of around sixty beats a minute, and tests have shown that the heart slows sympathetically to this relaxed rate.

The Silent Way

Teachers using the Silent Way run their classes with little or no speaking on the teacher's part. The teacher uses a set of 'rods' as prompts. These are small pillars of wood, of various colours and lengths, which can represent letters, words, sentences, etc.

The rods are used to form sentences, or stories, and to correct students' mistakes, either without speaking, or giving a model of the new language only once, and then lapsing into silence. It is claimed that the silence gives students time and space to work out and internalize language rules.

HELPING STUDENTS TO TALK

Probably the biggest challenge facing you will be getting your students to talk. They may be very motivated, and may have expressed an interest in learning English conversation, but the fact remains that, on the whole, they will not speak willingly or fluently when the chance arises; will not object if you choose to hog the limelight and lecture to them; and will clearly be much more content with their heads down reading or writing than looking at you and each other, listening and chatting. Students will also be reluctant to disagree with you or each other, or to offer their own ideas.

The temptation is great – and it does not go away – to take the easy way out, ie to have lots of teacher talking time and heads-down work. The alternative – trying to encourage them out of their shells – can be a long and tortuous process, but is ultimately more rewarding both for you and the students, and is what is really needed.

The reticence of the Japanese is less than surprising, bearing in mind the historical tradition of social control (see pp 82–85). Even today, in most schools, aspects such as the exact details of hairstyles and the school uniform are controlled and standardized to the nth degree, and learning is often little more than the rote learning of facts, to be regurgitated at exam time. Students are expected to listen and take notes only, usually not being allowed the luxury of questions should they not understand some point, and certainly not expected or encouraged to form an opinion or discuss the pros and cons of a topic.

So, what doesn't work, and how can we make it work? One technique to avoid is that of throwing a subject out for students to pick up – for example, writing 'Should married women work?', on the board. In general, this is a real no-no. Japanese society and the education system are so far removed from this approach that it is almost certainly doomed to failure. You usually have to prepare the ground carefully and painstakingly if you want to get any kind of discussion off the ground. The preparation might include:

- Preteaching the vocabulary.
- Kicking off with a reading or listening passage.
- Allowing students time to prepare their points of view, either individually in class or as homework, or in pairs or small groups.
- Exposing students to a number of possible opinions for them to accept or reject, and hopefully personalize or develop.

Even with all this work beforehand, you may achieve only five or ten minutes of teacher-dominated discussion after 90 minutes of lead-in. You might ask yourself whether it is worth it. Although it benefits the students in the long term if you have a number of sessions like this, it probably is not worth the effort involved from both you and the students to have discussion in classes as frequently as you would with students in the West. However, if you do persevere, it gets easier the more you expose them to this method.

Begin a conversation gradually

It is probably more realistic to think of less ambitious ways of encouraging fluency. Let's start with the worst-case scenario. The students are reading aloud a dialogue from their books. How can you wean them away from the security of the text? First, encourage them to look up and down as they speak, making eye contact with their partner perhaps once a sentence. (Apart from anything else, this simple step should improve their intonation considerably.)

As a next step, write prompts on the board. These can consist of either one or two words from each sentence in the dialogue, or a description of it. For the sentence 'Would you like to come round for dinner?', you could write 'like/dinner' or 'Invite him to your house for dinner'.

Students should not be forced to memorize a dialogue. For each prompt, suggest one or two other possible sentences with the same or similar meaning.

A recommended source book for ideas on teaching conversation is *Conversation* by Nolasco and Arthur.

Closed pairs

Undoubtedly one of the most useful tools in the teacher's armoury when it comes to helping Japanese to speak English is closed pairs. The students are put into pairs, and each pair has the same, or a similar conversation, while the teacher walks around the class and monitors them. Many of the problems normally associated with Japanese students disappear when they have the chance to work in closed pairs. Shy, silent students, afraid of making mistakes, will be magically transformed into voluble chatterers. Believe me!

At first, closed pairs can be a new and frightening idea for everybody in the classroom – you, the Japanese team teacher (if there is one) or management, and of course the students. It is vital for everybody to believe in closed pairs, so let's look at how to help each of the above to overcome any possible reservations or resistance to this form of practice.

You

To convince yourself that closed pairs work, I suggest you try to brainstorm (try to get the students to throw out ideas) first with the whole class, and then in closed pairs. Ask the whole class a question like 'Tell me three parts of the body' or 'What's wrong with this sentence?' (write 'I go shopping yesterday' on the board). If it is a normal Japanese class, there will be dead silence.

Now say 'Talk to the person beside you'. If necessary, walk round the class, gesturing them into pairs. After a small initial shock, if this is their first experience of closed pairs, they will start to talk to their neighbour, and the change in noise level will be remarkable.

Trying closed pairs may require a certain leap of faith, and you may feel unconvinced at gut level, even if you think it's a good idea at the intellectual level. The idea of letting go can be scary, but you must do it with complete confidence. Teachers often have two worries:

- What if it becomes a riot? (Obviously more of a concern with children.)
- Won't they all be making lots of mistakes without me being there to hear and correct them?

On discipline, it is normally true to say that unless you are having major problems in whole-class teaching, you are unlikely to have problems in closed pairs. The ones who do not talk normally because of lack of motivation may not put much into closed pairs, but you have not really lost anything, have you? Rather than causing discipline problems, many teachers find that they can in fact tighten up their control in closed pairs by zooming in on problem students and giving them the benefit of a steely glare, or just standing near them.

On the second point, not being able to correct every mistake, remember that it is better for a lesson to be a continuum from the rigidity of total control towards the absolute freedom students will have to succeed or fail when they use English in free speech outside the classroom. So you should 'loosen the reins' a bit during parts of the lesson.

One extra advantage of closed pairs is that they are an excellent way of discovering whether students have really absorbed what you have taught them without embarrassing them in front of the whole class. The fact that you 'teach' a class something does not necessarily mean that they have learnt it. If, in listening to the students in closed pairs, a large part of the class demonstrates that all or part of a lesson has not 'gone in', don't panic. Just think of closed pairs as a useful diagnostic tool. For you, it shows which areas still need to be worked on – and for the students, it should help to remove any resentment at having to spend more time on points already 'taught'.

Japanese teachers or management

If you are working with a Japanese teacher, set out the advantages of closed pairs. The first is that students will actually talk! First, it is much more natural to speak in a normal projection to one person instead of in a loud voice in front of a large group. Second, the time each student will have for talking will be vastly increased – for example, in a 40-minute class with 40 students, the average time each student will normally speak for is just 30 seconds, assuming the teacher speaks half the time. This figure rises dramatically using closed pairs.

One reason Japanese teachers give initially for disliking closed pairs is that the school has gone to a lot of time and trouble to import a native speaker, and that you are being wasted if you are not talking to the whole class all the time. The answer to this is that, even using closed pairs at every possible opportunity, there will still be plenty of teacher-talking time in the lesson. You should also assure the Japanese teacher that you will, of course, ensure plenty of modelling, drilling and correction before putting the students into closed pairs.

If your boss is Japanese, it is probably easier not to go into exact details of your teaching methods if they include radical ideas such as closed pairs, unless you are sure that you will receive a sympathetic hearing.

Students

The golden rule with regard to the students is to make sure that they know exactly what to do. First, they need to know clearly what they are supposed to do when they are in closed pairs. Usually, the best way to ensure this is to begin by having students speak in open pairs first (ie two students speak while the rest of the class listens). This is generally better than explaining what to do.

Next, the logistics of who does what to whom must be made clear. Walk round the class, gesturing them into pairs.

Put the class into closed pairs as soon as you feel that you have done enough open pairs for most students to have the idea of what is required. At the start of closed pairs, it is often a good idea to listen in briefly on any weak students to make sure they are getting on all right.

You may wish to have one or two more open pairs when the students have finished a closed-pairs session. This should give the students a chance to give and observe a more polished performance than the often stumbling attempt which is all they could produce in open pairs before practising in closed pairs. Working in closed pairs is a good way to give students confidence before asking a pair to get up on the floor to perform in front of the class.

While students are in closed pairs it is also useful to monitor the weaker students to see if they will be able to handle the spotlight of being in an open pair during this second session of open pairs. Indeed, probably the most appropriate time to ask weaker students to come out on the floor is after they have shown you and themselves in closed pairs that they can manipulate a new language item competently and confidently.

If, once they are in closed pairs, you suddenly realize that you want to interrupt and say something to the whole class, a sharp handclap is usually enough to get attention. This is also the best way to signal the end of closed pairs.

What should you do during closed pairs? You should monitor, of course, but should you correct? As a general rule, only correct errors associated with that day's teaching points, unless there is a severe problem (eg communication breakdown). It is good to wean dependent students off your control. However, this time is also useful for giving weaker students general help. Bear in mind what was said before – that if a number of students are having difficulties it may be necessary to re-teach something.

An important point about closed pairs is that they can be as long or short as a piece of string. It is sometimes thought that they should only be used at the end of a lesson, as a kind of grand finale, to practise all the new language taught in one long session, lasting perhaps five or ten minutes. In fact, as the initial examples show, closed pairs can be used in very short bursts of even five or ten seconds.

To see closed pairs used in the context of a lesson, take the following six-line dialogue:

> **A:** What did you do last weekend?
> **B:** I went to Harajuku.
> **A:** Oh, who did you go with?
> **B:** Junko and Kyoko.
> **A:** How long did you stay there?
> **B:** Oh . . . about three hours.

The teacher presents the first exchange:

What did you do last weekend?/I went to Harajuku.

Cover form and meaning (see p 113); modelling; chorus drilling; and individual drilling. The first exchange is then practised a few times in open pairs. Now the students are put into closed pairs to practise the exchange twice, swopping roles after doing it once. Then one or two pairs repeat the exchange in open pairs.

The next exchange is similarly presented and practised. Then the first and second exchanges are done together, in open and then closed pairs.

The third exchange is then covered, and finally the whole dialogue is done in open and closed pairs.

You can now go on to substitute and personalize the dialogue in open and closed pairs. The important point is that during the presentation of the basic dialogue, the students have had five short closed pairs sessions.

TEACHER–TALK: WHEN, HOW AND HOW MUCH?

One of the major roles of an English teacher in Japan is as a model for students to listen to and try to understand and imitate. Hopefully you will achieve more aims than just this, but if you are assisting a Japanese teacher in a high school, this may be your lot! Several aspects of teacher-talking are important, so let's look at some of these.

First, how much of the lesson should the students spend listening to your dulcet tones? Well, do you want your lessons to be lectures or do you want to encourage students to speak? Unless you are giving a talk about, for example, cultural differences or recounting an episode in your life, it is a good exercise for you to see how little speaking you can do and still run a successful lesson. The less you talk, the more chances the students will have to speak.

Second, how should you simplify your speaking so that lower-level students can understand you? You can do it in two ways: by slowing down your rate of delivery and by using simpler words. As pointed out later in more detail in the section on pronounciation, you must be careful that slowed-down speech keeps the other factors which make it natural – don't separate each word, or over-enunciate.

There are a number of elements in speaking more simply. Vocabulary can be made less sophisticated, idioms can be avoided, and more basic grammar forms can be used (see the box below for examples).

	INSTEAD OF	YOU COULD SAY
VOCABULARY	awful	very bad
	fascinating	very interesting
IDIOMS	get over	recover from
	come across	discover
SENTENCES	Perhaps it might be better if you did it this way	(Why don't you) do it this way.
	All I want you to do is to name an occupation.	Tell me a job.
	I wouldn't do that.	Don't do that.
	If you wait here at the end of the lesson.	Wait here at the end of the lesson.

In addition, phrasal verbs (verb plus preposition) such as 'see to' ('arrange') can be very difficult to understand, and it is best not to use them when giving instructions or explanations.

Similarly, avoid 'throwaway' jokes or asides. These are a luxury which will either confuse the students, or waste a lot of class time when you try to explain them (and believe me, *nothing* is still funny after ten minutes of explanation). There is no harm in exploiting situations in a humorous way if the humour can be expressed simply or visually, but save your puns and sophisticated observations for when you are with other native English speakers.

As well as speaking at a level appropriate to that of your students it is important not to give out too much information at once. You must constantly check comprehension of what you say. It can be embarrassing to speak for two or three minutes to a group of beginners, only to find they did not understand your first sentence. So after every 'chunk' of information, it's a good idea to check that students have understood.

The amount of information in a 'chunk', and how you check comprehension will vary with the students' level and how well you know them. With beginners, you may have to check every sentence, or even several times a sentence.

The easiest way (from your point of view) to check comprehension is simply to ask the students a question, such as 'Do you understand?'. There are two problems with this. First, they may not be the best people to judge whether or not they understand. Second, and perhaps more relevant when teaching Japanese people, they may be unwilling to bite the bullet and admit that they do not understand.

Consider the sentence

John went to the bank yesterday.

Some ideas for checking comprehension are:

> *Specific questions:*
> **Where did he go?**
> **Who went to the bank?**
> *Negative checking:*
> **Did he go to the post office?**

When negative checking, be very careful not to phrase your question with a negative (eg 'He didn't go to the post office, did he?'). This should always be avoided because it is a very difficult concept for Japanese to grasp and will cause confusion.

One time it is vital to ensure that students understand you is when you want them to perform a task, or to work in pairs or groups. Usually the simplest way to explain a task is to do an example of it.

Having thought about all the ways to make sure students can understand you, there is the sometimes tricky element of ensuring that you are not talking down to them – treating them like little children or people of inferior intelligence. This is a difficult area to illustrate in concrete terms. What it is important to bear in mind is that just because someone is a beginner in English does not mean that he or she is not competent and successful in other areas of life. Especially when teaching business people older than yourself, you risk alienating students if you seem to be talking down to them. It is perhaps useful to try to imagine how you would like to be treated if you were a beginner student. If you study Japanese language or some aspect of Japanese culture during your stay, this could put you in that position and help you to appreciate life from the student's seat, especially if you are exposed to the 'laying down the law' approach of many Japanese teachers.

CLASS MANAGEMENT

Under the umbrella of class management, I have included seating arrangements in the classroom; discipline; how and what to write on the board; relationships with and between students; controlling the focus and pace of a lesson; and dealing with different group sizes.

Seating system

The ideal seating system for most classes, if the institution and class numbers permit, is for the students to be in a semicircle, with the teacher facing the open end of the semicircle. In this arrangement, every person in the room can speak directly to every other person in the class, and can see their lips to help understand them, and their face to see their emotional responses. It is the easiest arrangement in which to lead open-pair drilling, and students can change chairs and stand up easily for a mingling activity or role play. Every student can see the teacher and the board without looking over another student's head. It is also close to the natural position that a group of people would adopt to sit and chat socially.

If you are teaching in a high school, with the students in rows, you are a little more restricted. However, even with a traditional seating pattern, it is still possible to have closed pairs and students out at the front of the class, and you may be able to move some of the desks.

With businessmen, especially in-company teaching, classes are often round a table. This is another natural social way of grouping, and, in addition, it is a way the students will probably be familiar and comfortable with. It is a little more awkward for everybody to see the board without craning, and not so easy to get up on the floor, but there tends to be less play acting in business teaching, so this is not such a loss.

You may want to give each student an opportunity to talk to a student other than his/her immediate neighbours. One way is to name the students (either aloud or mentally) 'A', 'B', 'A', 'B', etc. Having done this, move each 'B' student two chairs along. Approach the first 'B' student, gesture to the seat of the second 'B' student, and say 'Could you sit there?'. Then approach the second 'B' student, gesture to the third 'B' student, and say the same thing. Go round the class in this fashion. Alternatively, write on the board 'If you are "B", move two seats to your left'.

Writing on the board

Some tips on using the board:

- Write as clearly as possible.
- Think about layout. Perhaps include a board layout in your lesson plan. Draw a vertical line or lines to divide the board into sections for different purposes, such as vocabulary and sentences.
- Use different colours for labelling, etc.
- Have pauses in your lesson for students to copy from the board.
- Ask students to tell you what to write as you build up a board display.

Nominating students

When you ask a question, you can ask the class in general or ask a student by name. Asking the class in general develops students' confidence and initiative. However, if a few confident students are answering all the time, nominate some quieter students, being careful not to press or embarrass them.

Asking students by name means that you have to know their names, or have a seating plan to hand. Establish when taking the first register which is their surname and which their given name, and the pronunciation (usually very easy, since Japanese words are spelt as they are said). Try to avoid pointing with an extended forefinger. This can be intimidating, and an open-handed gesture, as though you were introducing the student, is much softer.

Favouritism. It is inevitable that there will be students that you like more than others, for such reasons as intelligence, physical attractiveness, or diligence – and there will be students you do not particularly like. It is important that you give each student equal regard and attention, and do not reveal personal preferences. If you want to show that you are not pleased because, for example, a student has not done his homework, make it clear that your displeasure is directed at the lack of homework, and not at the student personally.

Changing the focus and pace

One simple way to make lessons more interesting for yourself and the students is to vary both what they focus their attention on, and also the speed at which the lesson moves along. It is much easier to have a stimulating, memorable and successful lesson if the students' attention has the chance to move around. No matter how fascinating you are to your students, they will eventually tire or get bored if the whole lesson consists of you talking to them and asking them questions.

The temptation is often to focus attention on either yourself or the textbook. However, the changes can be rung in a number of ways. At different points in the lesson, the focus can be on:

- The teacher.
- The textbook.
- The board.
- Students' notebooks.
- An audio tape.
- Flashcards.
- Real objects, such as a tin-opener or a tennis racquet.
- Other students, individually or as a group.
- Part of the classroom, either for what it is (say, a chair) or what it might be (say, a taxi).

An added bonus for you of having a change of focus is that you can take short breaks during the course of the lesson while attention is directed away from you. A plus point for Japanese students is that they have the chance to develop some autonomy, because everything is no longer being channelled through the teacher.

It is useful to think about changes of pace as well. If the students have been reading a long passage, they will need something light and fast moving to change the pace, such as a short game.

Large groups

Working with large groups, forty or even fifty students, requires some special techniques, or modifications to those outlined elsewhere in this book.

It is often not practical to rearrange the seating, and you must make do with serried ranks. This does not prevent you from using closed pairs, an especially useful tool with large numbers

You may have to project your voice considerably. In addition, your gestures may have to be wider and tend to the theatrical.

In view of the reduced intimacy and impersonal nature of such groups, it is helpful to make an added effort to learn and remember names. A seating plan is often useful – be careful that high school students do not swap seats for a joke. In a women's college where I taught, I asked the students to supply a passport-size photograph, and gave them a simple form to complete: name, class, age, hobbies etc. These were very useful in helping me to get to recognize individual students.

One-to-one

One-to-one teaching is where there is only one student being taught. This is sometimes referred to as 'private' teaching. However, I am reserving the word 'private' for work arranged by a teacher other than through a school or employer.

One-to-one teaching is much closer to normal interaction than teaching a group. It is also flexible, because there are no other student's needs to consider. You can break at any time, or change the course of the lesson as appropriate.

Furthermore, since there is only one student to consider, there can be considerable flexibility both in setting a syllabus, and in deviating from it. Ideas for the syllabus can come from both the student saying what he or she wants and needs, and the teacher's judgement of the student's needs and how to meet them. If the teacher's feelings about the student's needs do not tally with the student's own estimations, the teacher will have to decide to what extent he or she will accept the student's wishes (since it is the student who is paying after all), whether to try to persuade the student to accept all or part of what the teacher wants to teach, or whether to have a hidden agenda, and purportedly teach what the student wants while slipping in other teaching. In the end, there is often only the vaguest outline of a syllabus, with the teacher and/or the student deciding almost lesson-to-lesson what will be of interest and use.

COMMUNICATION – WHAT LANGUAGE IS FOR

Communication is the buzzword of English teaching in Japan. Everybody professes to want it, but few have more than a hazy idea what it entails, apart from the ubiquitous 'free conversation'.

One unfortunate side-effect of the way that English is typically taught in Japanese high schools – as a body of knowledge to be crammed into the students' heads like mathematical formulae – is that Japanese people are not used to using English as a vehicle for communication. Students are quite content when the lesson consists of everybody looking at their textbooks, but the simple command 'Close your books' can produce a visible onrush of panic throughout the class.

True use of language involves communication. This can come from reading or listening to information. Generally, Japanese students have a greater need to practise listening than reading. It is important to realize that if students have their textbooks open and are listening to you, or another student, reading aloud, then what is being communicated is only the sound of the language – they are almost certainly getting the meaning from the printed text: in other words, it is *reading* comprehension and not *listening* comprehension.

Listening practice is examined in more detail later. Here, we will look at interactive communication, where the student has to give and receive information.

Information gaps

One way to achieve this is through an 'information gap'. Each student has all or part of the necessary information, and has to speak and listen in order to communicate all the information. It can be done in pairs, when it is often in the form of a conversation or in larger groups, when it can take the form of a questionnaire.

In an information gap exercise, the teacher gives out two sets of sheets, each containing different pieces of information. Each pair or group of students has all the information between them, and has to ask and answer to find it all. The information can be in the form of a text or a picture, or in tabular form, such as a list, a grid or a diagram.

To look at some examples, one student could be a prospective traveller asking about train times, and the other student a travel agent with a timetable or one student could be a pop star and the other an interviewer. The information cards they might be given are illustrated in the boxes on the following page.

STUDENT A	STUDENT B
You want to go from London to Cambridge tomorrow morning by train. **Ask at the station for the times of the trains.**	**You work at the station. Here is a timetable:** **London (dep) Cambridge (arr)** **9.10 10.35** **11.20 12.45** **15.30 17.10** **18.20 19.50**

STUDENT A	STUDENT B
You are the pop star Vanilla. Your latest record 'All My Love' sold 3 000 000 copies. Your world tour is starting next week. The tour will reach Japan in October.	**You are a journalist. You are going to interview the pop star Vanilla. Ask about:** **Latest record – Can you tell me about . . . ?** **World tour – (1) When/start?** **(2) To Japan?**

Books covering information-gap activities include *Pair Work* and *Pair Work One* by Watcyn-Jones and *Tandem Plus* by Read and Matthews.

Personalization

Having students speak about themselves ('personalization') is a useful and stimulating method of moving on in a communicative way from repeating rote sentences. You might wish to assure students that they can choose to lie about or withhold personal information which they do not wish to reveal, such as their age.

Personalization can take the form of a questionnaire. (Japanese use the French word *enquête* for this, by the way, and many of them believe it to be an English word.) It is very easy to construct, or for the students to construct themselves, questionnaires to practise a language point. The questionnaires can take the form of 'Yes/No' questions; 'Wh' questions (what, when, etc); 'True or False' statements; or multiple-choice questions. For example:

> *Simple present tense:*
> **Do you smoke?**

Do you get up before 7 o'clock?
Do you like Mozart?

In a questionnaire, students can first ask their colleagues on either side. You can rearrange the seating (see p 127) or students can be standing, mingling freely.

Natural English

It is vital that Japanese students who can produce only very stilted English are exposed to a model of English from you which is as natural as possible.

You must make sure that, although you may speak more slowly and use fewer idioms, your speech retains natural intonation and grammar (no pidgin, please), and that such features as elision and the weak sound (see p 143) are not lost.

Levels of politeness

It is important to ensure that your students are exposed to more than one level of politeness of English. Probably the three most useful levels are:

- Formal.
- Informal.
- Slang (to a lesser extent).

It is likely that your students will have learned English which is too formal for most situations. Students will need to learn, for example, what kind of language is appropriate for making a dental appointment as opposed to arranging to meet a friend.

Because your students will often have been taught mainly formal English it is important to expose them to informal expressions. The idea of register exists in Japanese – and they often have many more levels than in English, so it is an easy concept to get across. A useful word is *teinei* – 'polite'.

Students will need to learn the first two of the above levels for both understanding and speaking. When trying to select what to teach, one rule of thumb is to imagine the kind of language which you use when you are talking to people other than family or close friends.

When you talk to someone you know very well, you are more likely to use very informal language. It is usually very difficult for Japanese students to use very informal or slang expressions in a natural way – one reason for this is that their diction is too careful for this purpose. So it is probably best to teach a few such expressions, and to stress that they are for reception (understanding) only rather than production (using). It is also advisable to introduce them only to more advanced students.

One form of slang which your students may well never have met is cursing or swearing. The concept does not exist in Japanese, with the sole exception of *kuso* (shit), and you may be met with incredulity, or at least find the idea difficult to explain. The concept is that we use words connected with sex or religion to express or emphasize emotions, such as anger, surprise or excitement. In general, in English, cursing (religious words) is less taboo than swearing (sex words).

On the whole, it is not useful to teach slang or swearing for productive use. Even if students are in a situation where other native speakers are using slang and/or swearing, it is most unlikely that they will be able to use these forms in a natural way, and will sound more out of place by trying to use them than by using language which is a little more formal than that of the other speakers. It is, however, useful to expose students to a limited number of slang expressions, so that they will understand them if they hear them. *Don't go overboard on this.* It is very easy to overload students in this area: they are often very eager to learn these types of expression, but it is best to impose a limit.

Sometimes there is a handy contrasting pair of formal and informal expressions (see below). Sometimes an expression simply stands on its own and you must just point out whether it is formal or informal.

FORMAL	INFORMAL
May I	**Can/Could I**
Would like	**Want**

Communicating culture

An important element in your teaching will be exposing students to, and explaining significant and interesting parts of your culture. This can take several forms:

- Talks on specific aspects of your culture, eg my sister's wedding.
- Discussions on differences and similarities in the two cultures (eg weddings in Japan or your country).
- Dealing with points of culture as they arise in your lesson.

The following list is just to get you started – you will have no trouble adding to it once you have been in Japan a little while:

- Using Christian names *v* titles ('younger son') or family names.
- Dating.
- When and how to give presents (eg *omiyage* (holiday gifts) *v* postcards).

THE FOUR SKILLS

There are four language skills – speaking; listening; reading; and writing. Two are productive and two receptive.

	PRODUCTIVE	RECEPTIVE
ORAL	Speaking	Listening
WRITTEN	Writing	Reading

It is worth considering the best order in which to go through the skills. Students' chances of producing satisfactory pronunciation will be improved if they hear and say before they read and write. This is borne out by the fact that tolerable pronunciation which students can produce when they imitate the teacher sometimes becomes worse when they see the word written down. The order, then, is – hear; speak; read; write.

The two skills which you will probably be asked to concentrate on are the complementary skills of speaking and listening. Speaking is covered throughout this book, and I do not include any special notes on it in this section. I will deal here in some detail with listening, and in rather less detail with reading and writing.

Listening

Listening practice generally takes three forms. Students can listen to you, to other students, or to a recording (usually an audio cassette). It can take place in the classroom or in a language laboratory. I will concentrate on listening in the classroom, as teachers are usually given fairly specific instructions by the school on how to work in a language lab – normally it is a matter of monitoring students one-by-one as they work their way through pre-recorded drills, and giving them individual correction and assistance.

In the classroom, everything you say is listening comprehension for the students. As far as your instructions are concerned, the acid test of their comprehension is whether they do what you want them to!

Personal anecdotes can provide useful listening comprehension. These can be true, adjusted, or totally fictitious accounts of your childhood or university life, what happened to you last week, where you went last night, etc.

It is important not to ignore students themselves as a listening source. This can take the form of an information gap (see p 131).

Audio tape

When doing a listening comprehension from a tape, some points to bear in mind are:

- *Set a task.* Don't play a tape without giving students a reason to listen. A task can take the form of questions – either for meaning or language, or a task such as drawing or writing something on a map, diagram or picture. It is usually better to preset the task, not to play the tape and then give them the task.
- *Move from general to specific.* Do not be afraid of exploiting the tape for different purposes. Each time you play it you can set a different task. Make your first task a general one to check overall comprehension, and then move on to more specific comprehension questions. After that, you can examine the kind of language used. (See the box below for examples.)
- Finally, of course, the students can be asked to *repeat* all or part of the utterances on the tape.

TYPE OF TASK	SAMPLE QUESTIONS	ANSWER
General comprehension	**Where is he?**	**(He's) in a shop.**
	What does he want?	**(He wants a) red pullover.**
	Does he get it?	**Yes (he does).**
Specific comprehension	**What does his friend suggest?**	**(She suggests) try(ing) on the cashmere pullover.**
Language focus	**How does she suggest it? (What words does she use?)**	**Why don't you . . .?**

With regard to checking answers, give students a chance to compare answers with a neighbour in closed pairs before checking with the whole class. When you do check with the whole class, do not be too eager to tell the students the right answer. When a student gives an answer, see if the class agrees with it, and write the answer (or possible answers) on the board. When all the answers are on the board, play the tape again for students to check the possible answers on the board. If a question still has a wrong answer, play that part of the tape once or twice to see if they can get the right one. However, don't prolong their agony too much. They can listen to a phrase only a limited number of times before further listening does not help any more.

In dealing with comprehension questions, do not insist on complete sentences when the students answer. In the boxed examples, the vital information is outside the brackets, and this is all students need to produce to show that they have understood.

Video

A few words about the use of video. Don't be in awe of it the first time you bring it into your lesson. You can use it at first as you would an audio tape. With repeated use, more and more ways of exploiting it will probably come to mind without conscious effort on your part.

Keep the length of video sequences about the same as those for audio tapes. Teachers sometimes play video sequences as much as ten times longer than they would play an audio tape. The danger here is that students can settle into a passive TV-watching mode. If you are using a long tape, try to pause every few minutes to check answers. If it is an authentic play or film, scenes usually last just a few minutes, and this is therefore a natural section to use in class.

It is a good idea to make sure everything is plugged in and switched on, with the tape cued if you are not starting at the beginning, and the tape counter set. Also, it may be handy to know where to get help if you have any technical problems.

Two techniques with video which are easy and productive: (a) use the freeze-frame for the students to describe the scene and to predict what will happen; (b) view the sequence with no sound and ask the students to imagine what is happening and what is being said.

If you are involved in the selection of video material to be used in your school, watch a good amount of the tape before selecting it. Check especially for sound quality. Makers of teaching videos are sometimes very ambitious, and include a lot of outside recordings. This is useful for displaying various aspects of culture and giving a natural context for the language, but the quality of the soundtrack suffers as a result. On an audio tape it is unusual to have more than 10% of the tape recorded with background noise, such as traffic, wind or other conversations going on. Many teaching videos, on the other hand, have a substantially larger amount of the recording done out of the studio.

Reading

If you are setting questions for a reading comprehension, make sure that the answers can be taken directly from the text. Japanese students are usually poor at inferring (reading between the lines) or giving an opinion.

Don't speak to students while they are reading anything. Even for native speakers it is difficult to take in two forms of information at once. Give them enough time to digest the reading before starting to speak. Better still, do your speaking before giving out the reading text.

Writing

Japanese tend to write English which is vague and lacks cohesion. One specific grammatical problem is writing incomplete sentences. Either there is no verb, or no main clause – for example, 'Because it was snowing'.

Essays often seem to wander around, with rather a lot of sentiment, but little logical development or resolution. Restrict your assignments to simple story-telling rather than letting their imaginations roam on descriptive or emotional topics.

Paragraphs are a new idea for many. It can take a long time to explain both the concept, and the mechanical rule for creating a new paragraph. Use an example of paragraphs in a book which they can look at to demonstrate this.

VOCABULARY

Learning vocabulary is a necessary part of learning a language, and indeed Japanese students often say that a lack of sufficient vocabulary is one of their greatest problems. However true this may be, and no matter how eager students may be to learn new words and expressions and note them down feverishly, there is a limit to the amount of new information that can be committed to memory, so try to restrain yourself and limit your teaching of vocabulary to a manageable amount – certainly less than ten completely new items per lesson.

Whether or not students are correct in their self-assessment that they need a lot of vocabulary, there is no doubt about the kind of new words they need to learn. They have learned lists of vocabulary which include many esoteric and dated words, but often the simplest of everyday words stumps them. However, don't overdo the teaching of idioms: it is very easy to overload them with these. In general, be selective in the vocabulary you teach and try to develop a feel for how frequently we use a certain word or expression, and concentrate on those which are used most often.

Vocabulary can be presented and explained in a wide variety of ways.

Pictures. You can either bring pictures to the classroom, or draw on the board. Try not to be too embarrassed about your poor artistic abilities.

If you can bear it, a good laugh at your attempt at, say, a bicycle, can work wonders in loosening up a class. It is good for the students' confidence to see your pathetic efforts, since most Japanese people can execute simple drawings at a high level of competence, due to years of practice with their complex picture writing system. As a result, they should lose some of their awe of you.

Although drawing is usually considered an art, there is a strong element of craft involved, and most teachers, if they are willing to persevere, become in the end reasonably competent, producing outline drawings which are recognizable, if not beautiful. There are a number of books with tips on drawing simple pictures, and basic stick figures to copy. One is *Stick Figure Drawing for Language Teachers* by F. Johnstone.

Objects. The actual object can be brought into the classroom. This provides interest and focuses attention on the subject. You are, of course, limited to words describing small and easily portable things.

Example. Giving examples is useful in the case of 'group' words. The word 'vehicle' can be explained by giving the examples 'car', 'train', and 'plane'. The word for 'for example' is *tatoeba*.

Explanation. This is perhaps the most common method. It can, however, be difficult to explain something, especially to lower levels, without using words which are at least as difficult as the term you are trying to explain.

Mime. This is often useful for verbs like 'run' or 'drink' and prepositions like 'to' or 'on'.

Opposites. Surprisingly often, the meaning of a word can be explained, or at least clarified, by giving the opposite. The word for 'opposite' is *hantai*, and the phrase for 'the opposite of *X*' is *X no hantai*.

Translation. This is usually a last resort. Translation can be done by you, by a stronger student, or the students can look it up in their dictionaries. If students use a bilingual dictionary, try to find one which gives an example sentence, to ensure that the correct sense of the word is being translated. Bear in mind, too, that many words or concepts cannot be translated easily, and some not at all.

CORRECTING MISTAKES

Making mistakes is a necessary part of learning a language, and, as mentioned previously, the Japanese sense of shame at making mistakes can hold them back. So it is vital that your treatment of mistakes is sensitive and appropriate, to encourage them to try things out in the presence of you and their peers.

Many Japanese students will apologize for making a mistake, but if you engender the correct spirit, and if you have the class for long enough, they will probably stop doing this.

How to correct. Gently! Japanese learners usually feel sensitive and exposed when they have made a mistake. It is almost always possible to avoid using the word 'No'. You can get your meaning across by saying 'Not exactly', 'Well . . . ' 'Hmm . . . ', or with a slight grimace, or even a thoughtful expression. The Japanese are used to subtlety, and it will not be difficult for them to work out that they have made a mistake.

When and what to correct. Don't correct every mistake. It is disheartening and self-defeating for students. If there are too many corrections, they will remember less than if you are selective. A rule of thumb is to correct most mistakes connected with that day's lesson, some mistakes relating to points covered in previous lessons, and hardly any that relate to points yet to be taught.

The amount of correction should normally vary as the lesson progresses. Correction is usually more comprehensive at the presentation and drilling stages. If the students are engaged in a communicative activity or a free-speaking exercise, it is sometimes a good idea to note some of the mistakes made, but to leave correction until the end of the activity. There is no need to name names when you discuss these mistakes.

Who should correct? The student who made the mistake should be given a chance to self-correct (often the student will do this without any prompting from you, so do not be too eager to jump in). Next, other students, either individually or the whole class, should be asked for the correct answer ('Can anybody help?').

Finally, if none of the students can correct the mistake, you should give the correct answer.

When seeking self or peer correction, isolate the mistake if necessary. You can repeat the mistake (although this method is frowned upon in some academic circles), say the sentence up to but not including the mistake, or refer to or define the mistake, by saying 'Tense' or 'Preposition'.

One other way to isolate it is to hold up or point to one finger for every word in the sentence. This is useful if the mistake is one of omission. It is worth practising this technique privately before you do it in class. Imagine you are facing the students. Hold up your right hand with the palm facing you, fingers extended. With the forefinger of your left hand, point to your right thumb and say the first word of the sentence. Point to your right forefinger for the second word and so on. If the sentence has more than five words, put your left hand beside your right hand in a fist, and lift your left little finger for the sixth word and so on. This is not the only way to do finger work, but if you use a slightly different method, remember to raise your fingers from your right to your left, so that the students see a sentence being formed from their left to right.

PRONUNCIATION

Pronunciation can be broken into three component parts – sounds, stress and intonation. Most pronunciation work deals with sounds.

Japanese people have two main problems in pronouncing English sounds. First, like all language learners there is the problem that the sound system of the target language (English) and that of the first language are different in some respects. However, an additional problem for the Japanese is that they learn English primarily by reading rather than listening, and this often means that they have had little or no opportunity to make a start on natural English pronunciation. When teaching in Japan there is often a strong element of de-teaching incorrect pronunciation rather than simply demonstrating the correct one. Some Japanese teachers use *katakana* to teach their students pronunciation, producing some very poor (and funny) Japanese English. Avoid using *katakana* in explanations.

Pronunciation practice should not go on too long – probably 10 minutes at most. It can be done as a separate unit in the lesson, or you can work on problem areas as they arise in the course of the lesson.

Don't set unattainable or unrealistic goals. Many adults have great difficulty in altering their pronunciation. You may ask yourself how much improvement is really necessary. Do you want them to sound like native speakers, or merely to be understood?

Although there is a wide variety of accents among different English speakers, there is a body of common sounds which Japanese often mispronounce, such as the 'schwa' or weak sound. The difference between the different varieties of English are largely a matter of vowel sounds. The debate about whether you should teach students your own accent or some form of 'standard' English is unresolved, but it is certainly useful for students to be exposed to more than the 'standard' accent.

The list of points below relates to areas which are I believe, common to all native speakers of English in most situations, rather than on how various authorities might say English should be pronounced – in other words it is *descriptive* rather than *prescriptive*. If you think that any of the examples do not apply to your accent, or are examples of 'bad' pronunciation, I would advise you to listen to your family or friends, or to the radio or TV before deciding not to teach them. Some teaching tapes in contrast are prescriptive, ie they tell students what English should be (whatever that means), rather than accurately reflecting how English is actually used by most native speakers. The main problem with this prescriptive approach is that students may not understand what they hear around them when they visit a country where English is spoken.

A subtle but useful skill to develop is that of being able to monitor yourself in natural speaking. If you want to check on the most natural pronunciation for a certain sentence, it is often helpful to give it a simple context by imagining a question to which the sentence would be an answer. This is especially useful for intonation.

At all times, when speaking to students, whether modelling pronunciation or talking to students of any level, try to ensure that the only thing that you alter is your speed of talking. If you have to change any other part of your speech, eg to let them recognize it by saying it as it would be written, remodel it with natural pronunciation before asking them to say it. There is sometimes a tendency, when speaking slowly, to change sounds, rhythm, linking, schwa, stress, etc – ie to fall into the trap of ignoring many of the points below.

Minimal pairs

The simplest way to work on pronunciation is to compare two sounds. Often this takes the form of going from the known to the unknown. Contrast a sound which exists in both languages with one which exists only in English – for example, 'b' and 'v'. Think of pairs of words which differ only by these sounds, like 'berry' and 'very'. Put the pair, or list of pairs, on the board under the headings '1' and '2':

(1)	(2)
berry	very
bowl	vole
ban	van
boat	vote

The first thing to do is to model (and if possible explain) the new sound. In this case ('v'), instead of the lips touching, the top teeth touch the bottom lip. Next, have the students repeat the new sound. Get them to look at each other's mouths if the formation of the sound is visible. Now have them repeat two contrasting words. Now write on the board,

(1) **berry, not very, berry**
(2) **very, not berry, very**

Explain that if you say the first sentence they should raise one finger, and if you say the second sentence they should hold up two fingers. Say the first sentence. If not all students hold up their hand, or if a large percentage hold up two fingers, repeat the sentence until most students are holding up one finger. Now say 'One' and hold up one finger. Go through the list in this fashion. Then have the students say the sentences to each other in closed pairs.

The exercise can be made more challenging by saying only one word, and not the contrasting phrase. Also, initially, students can be encouraged to look at each others' mouths if this will help in pinpointing the sound. Later, students who are modelling a sound can hold a sheet of paper over their mouth to hide it.

The weak sound – schwa

As is well known, English is not pronounced as it is written. The most common non-written sound is the weak sound, called 'schwa', written in phonetic syllabary as ə. This sound is used in most unstressed vowels. For example, compare the spelling of the following sentence with the pronunciation transcript with the schwas marked.

I went to the station to take some photographs with my new camera.

I went tə the statən tə take səm photəgraphs with my new camərə

Your students may have difficulty in producing this sound, either in isolation or within a sentence. Fortunately, one phrase which almost all Japanese can say naturally is 'rock 'n' roll' (rock ən roll).

Starting from this, they can move on to other examples of the schwa.

The following list shows common words which are pronounced with a schwa in sentences where the word is unstressed. This is in the great majority of cases. Examples are given of each word unstressed in a sentence and stressed. If you say these phrases aloud, the contrast should be clear.

WORD	WITH SCHWA	WITHOUT SCHWA
and	Mr ənd Mrs Jones	How do you spell 'and'?
of	A cup əf coffee	What's it made of?
to	I went tə the bank.	Where to?
for	I kept it fər a year.	What for?
that	A woman thət I know	That boy
can	Cən you swim?	Yes, I can
them	Cən I try thəm on?	No, not them

In addition, almost all words of three or more syllables have at least one vowel pronounced as a schwa. Some examples are:

> govərnment
> ovərnight
> forənər
> unpleasənt
> socəlize
> məjority
> Japənese

Different words from the same root often have different stress patterns, and have the schwa in a different place:

> Japən   Japənese
> photəgraph   phətogrəpher

Linking

Japanese people tend to pronounce each word separately, instead of joining words together within a sentence. This is especially noticeable with a word preceding one beginning with a vowel, as in 'big apple'. Write the phrase on the board, either drawing a slur (∪) between the words, or moving the final letter of the first word to the second word:

big␣apple or **bi gapple**

The letter 'n'

The letter 'n' causes problems of which, in many cases, Japanese people are unaware. There are three separate sounds which are all written as 'n' when Japanese words are transliterated into the Roman alphabet. If the letter is at the beginning of a word or consonant, it is pronounced as in English. However, if it occurs at the end of a word or consonant, the sound is either 'm' or the French nasalized 'n' as in *un* – the closest equivalent in English would be 'ng'. So when Japanese say the word *Nippon*, the first letter is pronounced as in English, and the second 'n' as an 'm' or nasalized 'n'.

One way to work on this problem is to put words which end in 'n' in sentences where they are followed by a word beginning with a vowel. The two words are joined together, as was done in the previous example on linking. The word can then be practised in isolation, with the memory of how it was pronounced in the sentence helping the student to pronounce it correctly in isolation. For example, first practise a sentence such as 'There's a man␣at the door', and then practise the word 'man'.

Consonant clusters

Most Japanese words have the simple pattern of consonant/vowel/consonant/vowel, etc. If you look at words such as *karate, jūdō, sumō*, Nagasaki, you will see what I mean.

It may help your students get over a block with consonant clusters if they realize that, although Japanese is often said not to have consonant clusters, it is more true to say that it does not have them for 'hard' consonants, like 't', 'k', and 'p'. However, consonant clusters are certainly used after 'soft' consonant sounds, like 'n', 'sh', and 's'.

Ask the students to pronounce the following words:

> *tansu* ('n' and 's' together)
> *desu ka?* (the 'u' is silent)
> *shita* (the 'i' is silent)

You will immediately notice that they are producing a consonant cluster. However, they may not be aware that they are swallowing the vowels, and you may need to point it out.

The most common Japanese strategy for dealing with consonant clusters, and this can be observed when English words are borrowed by Japan, is simply to insert a vowel sound between every pair of consonants or after a final consonant. So the monosyllabic 'strike' becomes the five-syllable monster '*su to rai ku*'.

Apart from simply modelling the correct sound three other strategies are suggested below.

(a). In a consonant cluster, the first consonant is usually not released. Tell your students to try to hold their mouth in the position of the first consonant and move their mouth directly into the shape of the second consonant without inserting an intrusive vowel. For example, in the word 'backbone', keep the throat closed for the 'k' and close the lips for the 'b'.

(b). If there are three consonants together, either in a word or a phrase, and especially if the middle one is 't' or 'd', this middle consonant often disappears:

Spelling:	Pronunciation:
next month	**nex month**
last week	**las week**
West Germany	**Wes Germany**
asked	**ast**
clothes	**cloze**

(c). If the last consonant of a word and the first consonant of the following word are the same, the mouth is held in the closed consonant position for a fraction of a second longer before being ploded. This action is also a feature of Japanese words with double consonants, so the following similarities can help students not to insert an intrusive vowel:

Japanese word:	English phrase:
natto	**What time**
Nikko	**Take care**

Note that this rule does not apply to English words with double consonants. The two 't's in 'batter' are not held as the two 't's in 'Bat two' are.

Middle 'e' or 'i'

A number of words, usually of three or more syllables, drop the sound of an 'e' or 'i' in the middle: for example,

'e' dropped:	'i' dropped:
int<u>e</u>resting	**med<u>i</u>cine**
veg<u>e</u>table	**asp<u>i</u>rin**
diff<u>e</u>rent	**bus<u>i</u>ness**

Elision

Very often we shorten words by dropping a sound, usually a vowel. This is called 'elision' or contraction. Both 'has' and 'is' have the elided form using ''s'. This can cause confusion in both reading and listening.

WORD	UNELIDED EXAMPLE	ELIDED EXAMPLE
is/am/are	My name is . . .	My name's . . .
have/has/had	I have done it.	I've done it.
will	He will do it.	He'll do it.
not	She did not go.	She didn't go.

Elision usually, but not always, reduces the number of syllables:

My father is a doctor. My father's a doctor.
My parents are doctors. My parents're doctors.

In the second example, where the number of syllables remains the same, the effect of elision on pronunciation is to change the 'a' to a schwa.

Other mispronunciations

Some other examples of words which are commonly 'mispronounced' are:

going to/gonna
want to/wanna
did you/didja
do you/dəyə

Finally, the initial 'h' in personal pronouns – he, his, him, her, etc, is often dropped in the middle of a sentence.

Intonation

In general, intonation is difficult to describe or to give rules on. The best practice is to speak as naturally as possible and ask the students to imitate you.

One specific example where clear instruction can be given is in the intonation of questions. There are two kinds of questions.

Do I know you?

This is an example of a Yes/No question (sometimes called a 'closed' question).

What's your name?

This is an example of a question-word question (sometimes called a 'Wh' or 'open' question).

The final intonation of a Yes/No question is usually upwards, and the final intonation of a question-word question is usually downwards. Japanese speakers tend to use upwards intonation on all questions.

Footnote

Although I have in some cases gone into the details of problems of pronunciation and how they might be worked on, in the final analysis your greatest strength is that you are a native speaker, and simply modelling your natural pronunciation will help students tremendously. In fact, there is a point after which, and there are certain students with whom, technical explanations may just get in the way and be self-defeating.

GAMES

Games are a stimulating way to get students to practise painlessly. They are useful at the end of a class, when students might otherwise find other forms of practice boring, and they often ensure a positive and cheerful end to a class. It may be necessary to use games with care with certain students. Some adolescents are touchy about engaging in activities which they perceive to be childish. And some adults may consider that if they are playing a game no serious language study is going on. However, as long as this activity is approached with sensitivity by the teacher, and not overused, very few groups will resent playing games.

As well as explaining the rules, it is usually best to have a dry run of a game before starting it in earnest.

The most common type of game is a *quiz*. Students are divided into teams, and each team prepares a list of questions. As for questionnaires (p 132), it is not difficult to construct quizzes round specific language points. There are also a number of other useful games.

Noughts and crosses can be easily adapted for the classroom. Different cues, in the form of a word, phrase or picture, can be put into each part of the grid. A student or team selects a cue and, if they can construct a correct sentence from it, can put a nought or cross in its place:

often	sometimes	rarely
rarely	sometimes	never
never	often	always

Simon Says. Give a command, such as 'Stand up' or 'Touch your nose'. If you precede your command with 'Simon Says', students should obey. If you simply give the command, they should ignore it.

20 Questions. Students can ask 20 questions to guess a word (usually a noun). Examples of questions are: 'Is it big?'; 'Is there one in this room?'; 'Have you seen one this week?'

Crosswords. Make a simple crossword, perhaps using vocabulary already taught. Make two copies, one with the across answers completed, and one with the down answers completed. Use this as an information gap, in which students have to define or explain their answers:

> **Student A:** What's 1 Down?
> **Student B:** It's the opposite of black/It's the colour of my shirt.
> **Student A:** Is it 'white'?

Hangman. Draw a line of dashes on the board, one dash for each letter of a word to be guessed. If students guess a correct letter, fill it in. If they guess an incorrect letter, draw a line of the scaffold. You may want to write a clue (*hinto*) on the board to help students along.

Songs

Songs are an enjoyable, memorable and painless way for students to practise. They can be sung or listened to over and over, and whereas you would find it difficult to repeat exactly the same dialogue in several lessons, songs actually become more enjoyable, accessible and attractive to the students the more they hear them.

The rhythm of songs helps to reinforce and practise natural sentence stress. In addition, your Japanese students will have been widely exposed to English songs, and will be delighted to have a song unravelled for them.

You can present songs either on tape, or if you play an instrument and are willing to perform in front of the class, you can use that.

Not all songs are suitable for use in teaching, and the ones chosen should generally fit at least some of the following requirements:

- *Not too long.* A song should be fairly short, with plenty of repetition, whether in the form of a chorus, or verses with similar patterns.
- *Clear lyrics.* Most heavy metal songs would fail on this count. It is usually more difficult to hear the lyrics of a song than the spoken words in a dialogue, and you need therefore to choose songs where the lyrics are comparatively clear.
- *Strong melody.* This will help to make the song enjoyable, memorable and singable.
- *Relevant* (either in content or style). Most people enjoy certain distinct styles of song, often depending on their age. The issues dealt with, or the theme of the song, should be relevant to them. Songs which the students have already been exposed to are often the most popular.

You should not, however, be too fussy about selecting songs: for example, if most of your students like heavy metal, their enjoyment and motivation will outweigh the consideration of clarity of lyrics.

If you want to get an idea of which songs have become classics in Japan, and will certainly go down well with students in their thirties and over, just spend an evening or two in your friendly local *karaoke* bar. One or two to start you off are: Beatles songs such as *Yesterday*; Elvis songs, especially ballads; and *My Way* (the all-time *sarariman*'s favourite).

REVISION

This is something which hardly any teacher does sufficiently. One advantage of using a coursebook is that a lot of the material is normally recycled as the book progresses. There is no doubt about the usefulness of revising material. Some suggestions for doing this are:

- Give homework, and check it with the whole class in the next lesson.
- At the start of a lesson, briefly run over the previous lesson.

Ask 'What did we do in the last class?' A valid reason for this somewhat artificial question is provided if one student was absent from the previous class.
- Vocabulary revision can be turned into a game of Hangman (see above), with students taking turns to be Hangman.

Whether or not you manage to include planned revision in your teaching, it is worth developing the skill of going into a short sub-routine of the main points, when a student cannot produce language previously taught correctly, and other students cannot correct him or her satisfactorily. Quickly build up a board diagram or layout highlighting the rule(s), and do a brisk drill.

12 | Specific Japanese problems

This chapter is divided into three sections: (a) What students don't use; (b) What students overuse; and (c) What students confuse. In some cases, the choice of section is rather arbitrary. Articles ('a', 'an' and 'the'), for example, are in the third section, but could perhaps equally have been in the first.

The second section, 'What students don't use', covers problems in production – students do not use certain constructions in English. However, since they do not use these expressions, there will be an added problem in comprehension – they will perhaps not understand them when they hear them.

Like all non-English speaking nationalities, Japanese have particular problems in trying to use English, and there are typical mistakes associated with these. The fairly long list of these typical mistakes is not meant to be memorized. Rather, it is intended initially as a source of reference, to help familiarize you with Japanese problems. Secondly, as you gain experience in teaching in Japan, this chapter will help you to organize in your own mind their language learning difficulties, and will hopefully go some way towards providing you with strategies to deal with them.

As has been stressed elsewhere in this book, your main strength as a native speaker is that you can instinctively tell when a mistake has been made. Any classification or organization of error-correction is icing on the cake, so don't worry about trying to recognize and deal specifically with all these mistakes at the beginning of your teaching. Even when you are familiar with the background to a mistake, it is not always necessary to explain the rules – simple correction and drilling is often all that is needed. Remember too that you should not automatically correct every mistake (see p 140).

Some problems may be the result of incorrect, misguided or old-fashioned teaching. If students say that they were taught a form which you regard as incorrect or unnatural, try to be sensitive about how you treat correction. Don't denigrate or belittle their previous teacher or teaching. This, of course, is especially pertinent if the teacher concerned is still teaching the students (for example, if you are an Assistant in a high school).

An (**x**) after a sentence denotes incorrect or unnatural English: for example,

He go to work (**x**)

An (*x*) denotes a sentence which is correct grammatically, but awkward or unnatural:

An accident happened (*x*)

WHAT STUDENT DON'T USE

To be. The various forms of the verb 'to be' (am, are is, was, etc) are often omitted:

He rich. (**x**)

Comparatives. Japanese people will use the simple sentence 'Bob is rich' in the middle of a discussion of Bob and Ted, when the comparative sentence ('Bob is richer than Ted') would be much more natural in English. In fact, although a comparative form exists in Japanese, the full form is rarely used, and this practice is carried over when Japanese speak English.

Two reasons have been suggested for the Japanese avoidance of the use of comparatives, even in their own language. First, it is an awkward structure to use in Japanese. Second, Japanese people may not wish to denigrate one of the parties (in the above example, Ted).

Students may need considerable encouragement to use comparatives, and producing a complete comparative sentence can take a painfully long time, even for a non-beginner student.

How . . . ? (means of transport). Using 'how' to ask about transport is not really an obvious thing to do, if you think about it. It needs a fair bit of regular practice to get it to stick in students' minds:

How do you come to school?   By train.

I'm afraid/Well . . . actually . . . (introducing a problem). Japanese is a language where indirectness and subtlety rule supreme. Somewhat surprisingly, then, students can sound blunt to the point of rudeness because they fail to use softening introductory phrases so necessary to take the sting out of a negative utterance.

'I'm afraid' is a very useful softener before outlining a problem. The meaning is similar to 'I'm sorry', but is not so apologetic. Unlike 'I'm sorry' there is usually no intonation or pause on 'I'm afraid', the problem itself carrying the intonation:

I'm afraid there's been a mistake.

If you listen to the Japanese being spoken around you, you will soon notice the myriad expressions Japanese have of prefacing problems, such as *chotto, anno*, or *so desu ne*. These expressions, and English words like 'well' and 'actually', can each have several totally different meanings, depending on the intonation. One tip to help produce the right sound is to draw the words out, and almost to sing them on a low monotone.

Phrasal verbs. A phrasal verb (a verb plus a proposition) often has a meaning unconnected with either of its two component parts. The phrasal verb 'make up' has no evident connection with either 'make' or 'up':

He came across an old diary.
They kissed and made up.

On production, students will often use the moral formal Latinate verb (eg 'conciliate' instead of 'make up'). When they hear a phrasal verb, it will often not be understood. It is useful to practise phrasal verbs in a meaningful context. This will help to show the meaning and will aid remembering.

As with idioms or slang expressions, it is best not to overload students with phrasal verbs. A good book to start with is *Making Sense of Phrasal Verbs* by Martin Shovel.

Prepositions – at the end of a question. Students may well have been taught that a preposition must go at the beginning of a question, leading to stilted and old-fashioned sentences, such as 'To whom are you talking' instead of the more natural

Who are you talking to?

Pronouns. Pronouns are in many cases optional in Japanese, and as a result are often omitted. Students may say 'saw' instead of 'I saw it'.

There is. Japanese people tend to produce awkward-sounding sentences to avoid 'There is . . . ':

An accident happened. (*x*)
A red car is outside. (*x*)

instead of 'There was an accident' or 'There's a red car outside'. 'There was' is often a natural way to begin to answer a 'What happened?' question. A general rule is that 'happen' is used in questions and negative sentences, and 'There is/was' in affirmative (ordinary) sentences:

> **What happened?**
> **Nothing happened.**
> **There was an explosion.**

To (purpose). Japanese use the causative linker 'because', but rarely use its counterpart, 'to' indicating purpose (as in 'I went to the restaurant to have a meal'). If they do want to talk about purpose, they will often use the more formal 'in order to'.

It might help students to use 'to' more by pointing out diagrammatically that we can often talk about the same situation in two ways – by looking back to the reason, or forward to the purpose:

> **I went to the restaurant because I was hungry.**
> **I went to the restaurant to have a meal.**

```
                                              now
past ←──────────x──────────x──────────x──────────x──────────→ future
            hungry   I went to       have a meal
                     the restaurant
```

'You', 'They' – impersonal use. Both of these pronouns, when used to refer to unspecified people, are avoided by Japanese speakers:

> **You can hire cars at Hertz.**
> **They said it was going to rain today.**

'You' is a general use, meaning 'anybody'. It is usually unstressed, and pronounced 'yə', in contrast to the more usual personal use, which tends to be pronounced normally. 'They' means authority in general, and can mean the government, the media, the employing company, etc.

WHAT STUDENTS OVERUSE

Could. Japanese students will tend to say

> **We could take a lot of photographs.** (*x*)

While this is not an incorrect form, it implies that there was some difficulty overcome. Often when Japanese people use 'could', past simple tense on its own is more appropriate:

We took a lot of photographs.

A general rule is not to use 'could' for one occasion in the past. If there is effort or difficulty involved, use 'managed to':

We managed to escape.

Otherwise, just use past simple.

How . . . ? (for description). Japanese people overuse 'how' when asking for a description, in cases when an expression such as 'what . . . like?' would be more natural and neutral. In the following example, 'how' gives the idea that there has been some kind of change of circumstance, perhaps a crash:

How is your car? (*x*)
What's your car like?

How about? (past meaning). Japanese people use this instead of 'How was . . . ?' to ask about past situations – for example, they might greet you on your return from a trip with:

How about your trip? (*x*)

So. The English word 'so' is used at the expense of 'very':

It was so expensive (*x*)

The word *so* also exists in Japanese, and is used as filler or while the speaker is thinking what to say next. This function is carried out in English by the word 'well' or 'and' or by the sound written variously as 'Mm', 'Um', 'Hm', etc.

To. There are a number of nouns and pronouns in English which do not need the preposition 'to' when talking about direction to them:

I went to shopping. (*x*)
Are you going to home? (*x*)
We went to there last night. (*x*)

Too. 'Too' is used instead of, or as a stronger form of 'very' (as in 'too cheap'). The rule is that 'too' means that there is a problem. In simple situations, 'too cheap', 'too beautiful' and 'too delicious' are wrong.

You'd better. A Japanese student might say:

You'd better go to the Picasso exhibition. (*x*)

This is a direct translation of a structure which in Japanese is a suggestion, but in English is much stronger – a warning. A more natural sentence would be:

Why don't you go to the Picasso exhibition?

Repeating verbs and adjectives. Japanese people tend to repeat an adjective or a verb from a question, when a simple 'Yes' or 'No' would be appropriate:

Are you going? **Going.** (*x*)
Are you happy? **Happy.** (*x*)

WHAT STUDENTS CONFUSE

Almost/Almost all/Most. For example:

Almost Japanese people like fish. (*x*)

The rule is that we can use 'almost' on its own before an adjective or a number:

My grandmother is almost blind.
It was almost 3 o'clock.

However, before a noun we need to add the word 'all':

Almost all Japanese people like fish.

In fact, in many situations, a simple 'most' is more natural than the rather emphatic 'almost all'.

Come/go. The Japanese word for 'come' means strictly from there to here. In English, the word 'come' has another meaning connected with movement *away* from the speaker. When referring to movement from where the speaker is to where the listener is, Japanese people will say

I can't go to your party. (*x*)

instead of

I can't come to your party.

Continuous v passive. This is usually a problem of form rather than meaning:

He was phoning. *v* **He was phoned.**

'ed'/'ing'. A persistent problem is the confusion between present and past participles when used as adjectives:

He was interesting. *v* **He was interested.**
The movie was interested. (*x*)
I am interesting in jazz. (*x*)

The concept to get across is that 'ing' is the *reason* which makes the *result* 'ed'. If a teacher is interesting, his students are interested. If he is boring, his students are bored. Outline it in tabular form on the board, with an arrow going from 'ing' to 'ed':

REASON ⟶	RESULT
Interesting	**Interested**

Forget/forgot. For example:

> Where's your umbrella? **I forget it.** (*x*)
> What's your phone number? **I forgot (it).** (*x*)

A basic rule, which works for most situations is to use 'forget' for information (the verb has no object) and 'forgot' for things (the verb needs an object):

> What's your phone number? **I forget.** (information – present tense, no object)
> Where's your umbrella? **I forgot it.** (thing – past tense, object)

Is + adjective/Has + noun. This distinction crops up in all sorts of descriptive language – people, houses, illness, possessions, etc, and needs continual reinforcement:

> **It has beautiful.** (*x*)
> **I am headache.** (*x*)

's/of. Most other foreign speakers of English overuse 'of' at the expense of 's, because their possessive is always formed with 'of', as in French (*La plume de ma tante*). However, the possessive in Japanese is formed like the English 's, and Japanese people have a different problem with its use. They overuse it because its use is wider in Japanese than in English. They do so in three situations – for inanimate objects,

> **The table's leg.** (*x*)
> **The leg of the table.**

for manufacturer's products,

> **A Toyota's Corolla** (*x*)
> **A Toyota Corolla.**

and for possessive adjectives,

> **My's house** (*x*)
> **My house.**

Like/would like. 'Like' and 'would like' (meaning 'want') are confused, especially in questions, where 'do' is used instead of 'would'.

> **Do you like a drink?** (*x*)
> **Would you like a drink?**

Make/Do. The meanings of these two words are covered by one verb *shimasu* in Japanese. The basic difference in English is that 'do' describes the action (what you do), and 'make' describes the result (what you make).

'DO' (ACTION)	'MAKE' (RESULT)
baking	cake
cooking	pizza
woodwork	a table

One example which might help make the distinction clear is this. A kindergarten teacher hands out plasticine to the children and says 'Do something with it', and they variously bend it, stretch it, roll it into balls, etc. Then she says 'Make something with it', and the children begin to form a house, a car, etc.

This rule holds true in about 80% of cases. Other uses have no apparent underlying reason, and must simply be memorized. Common examples are:

> **do a favour**
> **make the bed**
> **make a noise**

Make/let. Surprisingly, perhaps, the Japanese have the same word *saseru* for the concepts of 'make' and 'let', and commonly confuse the two in English. Both words are in the area of having control – having the power to make or let someone do something. Contexts which can generate clear examples are parents/children; teachers/pupils; warders/prisoners; hijackers/passengers.

Make sure you teach both affirmative and negative forms of both verbs. A good starting definition is that 'make' is for something you *don't* want to do, and 'let' is for something you *want* to do:

> **My parents made me study the violin.**
> **They didn't make us wear a school uniform at my school.**
> **The warders let the prisoners talk during exercise.**
> **The hijackers didn't let the passengers go to the toilet.**

Used/be (or get) used to/used to. The word 'use' can be part of three different structures:

> (a) **I used a hammer.**
> (b) **I'm used to Japanese food.**
> (c) **I used to smoke.**

In (a), 'used' is simply the past tense of 'use'. The 's' is pronounced as a 'z'. In the other two examples, the 's' is pronounced as an 's'. In (b), 'used to' describes being or becoming familiar with a new experience, such as a different living or working environment. In (c), 'used to' is not a tense, but can be thought of as if it were.

There are three components to the meaning of 'used to' as exemplified in (c): it happened in the past; it happened more than once, or for a period of time – it was not a 'one-off'; and it does not happen now. These will be useful in explaining the meaning to your students. The form is: 'used to' + basic verb (infinitive without 'to').

Adjective order. For example:

> **It's a white big house. (*x*)**

Word order is much less strict in Japanese than in English. For adjectives, a basic order is *size, shape, colour, material*:

> **a small, square, red, wooden box**

Come/came from. For example:

> **I came from Japan. (*x*)**

This is a direct translation from the Japanese, which uses the past tense where English uses the present ('I come from Japan'). Explain that the meaning is 'I was born in Japan'.

If. In Japanese there is only one form for the three or more constructions available in English. There is as a result general confusion about the various tenses to be used in sentences beginning with 'if' (see p 175):

If I am born in America I can speak good English. (*x*)

Negative questions – answering. The logic of answering negative questions is directly opposite in Japanese.

Didn't you go?	**Yes, I didn't (go).** (*x*)
	No. I went. (*x*)
Didn't you go?	**No, I didn't (go).**
	Yes, I went.

Even when students have understood the problem and say the correct words, they may continue to nod or shake their head with the opposite meaning. You may find that the only way to correct this is to move their head in the correct direction with your hands. However, remember my advice about touching students, and do this only if you have developed a trusting relationship with them.

Numbers. Japanese have some different methods of counting, which means that in order to express Japanese numbers in English, they not only have to formulate new words for the numbers themselves, but also have to reorganize the basis on which the numbers are put together. One, followed by eight zeros in English and Japanese is, respectively:

100 000 000 and 1 0000 0000

Where we split numbers into groups of three digits, putting a comma or a space between each group, the Japanese split numbers into groups of four. So, we get to a thousand and then in effect start again, until we get to the next thousand, which we call a million. The Japanese, on the other hand, continue up to ten thousand, for which they have a specific word – *man*. So 20000, which for us is twenty thousand, is for them two ten-thousands. The number 4 520 000 is for us four million, five hundred and twenty thousand, but for them is written as 452 0000 (ie four hundred and fifty two ten-thousands). Large numbers around a billion are virtually impossible to switch over without resorting to pen and paper.

The Japanese method of calculating dates is also different. Whereas our dating system has been constant for 2000 years, in Japan it changes every time there is a change of emperor. The present emperor is the fourth this century, so asking a Japanese person when his grandfather was born can involve a fair degree of head scratching. He or she will know it was in year 43 of the Meiji era, but to give an answer in AD involves some addition and subtraction. Transposing dates from Japanese history is all but impossible without a reference table.

Whether these two different reference systems and their associated problems have given Japanese a mental block about numbers, I don't know, but it is certainly true that numbers need a lot of practice. Some specific difficulties, apart from general lack of confidence and familiarity with numbers in English are:

- Twelve is often confused with twenty.
- Seven is often confused with nine, since the Japanese word for seven is *nana*.
- '–teen' is confused with '–ty'. A good way to highlight the contrast is to demonstrate that thirteen has two almost equal strong stresses, and thirty has only one strong stress. This point can be taught as a minimal pair (see p 142).

Phoning. Identifying oneself ('This is . . . ' or 'It's . . . ') and the other party ('Is that . . . ?') are different when speaking on the telephone from face-to-face conversation. ('I'm . . . ' or 'Are you . . . ?'):

    I am Yoko. (*x***)**
    This is Yoko.

13 Teaching grammar and functions

Grammar is the structural make-up of language in terms of subjects, nouns, tenses, etc. We can examine the following sentence in terms of grammar:

John ate a hamburger.

'John' is a noun (a person, place or thing); 'John' is the subject (the doer of the action); 'ate' is the verb – past simple tense (one action viewed in total in the past); and so on.

Another way to dissect language is to look at it in terms of what it is used for. This breaks it up into *functions* – the practical uses of grammar. Some functions are:

- Inviting. (**Would you like to . . . ?**)
- Suggesting. (**Why don't you/What about . . . ?**)
- Advising. (**Perhaps you should/If I were you I'd . . .**)

A list of important structures (ie grammar) and functions is given in this chapter, together with ideas on how to teach them, and associated problems for Japanese students. The list is by no means comprehensive, but it covers the main areas useful to Japanese students. There is a glossary of teaching terms in Appendix 3.

GRAMMAR

As I have mentioned previously, Japanese people study English in an almost purely grammatical way for at least six years. They therefore do not need nearly as much grammar teaching as other nationalities learning English.

This section is intended primarily for your reference; secondly to help you correct students when they make mistakes; and finally, if you want to teach a grammar lesson, to help you do it in a natural and communicative way.

If you have not previously studied grammar, remember that the fact that you are a fluent speaker of English means that you have successfully internalized a knowledge of English grammar. You automatically know that 'he go' is incorrect and 'he goes' is correct. Your greatest value to your students is as a model and a touchstone of natural English.

The following grammar summary explains the basics of English structures to you as a teacher, detailing both the form and meaning of each structure. 'Form' is the words which make it up, and 'meaning' is what the structure means. There are then ideas on how to teach each structure, together with notes on problems encountered by Japanese speakers.

There is not always a one-to-one relationship between form and meaning. One form, for example the present continuous, can have several meanings:

> **She's having a shower at the moment.** (present meaning)
> **She's going to the dentist tomorrow.** (future meaning)

And one meaning, for example 'future', can be expressed using several forms:

> **I'm going to Okinawa next week.**
> **I'll go to Okinawa next week.**

It is often helpful to build up a *time line* on the board to give visual help in making clear the relationship between an event and another event or time. A time line is simply a horizontal line, in which the left is past and the right is future, and on which events and times can be shown:

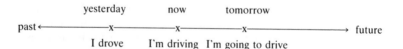

You can complete your time line, and then explain it to your students. Alternatively, as you build up your time line on the board, you can keep up a simple running commentary with gestures.

Tenses

There are six tenses in English, and each has a simple and continuous form (see the box below). The past perfect and future perfect are much less common than the other tenses. The future perfect in particular is so rarely used that some teachers do not present it as a formal lesson, but simply give a brief explanation if it comes up.

TENSE	SIMPLE	CONTINUOUS (or PROGRESSIVE)
Present	I drive	I am driving
Past simple	I drove	I was walking
Present perfect	I have driven	I have been driving
Past perfect	I had driven	I had been driving
Future	I will drive	I will be driving
Future perfect	I will have driven	I will have been driving

Three forms – affirmative/negative/interrogative

Each tense can be used in three forms:

- Affirmative (**He went.**)
- Negative (**He didn't go.**)
- Interrogative (**Did he go?**)

It is important to ensure that students are familiar with all three forms, especially at lower levels.

Simple present tense

> **I like *sushi*.**

Meaning. The present tense is used to describe habitual actions (**I go to work by train**); states (**I live in Tokyo**); general truths (**The sun rises in the East**); and future schedules (**I arrive in Hong Kong on Friday**).

Form. The tense uses the infinitive 'to walk' form without 'to'. For the third person singular – he, she, it – add an 's' (**He walks**).
  The interrogative (question form) and the negative form use the auxiliary verb 'do' (or 'does' in the third person singular):

> **Do they live there?**
> **Does he like *sumō*?**
> **I don't know her.**
> **She doesn't look very happy.**

Teaching. This is usually the first tense students learn. Teach only the present meaning to beginners. Leave the future use until you are teaching futures. Use the word 'always' to get the meaning across. The Japanese word *zutto* gives this idea.

Time line:

```
              yesterday      today      tomorrow
past ←————————x———————————x——————————x————————————→ future
                 go            go           go
```

Situations. Used for daily routines (for habitual actions), and habits.

Problems in teaching. The 's' in the third person singular is often omitted. There is also confusion in meaning with the present continuous (see below).

Present continuous tense

I am sailing.

Meaning. The present continuous tense is used to describe actions happening now (**What's he saying?**); temporary situations (**I'm doing a lot of overtime this month**); and arranged future (**I'm meeting Akiko tonight**).

Form. The tense uses the auxiliary 'be' plus the present participle:

I'm trying to find it.
Are you listening?
They aren't helping much.

Teaching. For the first use (actions happening now), the point to get across is that it's happening *now*.

The usual way to present this tense is to look at and describe an action picture or talk about what you and the students are doing during the lesson. However, using such situations for presenting or explaining the present continuous has been criticized as unnatural. We do not usually look at someone and say, 'He's sitting on a chair'. This may be being over-fussy. However, if you want to be more communicative, think of situations in which we normally use the present continuous. These are usually cases where the listener cannot see the action (she or he may be in another room, or on the phone).

For details on teaching the third use (arranged future), see 'Futures' (p 171).

Time line (first use):

```
                            now
past ←———————————————————————x————————————————————→ future
              I'm reading a book
```

Problems. First, the auxiliary tends to be omitted ('I writing'). Second, students often do not elide: 'I am going there' sounds less natural than 'I'm going there' in all but the most formal situations. Finally, there is confusion with the present simple. Japanese has the two forms with different concepts.

Simple past

I saw her again last night.

Meaning. This tense is used to describe a completed action in the past. (**He walked into the room**).

Form. The second of the three parts of the verb is used (see, saw, seen). This part can be regular, ending in 'ed', or irregular (eg saw, went, came, etc).

Teaching. Narration is the easiest way to introduce a lot of verbs in the simple past in a short space of time. You can introduce a story about daily routine in the simple present, starting with 'Every day John gets up at 7.30. He has a shower, and then has breakfast'. Having gone through the story in simple present, you can change the beginning to 'Last Monday John got up at 7.30', and change all the verbs to simple past.

Problems. The main problem is pronunciation of 'ed'. Japanese people often pronounce it as it is written. However, although the spelling is regular, the pronunciation varies, and is never the sound 'ed' as in Ed Sullivan. The three possible pronunciations are 'walkt', 'pulld' or 'plantid'. It depends on the pronunciation of the last letter of the present tense of the verb.

VOICED LAST LETTER	UNVOICED LAST LETTER	LAST LETTER t OR d
t	*d*	*id*
walked	**pulled**	**waited**
stopped	**roamed**	**landed**
missed	**trained**	**boarded**

Have the students put one or two fingers on their throats and feel their voices disappear at the end of 'walk' and 'stop', because the last letter of each is unvoiced. In contrast, at the end of a word like 'pull', you can hold the 'l' and feel it, because it is voiced.

Past continuous

I was dreaming of the past.

Meaning. The past continuous is used to describe a continuing action at a specific time in the past. (**I was having a bath when the phone rang.**)

Form. The tense is formed by the past of the auxiliary 'be' plus present participle ('was having' in the above example).

Teaching. The past continuous is usually contrasted with the simple past, a single shorter event (in the simple past) happening during a longer continuous event (in the past continuous).
Time line ('I was having a bath when the phone rang'):

```
              bath          now

past ←──────────x──────────x──────────────────→
            phone
```

A generative situation for teaching the past continuous is one event which affects a number of people. Questions such as 'What were you doing when President Kennedy was killed?/the earthquake started?/the lights went out?' help illustrate the point. You could show an apartment block, in which all the occupants are variously engaged watching TV, talking on the phone, etc, when disaster strikes in some form.

Present perfect

Have you seen her?

Technically speaking, the present perfect is not a tense, but an aspect. However, for practical purposes, it can be considered a tense.

Meaning. The overall meaning is past connected with the present. There are three specific uses:

- *Unfinished past.* An action or state which began in the past and has continued until now. Use 'for' if you say the time period (a year, two days, etc) and 'since' if you say the starting time (yesterday, last October, etc) – **I've had my car for two years/since 1990.**
- *Experience.* Something that has happened in your life up till now (sometimes 'ever' is added for emphasis) – **Have you (ever) seen 'Gone With The Wind?'**

- *Present result.* Something which happened in the past, but you can see the result now. American English often uses the past simple instead of the present perfect in this situation, especially when adding 'just'. For example – **The taxi (has) (just) arrived (and it's at the door).**

Form. The present perfect is made up of 'have/has' plus the past participle (the third part of the verb – see, saw, seen):

I have (I've) landed on the moon.

The interrogative and negative do not need an extra auxiliary 'do/does', since there is already an auxiliary ('have/has'). The interrogative is formed by inverting the subject and 'have/has' – so 'She has' becomes 'Has she' (**Has she tried it?**). The negative is formed by adding 'not' after 'have' (**I have not (haven't) been to Hokkaido**).

Teaching. The present perfect is often confused with the simple past. We use the present perfect in situations which are connected in some way with the present, and the simple past with situations which are completely past.

Some contrasting sentences:

I've lived in Tokyo for 6 months. (and I live here now)
I lived in Paris for two years. (in the past)

Some time words can cause confusion here – since, for, ago and in/on:

She's lived in Tokyo since March.
She's lived in Tokyo for four months.
She moved to Tokyo in March.
She moved to Tokyo four months ago.

Note, in the last example, the position of 'ago', after the time period 'four months'. The choice of which word is used depends on the tense, and whether the time is a period or a point.

	POINT IN TIME (1988, 3 o'clock, May)	PERIOD OF TIME (3 days, 2 years)
PRESENT PERFECT: the situation is still happening	**since**	**for**
SIMPLE PAST: the situation is finished	**in/at/on**	**ago**

Problems. The form 'Have you ever . . . ?' exists in Japanese, and this is overused at the expense of 'Have you . . . ?'. 'Ever' is an intensifier, and is used with an unusual event (eg 'Have you ever seen a ghost?').

Encourage students to contract 'have/has'. Note, however, that although contracting 'has' always means losing a syllable, contracting 'have' may drop the 'h' sound, but keep the same number of syllables:

> **The band's** (one syllable)
> **The band've** (two syllables)

Another point to note is that 's can be a contraction of either 'is' or 'has'. You might want to check that students know which word is being contracted in a particular case.

Present perfect continuous tense

> **I've been waiting for an hour.**

Meaning. The meaning is very similar to the first use of the present perfect simple above (unfinished action), and is often used with 'for' and 'since'. There is no substantial difference in meaning between these two sentences:

> **She's lived in Tokyo for two years.**
> **She's been living in Tokyo for two years.**

In this example, the present perfect continuous concentrates on the activity of the verb. This can be contrasted with the result of the activity, which cannot be expressed in the present perfect continuous, but only in the present perfect simple:

> **We've been driving for two hours.** (activity)
> **We've driven 100 miles.** (result)

Past perfect

> **When we arrived at the cinema the film had already begun.**

Meaning. This tense is used when we want to look back further into the past from a point already in the past:

> **When I got home, the postman had been.**

The postman's arrival was before my getting home, so we use the past perfect.

> **When I got home, I rang the office.**

Ringing the office was after my getting home, so we do not need the past perfect.

Problems. Japanese people often have the idea that this tense is used for events which happened a long time ago:

Millions of years ago, dinosaurs had lived on earth. (*x*)

Futures

He'll have to go.
I'm going to knock on your door.
I'm leaving tonight.

There are three ways of commonly expressing the future in English: 'I will' (**I will (I'll) fly to Osaka**); 'going to' (**I'm going to fly to Osaka**); and the present continuous (**I'm flying to Osaka**).

Situations. A businessman is arranging a business trip to Japan. He has to visit a number of locations in central Honshu, and has to decide whether it would be more convenient to fly initially to Tokyo or Osaka. He is talking to his secretary:

Secretary: I think it would be easier to fly to Osaka.
Businessman: All right. I'll fly to Osaka. (*He makes a decision*)

Later, he talks to his boss:

Boss: Have you decided your flight?
Businessman: Yes, I'm going to fly to Osaka. (*He's talking about a plan in his head.*)

Later, he receives his flight ticket. At home that evening, his wife asks him about the trip:

Wife: Have you arranged your trip to Japan?
Businessman: Yes, I've got the tickets. I'm flying to Osaka. (*He's talking about an arrangement – the tickets have been bought.*)

Problems. Japanese people use 'will' almost exclusively. Encourage them to use 'going to' or the present continuous when they are talking about a plan or an arrangement. Note that the difference between 'going to' and the present continuous is not great – in many situations you can use either. The important difference is between these two and 'will'. In the above situations, somebody has control over the future. In most neutral situations, 'will' is generally used.

Articles

'A' is used for any one of a number:

Can I have a cigarette?

'An' is used in place of 'a' when the noun begins with a vowel:

Would you like an aperitif?

'The' is used for a definite noun, when we know which one, or when there is only one:

The restaurant where we had dinner was very nice.
I live about three miles from the city centre.

In the first of the above two examples, we know which restaurant – the one where we had dinner. In the other example, there is only one centre in the city.

There are a lot of small rules, groupings and exceptions when dealing with articles, and it is not always easy to explain the reason for students' mistakes. You may have to rely on your ability as a native speaker to 'feel' whether something is right or wrong.

There are two basic rules. First, a single, countable noun needs an article. The following sentence is always incorrect:

This is pen. (*x*)

This rule is rather negative – it does not tell you which article is required, but at least 'a' or 'the' might be right, whereas no article is definitely wrong.

The second basic rule is 'first time "a"; second time "the" ':

We stayed in a hotel in Honolulu. The hotel was very comfortable.

This rule is not complete. It assumes that the first article is 'a'. Of course, the first time you use a noun, it may take 'the' or no article. A fuller rule might be 'If the first time you use a noun, the article is "a" (or "an"), the second use of the noun will require "the" '.

Comparatives

Comparatives are used to compare two things:

Moon river, wider than a mile.
Sally is taller (than Mary).
Origami **is more interesting (than gardening).**

The comparative is formed by adding 'er' to short adjectives, and putting 'more' before longer ones. The word 'than' is added after the adjective.

SYLLABLES	ADD	ADJECTIVE	COMPARATIVE
One	'er'	**big**	**bigger**
Two, last letter 'y'	'er'	**happy**	**happier**
Two, not ending in 'y'*	more	**modern**	**more modern**
Three or more	more	**beautiful**	**more beautiful**

*Exceptions include 'quiet'; 'narrow'; 'simple'; and 'clever'.

The following spelling rules for adding 'er' will be helpful:

● For one-syllable words ending 'consonant-vowel-consonant', double the final consonant – **bigger**.

● For two-syllable adjectives ending in 'y', change the 'y' to 'i' – **happier**.

Some Japanese words to make explanations easier: syllable (*onsetsu*); consonant (*shiin*); and vowel (*boin*).

Questions

There are two kinds of ordinary questions: 'Yes/No' or 'closed' questions (**Are you Japanese? Is today Tuesday?**); and 'Wh–', 'question word' or 'open' questions (**What are you doing? How old are you?**).

Japanese people sometimes begin an answer to a 'Wh' question with 'Yes'.

What did you do yesterday?   **Yes, . . . I went shopping.** (*x*)

This 'yes' means something like 'I hear and understand the question'.

Indirect questions/statements

Questions can be preceded by a group of words such as 'Do you know', 'Can you tell me', or 'I wonder if you can tell me'. These longer questions are called 'indirect' or 'embedded' questions:

Do you know if this train goes to Shinjuku?
I can't remember where I put the key.
Can you tell me where Susan went?

In an indirect question or statement, the verb is re-inverted back to its original position:

He went to Australia. (uninverted)
Did he go to Australia. (inverted)
I don't know if he went to Australia. (back to uninverted)

AFFIRMATIVE	He went to Australia.	Uninverted 'he went'
ORDINARY QUESTION	Did he go to Australia?	Inverted 'did he go'
INVERTED QUESTION	Do you know if he went to Australia?	Re-inverted to original 'he went'

Meaning. Indirect questions tend to be softer and more tentative than direct questions, and are often preferable for asking for information or directions. Compare **Where is the . . . ?** with **Could you tell me where . . . ?** or **Do you know where . . . ?** The last two are less direct and aggressive.

If the original question is a Yes/No question (ie without a question word), we need to add the word 'if' or 'whether':

> **Is the station near here?**
> **I don't know if the station is near here.**

Tag questions

Tag questions are statements which are turned into questions by adding a 'tag', such as 'didn't you', 'hasn't he' or 'would they':

> **You're Japanese, aren't you?**
> **It's a lovely day, isn't it?**

The two rules are simple, but there are so many possibilities that students can become confused and find it difficult to produce the tag at anything like natural speed. There are two rules: (a) add the auxiliary, or what would be the auxiliary in the case of a question or a negative sentence; (b) use a positive tag for a negative sentence, and a negative tag for a positive sentence. Examples:

> **You've been to Guam, haven't you?** (a) use the auxiliary 'have'; (b) positive first verb, negative tag.
> **You went there last month, didn't you?** (a) use the auxiliary 'did', which is the auxiliary we would use if we turned 'You went there' into a question ('Did you go there'); (b) positive first verb, negative tag.

Conditionals

Conditional sentences, or 'conditionals', are sentences beginning with the word 'if' (so imposing a condition). There are three conditionals:

(1) **If it rains tomorrow, we won't play tennis.**
(2) **If I had a hammer, I'd hammer in the morning.**
(3) **If I had seen him, I'd have told him.**

Meaning. Conditionals are used to describe conditions under which outcomes will happen, would happen or would have happened. The first conditional considers a likely or possible future:

If I see her, I'll give her the message.

The condition, seeing her, is likely or possible.

The second conditional considers an unlikely future, or an untrue present (or future):

If I went to the moon, I'd bring back some moon rock.

The condition, going to the moon, is unlikely.

The third conditional considers an untrue past:

If you'd come to the party, you'd have had a good time.

The condition, coming to the party, did not happen.

Form. The first conditional is formed by the present tense, with future meaning, followed by the future tense (**I'll give her the message**).

The second is formed by the past tense, with present or future meaning (**If I went to the moon**), followed by 'would' plus the present tense (**I'd bring back some moon rock**).

The third conditional is formed by the past perfect, with past meaning (**If you'd come to the party**), followed by 'would have' plus the past participle (**I wouldn't have been late**).

The clauses can be reversed, with no change of meaning. However, the comma is usually omitted when 'if' comes in the middle of the sentence: **If I see her, I'll give her the message** or **I'll give her the message if I see her**.

There are two principal variations. First, take:

If I drink brandy, I get a headache.

'If' here can usually be replaced by 'When', 'Whenever', or 'Every time'. Both verbs are in the present tense. This is sometimes called a 'zero conditional'.

Secondly:

If I had gone to medical school, I'd be a doctor.

This is a 'mixed conditional'. The first part is from the third conditional (untrue past), and the second part is from the second conditional (a present result). It is probably too confusing to present this form – just deal with it in passing if it comes up.

Teaching. It is normally best to teach each conditional separately, leaving plenty of time between each presentation, and contrasting each new conditional with previously taught one(s). Make it clear in your explanation and board display that the form of the tenses used is often different from the meaning or the time. The first conditional is necessary. The second is extremely useful at intermediate level for discussion, imagining, hypothesizing, refuting ideas, etc. The third is less common and useful, and might be too much of a load, as it is complicated and difficult to learn, and may cause confusion with the first two. Because of this you may wish to restrict your teaching of it to long-term higher-level students.

There are many songs which contain conditionals, and these can be useful ways for students to internalize the different and confusing tenses used in them. There are, in particular, very many 'hopeless love' songs which contain the second conditional.

Modal auxiliary verbs

'Modal auxiliary verbs', 'modal verbs', 'modals' are extra verbs which add meaning, such as 'can' or 'must'. This is in contrast to ordinary auxiliaries, such as 'do' or 'have', which help with form, but carry no meaning.

Modals are not particularly difficult to understand. However, the number of modal auxiliary verbs, and the variations on their use can sometimes make the area seem a little like a maze, both in terms of structure and meaning.

The modal auxiliaries are:

> **can/could**
> **may/might**
> **must**
> **shall/will/would**
> **should/ought**

Meaning. A starting rule is that modals tell us about the speaker's attitude to the action in the main verb – whether the speaker thinks the action in the main verb is carried out. We can take this simple sentence:

> **Kyoko lives near the station.**

By adding modals we can add:

> *possibility* – **She might live near the station.**

advisability – **She should live near the station.**
futurity – **She will live near the station.**

In summary, modal auxiliary verbs can add:

possibility – **She might do it.**
ability – **She can do it.**
necessity – **She must do it.**
advisability – **She should do it.**
future – **She will do it.**
permission – **You may sit there.**

The first difficulty, or confusing factor, is that many modal auxiliaries can have more than one meaning, depending on the context. For example, take the modal auxiliary 'must':

I must be going.　　(*obligation* – I am obliged to go).
You must be joking.　(*possibility* – there is a strong possibility that you are joking).

Here are the main different meanings of modal auxiliaries:

can　　*ability, permission, possibility*
may　　*permission, possibility*
might　*possibility*
must　　*obligation, possibility*
should　*obligation (possibility)*
will　　*future*

An added point to note is that opposite meaning is not always formed with a negative of the affirmative. The opposite of 'He can swim' is 'He can't swim'. However, the opposite of 'It can't be her' is 'It must be her'.

Form. Add the simple verb (infinitive without 'to') to the modal:

I can swim.

Modal auxiliaries do not need another auxiliary to form a negative or interrogative, and do not need an 's' for third person singular:

He can't swim.
He doesn't can swim. (*x*)
Can he swim?
Does he can swim? (*x*)
He can swim.
He cans swim. (*x*)

There are only two tenses possible with modal auxiliaries – present, which carries present and future meanings; and present perfect, which carries past meanings. To form the present perfect, use 'have' plus the past participle:

He might have gone.

Two exceptions to this are 'can' for *ability*, and 'must' for *obligation*, both of which can be expressed in the simple past: 'can' for *ability* has the simple past 'could'; and 'must' for *obligation* has the simple past 'had to'.

Teaching. The two principal approaches are to group modal auxiliaries by meaning or by form. If you group by meaning, you introduce one meaning at a time (eg *ability*), and when you teach a form in a later lesson with a different meaning, contrast it briefly with the previously taught meaning. So, for example, students would learn 'can' for *ability*, and later for *possibility*. In the second lesson (*possibility*), the meanings would be contrasted (**She can't swim** *v* **It can't be her**). This approach is probably best for teaching.

Another approach is to teach all the meaning of one form (eg 'could') together. However, such a method of presentation can be confusing at first, so this way of grouping is probably most suitable for revision.

A suggested teaching order is:

(1) *ability* (can/can't, could/couldn't). Situations to illustrate use – sports and pastimes.
(2) *permission* (can, may). Situations – social settings, visiting friends, etc.
(3) *obligation* (should/must, ought to/have to). Situations – related to figures of authority (eg school, doctor).
(4) *possibility* (must, could/may/might, can't). (Don't distinguish between could/may/might.) Situations – identifying objects and people.

Reported speech

Reported speech is what you get when you explain what somebody said without using quotation marks. In 'He said "I'm hungry" ', you are using direct speech – you say directly what he said. 'He said he was hungry' is reported speech. You report the meaning, but do not give the actual words. The main rule for reported speech is very simple: put all tenses one tense into the past (see box on next page).

Teaching grammar and functions **179**

DIRECT SPEECH	REPORTED SPEECH
Present simple of 'be' (**am/are/is**)	Past simple of 'be' (**was/were**)
Present simple (**arrive**)	Past simple (**arrived**)
Present continuous (**am/is/are/going**)	Past continuous (**was/were going**)
Present perfect (**have/has done**)	Past perfect (**had done**)
Future (**will come**)	Would (**would come**)

A number of other words are also altered. For example:

I becomes **he/she**
you becomes **I/he/she**
this becomes **that**
here becomes **there**
yesterday becomes **the day before**
tomorrow becomes **the next day**

Reported questions follow the tense-shift rule above, as well as reinverting as for indirect questions (see p 173): **'Have you been waiting long?', she asked** becomes **She asked if I had been waiting long.**

FUNCTIONS

Functions are the uses we put language to, such as inviting or suggesting. When learning a function, students need to know *exponents* (ways of performing the function): *associated exponents* (for example, how to reply); and *register* (different ways of performing the function in different social situations).

Each function can be carried out using several forms, called 'functional exponents'. For example, two functional exponents for the function of suggesting are:

Why don't you go by taxi?
What about going by taxi?

As well as teaching these functional exponents, there may be 'associated exponents' which could usefully be taught at the same time. In the case of the function of suggesting, replies for agreeing or disagreeing to 'Why don't we go to a disco?' would be relevant. Some replies might be:

That's a good idea.

> **Sounds good to me.**
> **Well, I'm not very keen on discos.**
> **Actually, I'd rather go bowling.**

Several functional exponents may have the same meaning, but have different 'register' (ie level of formality or politeness). For example:

Exponent	*Register*
Hi	Informal/friendly
Hello	Neutral
How do you do	Formal

It is important to make differences in register clear, and to give students separate situations in which to practise them.

In the following notes, informal exponents are marked (*I*), formal (*F*), and all others are neutral. For each function, I give: the forms of the exponents; associated exponents (eg how to reply to the exponents); notes on the exponents (problems, things to point out, register, etc); and situations in which to set the language (in a restaurant, talking to a sick friend, etc). The functions covered are: greeting; introducing; inviting; offering; requesting; advising; suggesting; and asking permission.

Greeting

Functional exponents

> **Hello/Hi/How do you do/How are you?**
> **Fine, thanks/Not too bad (thanks).**
> **Nice to meet you/Nice to see you.**
> **Good morning/afternoon/evening/night**
> **Goodbye/Bye/See you (later/tomorrow/next week/in October)**

Notes on exponents. Point out register differences. Practise formal exponents with family names (surnames), and informal ones with given names. Do not use the term 'Christian name' – most Japanese people are not Christian – and demonstrate first and family names using one student as an example (Japanese typically say their family name first, eg Ono Yoko).

'Nice to *meet* you' is for the first time; 'Nice to *see* you' is for next time(s).

There are two differences between 'How do you do' and 'How are you?'. First, as above, one is for strangers and the other is for friends or acquaintances. Second, 'How do you do' is not a question. The response is the same – 'How do you do'. 'How are you?' is a question.

Situations. Party, airport, etc.

Introducing

Functional exponent

> **(Ann), this is (my colleague), Mary White.**

Associated exponents include:

> **How do you do.**
> **Nice to meet you.**

Notes on exponents. There are many other exponents for introducing – 'I'd like you to meet . . . '; 'I'd like to introduce you to . . . '; 'Have you met . . . '; etc. However, the fact that these have similar but confusing forms, coupled with the greatly heightened nervousness felt by Japanese people on an occasion such as introducing two people, means that attempts at other exponents almost invariably fail, *whatever the level of the student.* You have been warned!

Note that the replies to 'How do you do' and 'Nice to meet you' are to repeat what was said to you.

Situations. Party, having visitors, business meeting, etc. Practise in groups of three or more, using open-handed gestures (make sure students put their pens down).

Inviting

Functional exponents

> **Would you like to . . . ?**
> **Do you want to . . . ?** (*I*)

Associated exponents include:

> **(Yes,) I'd love to.**
> **(Yes,) that would be nice.**

Notes on exponents. Students may use 'Do you like . . . ?' instead of 'Would you like . . . '. They may also omit 'to':

> **Would you like go to the cinema?** (*x*)

Situations. Social and leisure events: cinema, disco, dinner, golf, etc.

Offering

Offering to do something – functional exponents

> **Shall I . . . ?**
> **Can I . . . ?**

Associated exponents include:

> **Oh, thank you.**
> **Yes, please.**
> **(Yes,) sure.** (*I*)

Situations. Problems: heavy case (carry); tight lid (open); office duties (fax, photocopy, take); etc.

Offering something – functional exponents

> **Would you like a/some . . . ?**
> **Do you want a/some . . . ?** (*I*)

Associated exponents include:

> **Yes, please.**
> **Thank you.**

Situations. Food and drink.

Requesting

Functional exponents

> **Can you . . . ?**
> **Could you . . . ?**
> **Do you think you could . . . ?** (*F*)
> **Can I have . . . ?**
> **Could I . . . ?**
> **Would you mind?**

Associated exponents include:

> *Agree*
> **Yes, certainly** (*F*)
> **(Yes,) of course.**
> **(Yes,) sure.** (*I*)
> **No, of course not.**
> *Refuse*
> **Well, actually . . . I'm going out.**
> **I'm sorry there aren't any left.**

Note that in the last two examples, the refusals, the exponents comprise an apology (**Well, actually . . .**) followed by a reason (**I'm going out**).

Notes on exponents. 'Can I have . . . ?' means 'Can you give me . . . ?', but is softer and usually preferable.

'Can you'/'Could you'/'Do you think you could' are followed by an ordinary verb (eg 'go'). 'Would you mind' is followed by the 'ing' verb (eg 'going').

The answer to 'Do you mind . . . ?' is 'No, of course not'. However, it is not uncommon to answer 'Yes, of course', and give a gesture, such as waving your hand.

Situations. Asking for help: after a party (tidy up/empty the ashtrays/hoover the floor) or in an office (send this fax/copy this letter/phone the Paris office).

Advising

Functional exponents

> **(Perhaps) you should . . .**
> **If I were you, I'd . . .**
> **Have you tried . . . ?**

Associated exponents include:

> *Accepting*
> **Yes, (I think) I'll do that.**
> **(Yes,) I'll try that.**
> **That's a good idea.**
> *Refusing*
> **Yes, but it would take too long.**

Note that in the last example, the refusal is again followed by a reason.

Notes on exponents. 'You should' can often sound brusque or bossy unless preceded by a 'softener', such as 'I think', 'perhaps', or 'maybe'.

'If I were you' may be omitted, and only the second part of the sentence spoken.

'Have you tried . . . ?' is followed by the 'ing' verb (eg 'putting'). The other two exponents use the ordinary verb (eg 'put').

'You'd better' is a direct translation of a way to give advice in Japanese, and students often use it. However 'you'd better' is a warning, and too strong for most advice situations.

Situations. Problems (illness, business decisions); talking to someone who is going abroad or who doesn't like their job.

Suggestions

Functional exponents

> **Why don't you/we go to a disco?**
> **What/How about going to a disco?**

Associated exponents include:

> *Accepting*
> **That's a good idea.**
> *Refusing*
> **I don't really like discos.**
> **I'm not very keen on going to a disco.**
> **I don't really feel like going to a disco.**

Notes on 'exponents. 'Why don't we . . . ' is followed by the ordinary verb (eg 'go'). 'What/How about . . . ' is followed by the 'ing' verb (eg 'going').
　'I don't really like' and 'I'm not very keen on' can be followed by a noun or 'ing' verb. If it is a noun, it must be plural if it is countable ('discos' is countable and 'French food' is uncountable).

Situations. Arranging outings, trips, social events; choosing a restaurant.

Permission

Functional exponents

> **May I . . . ?** (*F*)
> **Could I . . . ?**
> **Can I . . . ?** (*I*)
> **Is it all right if I . . . ?**
> **Do you mind if I . . . ?**

Associated exponents include:

> *Giving permission*
> **Yes.**
> **(Yes,) certainly.** (*F*)
> **(Yes,) of course.**
> **Yeah, sure** (*I*)
> *Refusing*
> **I'm afraid . . .**
> **Well, actually . . .**

The refusal should take the form of an apology (**I'm afraid**) followed by a reason (**someone's sitting there**).

Notes on exponents. The answer to 'Do you mind . . . ?' is 'No, of course not'. However, it is not uncommon to answer 'Yes, of course', and give a gesture, such as waving your hand.

'*Would* you mind if I *sat* here?' is a more polite alternative to '*Do* you mind if I *sit* here?'. However, because of the confusing tenses, it is probably best not to teach it.

You may wish to teach 'Yeah' for understanding only, if students sound unnatural when they say it.

Situations. Visiting someone's house or office: use the phone, have a shower, make a cup of tea, turn on the TV.

This chapter is concerned with planning lessons, using a textbook, and planning a course.

LESSON PLANNING

Having a lesson plan gives you a clear framework for the lesson. It is not essential to have one and if you do have one, it is not a binding contract – if necessary you can and must step outside a lesson plan or amend it as you are going along. However, a plan gives you the chance to work out in advance a shape and order for the lesson, and to anticipate what problems might occur and what you might do about them.

Lesson plans, like lessons themselves, can and do vary widely depending on such things as the level, type and needs of your students, the type of lesson, and, of course, your own personality and style of teaching.

Some headings you might want to include in a lesson plan are:

- Aim of lesson.
- Specific language to be introduced.
- Materials.
- Assumed knowledge.

The following lesson plans are somewhat fuller than normal, to try to give you a more specific idea of the possible course of a lesson.

Lesson plan 1 – a beginner's lesson

Aim of lesson. Shopping language:

> **I'm looking for . . .**
> **Can I try it on?**
> **I'll take it (please).**
> **I'll leave it (thanks).**

Assumed knowledge. Basic clothes vocabulary.

Materials. Role cards: jacket – yes; shirt – no; etc.

Introduction. Revise clothes vocabulary by brainstorming:

Teacher: What's this? (*Gesture to your shirt.*)
Student: Shirt.
Teacher: Good. A shirt. (*Write 'shirt' on board.*) Tell me another kind of clothes.
Student: Shoe.
Teacher: Good. A shoe. (*Write 'shoe' on the board.*) Together (*gesture students into closed pairs*) write down three more kinds of clothes. (*Gesture to a few more items of clothing being worn by teacher and students.*)

Presentation

Teacher: OK. You want to buy a jacket. You go into a shop. What do you say? (*Write ' . . . jacket' on board.*)
Student: I want jacket.
Teacher: Maybe . . . A different sentence? . . . OK. Listen. I'm looking for a jacket. I'm – I am – looking for a jacket. I'm looking for a jacket. Everybody . . . Akiko . . . Keiko . . . (*Drill – choral and individual*; substitute drill – shirt, sweater, T-shirt.*)
Teacher: OK I'm the shop assistant. You're the customer, Keiko. You want to buy a jacket . . . Can I help you?
Student: I'm looking for a jacket.
Teacher: Yes.

> *Open and closed pairs for these three lines. Then re-do the three lines.*

Teacher: What about this one? . . . You want to. (*Gesture trying on.*) What's this? . . . Listen, try on . . . try on. (*Drill – choral/individual.*) Make a question. Use 'try on' . . . Listen. Can I try it on? (*Say again slowly, using fingers to isolate words, then again at natural speed. Drill – choral/individual. Add response 'Yes, of course'.*)

> *Put cues on board and do open and closed pairs of the partial dialogue:*

Shop assistant	Customer
Help?	Yes, . . . looking . . .
What/this one?	Try?
Yes	

Teacher: OK. So, you try on the jacket and you like it. Now you want to buy it. What do you say?

Student: I want to buy it.

Teacher: Well . . . a different sentence? Use the verb 'take' . . . Listen. I'll take it. (*Say slowly, 'I will take it'; and then repeat it at natural speed. Choral/individual drill.*)

Add 'take' to the customer's cues on the board, and practise the complete dialogue in open and closed pairs.

Teacher: OK. Now, maybe you don't want to buy the jacket. What do you say? . . . What's the opposite of 'take'?

Student: Leave.

Teacher: Good. Sentence?

Student: I'll leave it.

Teacher: Good. (*Choral/individual drill.*) We also have to say 'Thanks'. Listen. I'll leave it, thanks. (*Choral/individual drill.*)

Re-do dialogue with different ending.

Practice. Hand out one card to each student. 'Yes' means they want to buy it, and 'No' means they don't want to buy it. For example:

Jacket – Yes   Shirt – No
Coat – Yes   Sweater – No

Practise in closed pairs. Then have one or two pairs get up and perform for the class.

Board display. Write on the board:

I'm looking for a <u>jacket</u>.

Can I try it on?

I'll take it (please). (I want to buy it.)

I'll leave it, <u>thanks</u>. ← important word
(I don't want to buy it.)

Tell the students to write this in their notebooks, and have them write two complete dialogues in class or for homework.

Lesson plan 2 – an early intermediate lesson

Lesson. Refusing invitations.

New language. **Well, actually,/I'm sorry, I'm having dinner with John** (apologizing, or expressing regret, and using present continuous for future arrangements).

Assumed knowledge. **Would you like to . . . ? Yes, I'd love to** (previous lesson – making and accepting invitations).

Presentation. Set the scene with:

> **Mr Suzuki, you want to have a drink tonight with Mr Shimoda.**

Teacher: What do you say to Mr Shimoda?
Student: Would you like to have a drink tonight?
Teacher: Good. This is Mr Shimoda's diary for this week. Today is Monday. (*Copy diary onto board, writing 'dinner with John Miller' against Monday.*)
Teacher: Tell me about this evening.
Student: He will have dinner with John Miller.
Teacher: Mm . . . It's in his diary. It's decided. It's arranged. How do we talk about the future when it's arranged . . . Listen. He's having dinner with John Miller. (*Quick drill.*)
Write sentence on board.
Teacher: What's the tense – present or future?
Student: Present.
Teacher: Yes. What's the meaning – present or future?
Student: Future.
Teacher: Yes. (*Add to the board display as you speak*) So we've got present continuous tense with future meaning. And it's arranged, it's in his diary. (*You have added: 'He's having dinner with John Miller'; 'Tense – present continuous'; 'Meaning – future (arranged)'*).
Teacher: Any questions? . . . No? . . . OK. Copy that into your notebooks.

> *Clear board (except for diary)*

Teacher: OK. Mr Suzuki, invite Mr Shimoda to have a drink tonight.
Student A: Would you like to have a drink tonight?
Student B: I'm having dinner with John Miller.
Teacher: Good. Mr Hashimoto, invite me.
Student C: Would you like to have a drink tonight?
Teacher: Well, actually . . . I'm having dinner with John Miller

. . . What did I say before 'I'm having dinner'?

Student: Well, actually.

Teacher: Good. I want to show my feelings, that I'm not happy. Listen to my intonation. Well, actually (*say with apologetic intonation*).

Choral/individual drill 'Well, actually', then 'Well actually, I'm having dinner with John Miller'. Introduce, model and drill 'I'm sorry' in the same way. Build up a dialogue with a refusal for tonight and an acceptance for tomorrow night. Complete the lesson with a final dialogue.

A: Would you like to have a drink tonight?

B: I'm sorry, I'm having dinner with John Miller.

A: Would you like to go (to the cinema) tomorrow night?

B: Yes, I'd love to.

Lesson plan 3 – a song

Song – Yesterday (Beatles)

Assumptions. Students are familiar with the past simple tense.

Anticipated problems. The song has a poetic word order: 'Why she had to go I don't know' (I don't know why she had to go).

Some of the vocabulary will be unknown: 'long for'; 'hide' (away); 'hang' (over). There will also be unfamiliar constructions: students will not know the construction 'There's a shadow hanging' or the use of 'wouldn't' for 'refused'.

Dealing with problems. With regard to the poetic word order, the meaning should be clear: leave this until the end when you can unscramble and explain the idea of poetic word order. The unknown vocabulary should be pre-taught. The meaning of 'There's a shadow hanging' should be clear. Ignore unusual grammar unless asked. If asked, it means 'A shadow is hanging'. Finally, the meaning of 'wouldn't' should be pre-taught as 'didn't want to'.

Materials. You will need a cassette and tape recorder, and partially blanked out copies of the lyrics.

Pre-teach vocabulary and story of song. Draw a sad face on the board, and begin the lesson.

Teacher: Is he happy?

Student: No
Write 'Today' under the picture
Teacher: When is this?
Student: Today
Draw a happy face to the left of the sad face. Write 'Yesterday' underneath.
Teacher: When was this?
Student: Yesterday.
Teacher: How did he feel yesterday?
Student: Happy.
Write 'Paul' on the board.
Teacher: His name's Paul. Yesterday he was happy, but today he's sad.
Draw a dark cloud over the sad face, and shadow underneath (draw slanting lines over it).
Teacher: (*Point to cloud.*) What's this?
Student: Cloud.
Teacher: Good. (*Point to shade.*) What's this?
Student: ??
Teacher: It's a shadow. Shadow. Listen, sha-dow. Everybody, shadow.
Students: Shadow.
Choral/individual drill.
Teacher: The dark part under the cloud is a shadow. (*Point to cloud and face.*) Where's the cloud?
Student: Over him.
Teacher: Good. The shadow's heavy and it isn't moving. Can you tell me a word for what it's doing?
Students: ??
Teacher: In some countries, if a bad person is killed in prison, they do it like this (*mime being hanged*). What do you call that?
Students: ??
Teacher: Hang. It's called hanging. Hang. Listen, hang. Everybody, hang.
Students: Hang.
Choral/individual drill.
Teacher: The shadow is hanging over him. (*Write 'shadow hanging over him' on board.*) He's sad. Why is he sad? Why is the shadow hanging over him? (*Draw a girl waving goodbye to the happy face, and change it to a sad face.*)
Student: His girlfriend went away.
Teacher: Good. His girlfriend went away.
Draw in speech bubble for Paul. 'Why are you going away?'
Teacher: What did Paul ask her?
Student: Why are you going away?
Teacher: Yes.

> *Draw an empty speech bubble beside girl.*

Teacher: What did she say?

Student: Nothing.

Teacher: Good . . . Why not?

Students: ??

Teacher: Why didn't she say anything? . . . She didn't want to . . .
Can anybody say that a different way? . . . She wouldn't say.
Listen, she wouldn't say. Everybody, she wouldn't say.
Choral/individual drill. Write 'She wouldn't say' on board.

Teacher: She wouldn't say . . . What does that mean?

Student: She didn't want to say.

Teacher: Good. Yesterday, Paul was happy. He was in love. His
life was very easy. It was like a game. Now he's sad. He
doesn't want to meet people.
Teach 'hide'.
*Teach 'long for' (he wants to go back to yesterday, but he
can't).*
Listen to the tape – hand out partially blanked lyrics.

Teacher: Listen to the song and try to write the words.
Play song.

Teacher: Check together. (*Gesture them into closed pairs.*)
Play song again.

Teacher: Check together. (*Closed pairs.*)
Play again if necessary.
Check answers open.

Explain poetic licence

Teacher: In a song, sometimes the words are in a different order, a
different position. Can anybody tell me a sentence with the
words in a strange position?

Student: Why she had to go I don't know.

Teacher: Good. Can you tell me the normal sentence.

Student: I don't know why she had to go.

Teacher: Good. (*Write on board.*)

USING A TEXTBOOK

Teaching from a textbook can make for an easy life. However,
there is a tendency for lessons to become boring for both you and
the students. Teaching from a textbook is easier because the
framework of the course, and of each lesson, has already been
thought out; and because there is often a teacher's manual to go
with the students' book to give specific ideas on how to present
and exploit the materials.

On the other hand, teaching from a textbook can become boring because the layout of each unit is usually very similar, and therefore predictable; and because there is often the temptation to stick to the book and not add anything (the commands 'Turn to page 57' and 'Turn to the next page' can become like dreaded dirges).

Students like course books because they feel they are studying a 'proper' course, as opposed to a series of one-off lessons. Course books also provide tangible progress for them to show their friends, and a tangible result at the end of the course for them to take away and look back on.

Teachers, on the other hand, tend to dislike course books because all classes are different, so no book is perfect or complete. A course book is inflexible (or can seem so).

DESIGNING A SYLLABUS

When designing a syllabus, or using one given to you in a book or by a school, don't be afraid of leaving out items of language. You could not teach everything there is to know about English, even if you knew it. As you get to know what students need, it is axiomatic that you will also get a feel for what aspects of English are so unusual that they are hardly worth the time it would take to teach them. In fact, one of the greatest problems about the English which is taught in Japanese high schools is that the teaching is not designed from a 'usefulness' point of view. Students have a vast amount of esoteric knowledge about English, but have great gaps in their knowledge of everyday English and how to use it.

If there is an aspect of language which you feel will be of more use of them on the streets of London or New York than, for example, the future perfect, then, if it is in your power, you should follow your instincts.

Frequency and usefulness, then, are important criteria to consider, but another one is difficulty. You might feel that, with some topics, students will take a disproportionate amount of time to reach any level of proficiency. In such cases, you may consider either not teaching the point at all, or else teaching it for understanding, but not insisting that they actually use the item of language. Two possible examples in point are the pronunciation of 'l' or 'r' and tag questions (isn't she? wouldn't it? etc).

15 | Business people and children

A large amount of the English teaching in Japan is English for specific purposes (ESP), such as teaching doctors the type of medical English which will be useful to them professionally.

Business people

By far the greatest amount of ESP in Japan is business-related, mostly to business people. The teaching can be done in different ways:

- *One-to-one*. Teaching one student requires a different approach to working with a group (see p 130).
- *In-company group*. An in-company group may study during the working day, or in the evening.
- *In-school group*. A group of business people, from the same company or from different companies, may study at a language school.

Business people studying in the evening, after a full day's work, may be very tired. It is unrealistic to expect to get through a significant amount of material with them, or for them to contribute much to the lesson. You will have to lower your sights in one or more of the following ways:

- Aim to get through less material.
- Use material which is less challenging.
- 'Feed' them the answers almost immediately if they are having problems.
- Discard the lesson plan, and move to free conversation.

Teaching business English in Japan means almost exclusively teaching men. Women executives are rare, and women in general hold low-status jobs, and retire when they get married.

If a company or section studies together, there is liable to be a wide range of English levels within the class. Teaching a split-level class calls for a bit of juggling on your part, to try to prevent the

194

more able students from becoming bored, while ensuring that the lower-level students do not get lost. In an in-company class, there is the added difficulty of trying to make sure that the boss does not lose face by having his mistakes corrected by a junior, or being otherwise embarrassed. In general, it is best to ask senior staff only questions to which you are fairly certain they know the answer.

What they need

Despite their demands for 'business English', what most business people seem to need above all else is the basic groundwork in using English naturally which other Japanese students of English need. Of course, it is better if it can be presented and practised in a business context. But if and when any of these students meet a foreign business person, what will be evident will probably be their stiffness and awkwardness with English generally, rather than the fact that they cannot conduct meetings with the correct phraseology.

They are more likely to have successful contact with foreign business people if they can have a normal conversation with them about their flight and the weather. This will probably be more important than not knowing the difference between a cif document and a bill of lading. In fact, Japanese business people often know the jargon for their line of business. If they do not, it is usually a fairly simple matter of learning the specific vocabulary which they need.

Many business books concentrate almost exclusively on pure business matters, and do not have enough social English. Such books are often designed for European business people who have much less need for instruction in conducting themselves socially in English.

That is not to say that there are no good or suitable business books available. There are, but there are also a lot of business books which need a considerable amount of supplementary material for general English to make them suitable for Japanese students.

There are some good business videos. These show business people interacting in a natural way, and can be very useful to your students.

Surnames

In contrast to general English teaching, where teachers usually encourage students to use their given names in class, it may be advisable to allow business people to use their surnames. There may be considerable embarrassment about revealing or using first names, especially in an in-company class.

Irregular studying

Business people usually have very busy schedules, and office duties often interfere with their studying. They may be late for a lesson, and may miss lessons completely – cancelling if it is a one-to-one lesson, or not turning up for a group lesson.

Children

There is a good chance that you will teach children, perhaps even of pre-school age, during your stay in Japan. Young children need rather different teaching methods to those suitable for adults. Teaching young children is great fun and very rewarding, as long as you approach the lessons in the right way.

It is vital to bear in mind that children have much shorter attention spans than adults. Don't spend too long on any one activity. As well as changing activities, change both focus and pace. Especially with younger children, having a complete change every ten or fifteen minutes might not be too frequent.

Often it is impossible to explain grammar rules to children – they might not have thought of the concepts in their own language, never mind in English! If you provide lots of varied practice, you can see the language being painlessly integrated into their consciousness, just as it is with native speakers when they are learning their first language.

Unlike Japanese adults, Japanese children, especially younger ones, are *true beginners*. This means that you cannot assume anything. If you go to teaching children after teaching Japanese adults, you might be surprised at the amount you previously took for granted, from ability to write Roman letters to understanding of basic words such as 'here' and 'there'.

It is much easier to make significant strides in *pronunciation* with children than with adults. Their mistakes have not yet fossilized, because normally they will not yet have been exposed to too much bad pronunciation.

Discipline is an addition to your duties when teaching children as opposed to adults. Your most important lessons in this respect are the first one or two. Do not get too friendly too fast. Whereas with Japanese adults, much of your early work is spent breaking down their barriers and getting them to relax, the same approach can spell disaster with children. You do not have to be gruff and strict, but leave it for a few lessons at least before you join in on class laughter or do anything too undignified. It is never a problem to make your class a little looser when you have clearly established your authority. But if things get out of hand at the beginning, you can have the devil's own job trying to re-establish control.

A good starting point with children, to show them that they can, in fact, speak English, is to lean heavily on the vast number of English *loan words* which are used in Japan. Some of these are given in Appendix 4.

In many classes, the sexes are separated and you will have to consider the wisdom of *mixing sexes*. While it might be useful linguistically to have the sexes working together, for example, to play the appropriate role in a role play, this might meet with resistance or awkwardness, and you will have to decide if you are willing to pay this price.

You can normally assume that adults bring a certain amount of *motivation* to your class (though this may not always be true with businessmen, if their companies are paying for their tuition). Children, on the other hand, may not automatically see any special reason to put any energy or enthusiasm into learning English. Fortunately, with younger children, just a little energy and input on your part is usually rewarded a hundredfold by the students.

Older children may not be so easy to motivate. In particular, they may consider your lessons an irrelevance to their all-important goal of passing the university entrance exams, for which your lessons may not be much help. They are also often the most difficult group to get to realize that English is a living vehicle of communication – younger children quickly realize it on a practical level, and adults usually understand it cerebrally.

Some suggested activities, and ways to practise language with children, are listed below.

Games. If possible, turn everything into a game of some kind. It will not take you long to become adept at designing a game with a list of rules, often on the spot in the middle of a lesson. Sometimes, however, there is a problem if you want to play the same game in the next lesson, and you cannot remember all your marvellous rules! The easiest game is simply to divide the class into two teams and play in the form of a contest. Suddenly the most mechanical and dreary of exercises becomes a game.

Memory tests. Japanese children have marvellous short-term pictorial memories. After working for a while with any written or pictorial material, just repeat the same language activity with the material covered.

Songs and chants. Songs, especially action songs, are enjoyed by children. They are also very fond of chanting, and choral drilling can be much more extensive than with adults.

Actions. If possible, have some sort of physical activity associated with language work. It might take the form of Total Physical Response (see p 118), with the children acting out the language being spoken or heard. Other possible actions are: cards (picking up, discarding, taking, giving, bringing, putting, etc); writing (having students write down some words or sentences after an activity gives a change of pace and focus, and allows everyone to calm down a little – writing is also a useful reinforcement of speaking, and a record of the lesson); and drawing (good for practising colours, numbers, shapes and general descriptive language).

Appendices

Appendices

Appendix 1 | Three case histories

When you come home from a stay in Japan, you may want to put your knowledge of Japan and the Japanese to some practical use. You may wish to continue teaching English as a foreign language, to find work with a Japanese company, or use your knowledge of Japan and the Japanese in a domestic company. Alternatively, you may simply be content to have a note of your experience sitting on your resumé – and there can be no doubt that having seen the workings of today's most powerful economy from the inside should increase your employability in a good many fields.

If you stay in TEFL, your Japanese experience will undoubtedly be seen as a plus. More and more Japanese are studying abroad and many schools are having problems integrating Japanese students, because of their different needs. As a result, teachers with experience of Japan are usually welcomed.

If you decide to try to find work with a Japanese company, you may well find that you are employable in a range of fields in which you have no previous experience. The fact that you know how Japanese companies are run (even if it is on the superficial basis of keeping your eyes open when teaching in companies, and talking to *sarariman* students) means that a Japanese employer may find you a more attractive recruit than an experienced or qualified person who may not 'fit in' because of his or her lack of exposure to the Japanese working routine.

The following potted case histories give an idea of the kind of opportunities which are available to returners.

Daniel Dickinson was born in London. He studied French and German at Oxford University. He then went out to Japan on the JET programme (see p 7) in 1986, and stayed there until 1988.

He taught in a senior high school in Osaka. He was the first *gaijin* ever to have taught in the school, and he introduced the teaching of English conversation. He studied Japanese while he was in Japan, and thinks it is not a difficult language to learn, as long as you are prepared to put in time studying *kanji* and vocabulary.

He returned to the UK in 1988, and found work as a reporter for the London bureau of the *Sankei Shinbun*, a Japanese daily newspaper. He had no previous experience as a reporter, and got the job on the strength of his Japanese experience, and knowledge of the language.

He reports to the London Bureau Chief, who is Japanese. He writes a monthly column on UK life, which is translated into Japanese. He does interviews and carries out research, which are used by the Bureau Chief as bases for articles.

He needs Japanese mainly to communicate with the desk in Tokyo in the absence of his manager. He thinks his experience in Japan has been invaluable in helping him work in a Japanese company. He finds Japanese people demanding but fair to work with.

Katrina Hunt comes from Medford, a small town in southern Oregon. She was selected by the Medford Rotary Club to represent them in Monbetsu in Hokkaido for one year as a high school student. That was the beginning of her involvement in Japan. She went on to study International Relations at Williamette University in Salem, Oregon, spending one semester of her senior year studying at Tokyo University.

After graduation she decided to go back to Japan to work, and spent two years teaching in a high school in Hiroshima under the JET programme from 1987 to 1989.

She returned to Oregon in search of a job in which she could use her language skills and working experience in Japan. The process took longer than she expected. Most Japanese companies were eager to hire her in a secretarial position. After several months, she was offered the opportunity to join Nissei Electric as the Office Supervisor.

Cathy Leek grew up in Hamilton in Scotland, and went to Glasgow University, where she studied History.

She went out to Japan to study *zen*, and found work teaching at a language school in Chiba, on the outskirts of Tokyo. She spent eighteen months in Japan and her interest in Japanese culture in general, and *zen* in particular, meant that she was able to make good progress with *Nihongo*, although she spoke no Japanese when she first arrived.

She returned to the UK in 1989, and, through her Japanese experience, found work as an assistant to the UK representative for Daimaru, which has a chain of department stores throughout Japan. She does market research on UK products which Daimaru may wish to sell in their Japanese stores. Part of her work is looking after Daimaru executives when they visit the UK, acting as a liaison between them and their UK companies.

Her knowledge of Japanese is useful but not essential in her work. Although it is not necessary to speak Japanese with her boss, she feels her working environment is more pleasant because she is able to talk some of the time in Japanese.

Appendix 2 Some English schools

Tokyo

Berlitz Schools of Language, 3F Capital Akasaka, 1–7–19 Akasaka, Minato-ku, Tokyo 107 (Tel 03 3584 4211)

The British Council Cambridge English School, 1–2 Kagurazaka, Shinjuku-ku, Tokyo 162 (Tel 03 3235 8011)

ECC, 4F Nisugi Building, 7–3–4 Nishi-Shinjuku, Shinjuku-ku, Tokyo 160 (Tel 03 5330 1440)

ILC International Language Centre, 9F Iwanami Jimbo-cho Building, 2–1 Kanda Jimbo-cho, Chiyoda-ku, Tokyo 101 (Tel 03 3264 7464)

IF Foreign Language Institute, 31–1 Higashi Matsushita-cho, Kanda, Chiyoda-ku, Tokyo 101 (Tel 03 3252 7747)

ELEC Eigo Kenshujo, 3–8 Kanda Jimbo-cho, Chiyoda-ku, Tokyo 101 (Tel 03 3265 8911)

Greg Gaigo Gakko, 1–14–16 Jiyuagaoka, Meguro-ku, Tokyo 152 (Tel 03 3724 0552)

Hampton School of English, 4F Dai 2 Komatsu Building, 2–14–17 Shibuya, Shibuya-ku, Tokyo 150 (Tel 03 3406 1231)

Linguarama Executive Language Service, 12F Kasumigaseki Building, 3–2–5 Kasumigaseki, Chiyoda-ku, Tokyo 100 (Tel 03 3581 6741)

Kanda Institute of Foreign Languages, 2–13–13 Uchikanda, Chiyoda-ku, Tokyo 101 (Tel 03 3258 5827)

Nichibei Kaiwa Gakuin, 1–21 Yotsuya, Shinjuku-ku, Tokyo 160 (Tel 03 3359 9621)

Simul Academy, 2–22–1 Yoyogi Shibuya-ku, Tokyo 151 (Tel 03 3372 3100)

Sony Language Laboratory, 1–6–2 Nishi-Shinbashi, Minato-ku, Tokyo 105 (Tel 03 3504 1356)

Tokyo Foreign Language College, 7–3–8 Nishishinjuku, Shinjuku-ku, Tokyo 160 (Tel 03 3367 1101)

Tokyo International College of Business, 1–14–6 Jiyugaoka, Meguro-ku, Tokyo 152 (Tel 03 3724 0551)

Tokyo Yamate YMCA, 2–18–12 Nishi Waseda, Shinjuku-ku, Tokyo 169 (Tel 03 3202 0321)

Osaka

Berlitz Schools of Languages, 6F NS Building, 3–2–5 Honcho, Chuo-ku, Osaka-shi, Osaka 541 (Tel 06 245 3621)

ECC, Esupasion Umeda, 12–6 Chaya-machi, Kita-ku, Osaka-shi, Osaka 530 (Tel 06 373 0144)

GEOS Language System, 6F Matsumoto Building, 1–1–26 Shibata, Kita-ku, Osaka-shi, Osaka 530 (Tel 06 359 1415)

ILC International Language Centre, 8F Shirokabe Building, Shibata, Kita-ku, Osaka-shi, Osaka 530 (Tel 06 376 2105)

Linguarama Executive Language Service, 3–4–10 Hon-machi, Chuo-ku, Osaka 541 (Tel 06 271 8978)

Osaka YMCA International College, 1–5–6 Tosahori, Nishi-ku, Osaka-shi 550 (Tel 06 441 0892)

Kyoto

The British Council Cambridge English School, 77 Kitashirakawa Nishi-machi, Sakyo-ku, Kyoto-shi, Kyoto 606 (Tel 075 723 3251)

Kyoto YMCA Gakuin, Yanaginobanba-kado, Sanjo-dori, Nagagyo-ku, Kyoto-shi 604 (Tel 075 255 3287)

Kyoto YMCA Kokusai Senmon Gakko, Karasuma-Imadegawa-Sagaru, Kamigyo-ku, Kyoto-shi 602 (Tel 075 432 3191)

Kobe

Kobe YMCA Gakuin Senmon Gakko, 2–1–3 Gakuen Higashi-cho, Nishi-ku, Kobe-shi, Hyogo 651–21 (Tel 078 793 7402)

Palmore Institute, 4–7–30 Kitanagasa-dori, Chuo-ku, Kobe-shi, Hyogo 650 (Tel 078 331 2949)

St Michael Kokusai Gakko, 3–17–2 Nakayamatedori, Chuo-ku, Kobe-shi, Hyogo 650 (Tel 078 221 8028)

Hiroshima

Berlitz Schools of Languages, 8F Kougin Building, 1–23 Tate-machi, Naka-ku, Hiroshima-shi, Hiroshima 730 (Tel 082 245 1521)

David English House, Porestar Hiroshima, 7–5 Naka-machi, Naka-ku, Hiroshima-shi, Hiroshima 730 (Tel 082 244 2633)

GEOS Language System, 8F Kurimura Building, 10–18 Teppo-cho, Naka-ku, Hiroshima-shi, Hiroshima 730 (Tel 082 223 8533)

Fukuoka

Berlitz Schools of Languages, 4F Ayasugi Building, 1–15–6 Tenjin, Chuo-ku, Fukuoka-shi, Fukuoka 810 (Tel 092 751 7561)

NOVA Gaigo Gakuin, Tenjin Sazan Dori Parusu Building, 2–6–32 Tenjin, Chuo-ku, Fukuoka-shi, Fukuoka 810 (Tel 092 725 8377)

Appendix 3 Glossary of teaching terms

Adjective A word which describes a noun (eg a **noisy** band, an **open** door).

Adverb A word which describes a verb or an adjective. Adverbs often end in 'ly', with an adjective as their root (eg **beautifully**).

Auxiliary (verb) A 'helping' or 'extra' verb. Auxiliaries help to form a tense ('**Do** you want a hand?' '**Are** you coming?' '**Have** you seen her?'). Auxiliaries are: **am, are, is, was, were, do, does, did, have, has, had**. Auxiliaries can also be modal – ie they can carry meaning (see **modal auxiliary**).

Conjunction A joining word (eg **and, but, although**).

Countable Of nouns, able to be counted. **Car** is countable: one car, two cars. Nouns such as 'rice' are uncountable.

Elicit To draw out language from the students without first giving them examples of it.

Elision Shortening a word by omitting a letter (eg **There is** becomes **There's**).

Infinitive The basic form of a verb, usually preceded by the word 'to' (eg **to run, to fly, to float**).

Modal auxiliary (verb) A 'helping' or 'extra' verb which carries meaning, such as 'can' or 'must' (eg 'He **can** swim', 'I **must** go'). Common modal auxiliaries are **can, could, may, might, must**.

Noun A person, place, thing or state (eg **John, Honolulu, chair, joy**).

Object The recipient of the action of the verb. Objects can be direct or indirect. Indirect objects are usually preceded by 'to'. In the sentence 'I gave **the book** to **John**', 'the book' is the direct object and 'John' the indirect object.

Participle Part of a verb ending in 'ing' (present participle) or 'ed' (past participle). It needs an auxiliary and a subject ('I am **sailing**', 'I have **started**').

Person There are three persons: First – **I**, **we**; Second – you; third – **he**, **she**, **it**, **they** or a **noun**, such as 'car'.

Preposition A word which goes before a noun, and relates the noun to the rest of the sentence (eg **in**, **after**, **through**).

Subject The doer of action (eg 'The **cat** sat on the mat').

Verb A 'doing' word, such as **go**, **walk**, **ask**.

Appendix 4 English loan words

A large number of English words have been borrowed by the Japanese, and are used in normal conversation. Two caveats are that the pronunciation is often changed almost beyond comprehension by a native English speaker, and also the words themselves may have partly changed in meaning after the crossover.

autograph book

baby car
baby shoes
baby wear
beach ball
bedroom
beef
beer
biscuit
black coffee
bell
boat
bonus
boots
boss
bowling
boyfriend
bucket
building
bulldog
bus
butter
buzzer
bye-bye

cake
camera

camp
candy
captain
card
cash register
cement
chain
chalk
chance
change
check
chicken
chocolate
Christmas (Eve)
cider
class
classic
club
coffee
coke
cola
collar
collection
collie
colour
commercial (TV)
communication
computer

concert
concrete
corduroy
corned beef
corner
cost
count
cream
crew
cup
curry
cushion
cut
cutlet

dark (blue)
date
denim
department store
dessert
door
double
doughnut
dry cleaning
dump truck
dynamite

egg

error
evening dress

fan
fight
film
focus
football
fork
fresh
fruit cake
fruit juice
fruit salad
fry

game
gang
gas
gasoline stand
gift shop
glass
glove
goal
Golden Week
golf
gossip
green
grey
group
gum

hairbrush
hairstyle
half-time
ham
hamburger
handbag
handkerchief
handle
happy end
heavy smoker
heavyweight
hello
highway
hit
home run

hose
hostess
hot coffee
hot drink

ice cream
image-up/down
ink
instant coffee

jet
juice

kick
king-size
kiss
kitchen

laboratory
lamp
league
lemonade
lighter
love

maker
mama
manners
mansion
mass communication
mass production
medal
meter
milk
modern
mood
motor

napkin
net
new face
noodle
note
number one

oil

overcoat

pyjamas
pants
papa
parking
parts
part-time
party
peanut
pen
pencil (case)
perm
picnic
pink
pool
pork
post box
present
print
pro
plastic
pudding
puncture

radio
raincoat
range
record
remote control
rice
rink
romance
room cooler
running

safe
sailing
salary man
sale
sandwich
service
set
sharp pencil
sheet
shoot

shirt
shop
shopping centre
short
shot
slipper
snack
snow tyre
socks
soda
sofa
soft
song
sports
stand
star
steak
speed

spelling
stocking
stove
strike
style
summer
supermarket
supertanker
sweater
sweetcorn

taxi
tennis
tissue
toast
tomato
T-shirt

unique

violin
volleyball

waitress
water
wedding cake
weekday
weekend
window
wool

yacht

zipper

Appendix 5   Selective bibliography

Japan

R. Christopher, *The Japanese Mind* (Tuttle)
P. Popham, *The Insider's Guide to Japan* (Moorland Publishing)
P. Tasker, *Inside Japan: Wealth, Work and Power in the Japanese Empire*
   (Penguin)
J. Woronoff, *Japan: The Coming Social Crisis* (Yohan)

Japanese language

Association for Japanese Language Teaching, *Japanese for Busy People*, 2
   vols (Kodansha)
Japanese for Beginners (Gakken)

English teaching

Course books

B. Hartley, *Streamline English* (Oxford University Press)
S. Molinsky, *Expressways* (Prentice-Hall)
M. Swan, *Cambridge English Course* (Cambridge University Press)

Course books (children)

B. Abbs, *Discoveries*, for over 10s (Longman)
J. Ashworth, *Stepping Stones*, for under 10s (Collins)

Other

C. Ford, *Cultural Encounters: What to Do and Say in Social Situations*
   (Pergamon)
C. Granger, *Play Games with English* (Heinemann)
P. Nicholson, *Explain Yourself* (Maruzen)
Nolasco and Arthur, *Conversation* (OUP)
M. Rinvolucri, *Grammar Games* (Cambridge University Press)

M. Shovel, *Making Sense of Phrasal Verbs* (Cassell)
P. Watcyn-Jones, *Pair Work* (Penguin)

Business

P. Brown, *Business Partners* (Language Teaching Publications)
S. Norman, *Financial English* (BBC)
Living and Working in the USA (Via Press)
A. Vaughan, *Ready for Business* (Longman)

Business videos

The Bellcrest Story (BBC)
Bid for Power (BBC)
The Sadrina Project (BBC)

References

Jeremy Harmer, *The Practice of English Language Teaching* (Longman)
F. Johnstone, *Stick Figures for Language Teaching* (Ginn)
A. Matthews, *At the Chalkface* (Nelson)
G. Moskowitz, *Caring and Sharing in the Foreign Language Class* (Newbury House)
Raymond Murphy, *English Grammar in Use* (Cambridge University Press)
W. Rivers, *A Practical Guide to TESL and TEFL* (Oxford University Press)
T. Rohlen, *Japan's High Schools* (University of California Press)
Peter Wilberg, *One to One* (Language Teaching Publications)
Keys to Language Teaching series (Longman)
Gower *Teaching Practice Handbook* (Heinemann)

Appendix 6 | Classroom Japanese

Although it is generally preferable to run classes entirely in English, sometimes a word or two in Japanese can oil the wheels of the lesson to make things run more smoothly. This is especially true with beginner or nervous students.

Parts of speech

noun *meishi*
verb *dōshi*
adjective *keiyōshi*
preposition *zenchishi*
article *kanshi*
pronoun *daimeishi*

Tenses

present *genzai*
present continuous *genzai shinkō*
past *kako*
present perfect *genzai kanryō*
future *mirai*

Other

question *shitsumon*
answer *kotae*

singular *tansū*
plural *fukusū*

syllable *onsetsu*
consonant *shiin*
vowel *boin*

polite *teinei-na*
questionnaire *ankēto*
opposite *hantai-no* (The opposite of black: *Black no hantai*)
clue or hint *hinto*
all the way *zutto*

Teacher speak

'Don't need'. **Student:** 'I went to shopping.' **Teacher:** 'To *iranai*.' ('You don't need "to" '.)

'Silently'. **Teacher:** 'Read this *moku doku*.'

'In Japanese?' Even after only a short time in Japan, your basic conversational *Nihongo* may be better than many students' English. **Teacher:** '*Nihongo de (nanai)?*' ('How do you say that in Japanese?')

'Either one is all right'. **Student:** '"The film *which* I saw" or "The film *that* I saw" '? **Teacher:** *Dochi demo ii.*

'Something'. **Teacher:** 'I *nantoka* to the station.' **Student:** 'Went?'
   Teacher: Yes.
'What do you/does that mean?' *Dō yū imi?*
'What do you call it?/How do you say that?' *Nan to yūka?*
'For example' *Tatoeba*
'How do you spell that?' *Spell wa?*
'Talk to your neighbour' (*in closed pairs*) *Futari de* (tonari no hito
   to)

Loan words

gesture: this is useful, for example, when encouraging students to
   use a gesture when introducing two people.
case by case: this phrase can be used when a student asks for a
   distinction to be explained, but there is no apparent rule.

Appendix 7 Japanese glossary

For grammatical terms see Appendix 6, for food glossary See Appendix 8

aikidō a martial art
aoi blue (the word used to describe traffic lights showing 'go')
apāto apartment
ashita tomorrow
ato later

ban a block, used in address
basho a *sumō* tournament
batsu a cross (x)
bonsai miniature trees
bunraku puppet theatre
burakumin untouchable caste (a taboo subject)
burikko teenage girls dressed super-cutely
byōin hospital

cha-no-yu the tea ceremony
chikan pervert or groper, usually on a crowded train
chikatetsu subway train
chimpira trainee *yakuza*
chiri gomi wastepaper
chōme area of a few blocks, used in addresses
chū-gakkō middle school
chotto a little bit
chū centre or medium

dai large
daigaku university
daimyō feudal lord
danchi council house
daruma lucky doll
densha train
denwa phone
depāto department store
desu is

enka a kind of song, popular among *karaoke* singers
eta a less polite term for *burakumin* (a taboo word)

fudōsan-ya estate agency
futon traditional mattress and duvet folded away in the daytime
futsuka-yoi hangover
Futsu resha ordinary stopping train

gaijin foreigner
gakkō school
gaman endurance
Gambatte! Go for it!
gerende ski slope
genkan small entrance hall where shoes are removed
genmai brown rice
go a traditional board game
gomen nasai sorry
gomi rubbish

gumbai uchiwa referee's fan in sumō

han half
hanko personal stamp
hari acupuncture
heya room, also training stable in sumō
hidari left
hiragana writing system used for small words and verb inflections
hoken health insurance
hon-ya bookshop

ichi one
ikebana flower arranging
Ikki! shout to encourage someone to finish a drink in one
imasen s/he's not t/here
imasu s/he's t/here
ippon one bottle
irasshaimase welcome (literally a polite form of 'is')
itadakimasu the word for *bon appétit*

jan ken pon scissors, paper, stone
ji hour
jikatabi soft, split-toed boots
Jikokuhyō master rail timetable
jitensha bicycle
jō the area of one *tatami* mat (about one metre by 500 cm)
joshidai women's university
jūdō a martial art.
juku cram school

ka added to a sentence to make it a question
kabuki traditional theatre, with all parts played by men
kaerimasu go home
kaisoku (densha) rapid train
kaisūken coupon ticket
Kampai! Cheers!

kana hiragana and katakana
kanamono-ya hardware shop
kanji traditional writing system of Chinese characters
Kansai Osaka, Kyoto and surrounding areas
Kantō Tokyo and surrounding area
karaoke singing along to a backing tape
karate a martial art
kashiwade clapping at a shrine to awaken the gods
katakana writing system for foreign words
kawaii cute
kendō a martial art
kissaten coffee shop
kōban police box
kōkō senior high school
Kokumin Kenkō Hoken health insurance organized through the ward office
Kokutetsu Japanese Railways
konro a gas table
kotatsu table with a heating element underneath
kome-ya rice shop
kosokudōro motorway
koto long stringed instrument
ku ward (of a district)
kubi gesture of cutting your throat, which means being fired
kuso shit
kusuri-ya chemist's
kyabarē cabaret
Kyodai Kyoto University
kyūdō archery
kyūkō express train

man ten thousand
maneki neko lucky cat doll
manga comic book
maru circle (it also means 'correct')

matsuri festival
meishi name card
migi right
minshuku traditional hotel, cheaper than a *ryokan*
moenai gomi unburnable rubbish
moeru gomi burnable rubbish
mokuzō wooden house
Moshi moshi Hello (on the phone)

nan? what?
nemawashi small meetings before a meeting to agree the outcome beforehand
Nihon or Nippon Japan (nihon also means 'two bottles')
noh traditional form of theatre
noren curtain over shop doorway to show that the shop is open
norikae change train lines

ofuro bath
omiyage holiday gift
omiai kekkon arranged marriage
onsen hot spring

pachinko kind of vertical pinball

rajio radio
reikin key money
reizōko fridge
rikishi a *sumō* wrestler
Rōmaji Romanized (Western) letters
roku six
ryokan traditional hotel (an up-market *minshuku*)

saka-ya off-licence
sakura cherry blossoms
sararīman businessman
sarakin loan from a loan-shark
saseru make or let
sayōnara goodbye
senmongakkō technical college

sensei teacher or doctor
sentō public bath house
Shakai Hoken national health insurance
shakuhachi a kind of recorder
shamisen a kind of banjo
shi city
shiatsu finger pressure massage (low-tech *hari*)
shichi-san literally '7–3' – a tradition *salariman*'s hair parting, three-tenths of the way up
shikikin deposit
shimasu make or do
shimbun newspaper
shinkaisoku extra rapid train
shinkansen the bullet train
Shintō traditional animist set of beliefs
shita under
shō–gakkō junior high school
shōgi a kind of chess
shōgun military dictator
shōji sliding paper door
sodai gomi bulky rubbish (impolite wifely term for layabout husband)
sumimasen excuse me
sumō traditional wrestling

tandai junior college
tatami straw mat
teikiken strip of eleven train or bus tickets
Tennō the emperor
terebi television
Tōdai Tokyo University
Tōkkyū super express train
tōyu stōbu paraffin heater
tsuyu the rainy season

ue above
unten menkyo driving licence

wa harmony
warikan splitting a bill equally

ya shop
yakkyoku   grammar-translation
   teaching method
yakuza Japanese Mafia
yakyo-ku chemist
yao-ya greengrocer
yōchien kindergarten

yon four
yukata light cotton *kimono*

zazen sitting crossed legged doing
   zen
zen Buddhist denomination

Appendix 8 Food and drink glossary

atsuage fried *tōfu*
aji-no-moto monosodium gluta-
mate
aka chōchin ordinary bar
anko sweet paste made from *azuki* beans
azuki red bean

bentō picnic meal or packed lunch
bīru beer (*nama*, literally 'live',
means draught, although, confusingly, this can sometimes be
in bottles)

chā han Chinese fried rice
chanko nabe stew traditionally
eaten by *sumo* wrestlers
chū jockey medium draught beer
chū hai highball with *shochu*

dai jockey large draught beer
dashi soup stock (with dried
shaved bonito it is *kat-
suodashi*)
daikon large white radish
donburi bowl of rice with a topping

eda mame soy beans cooked in
their pods, usually eaten cold

furai fried

gari pickled *shoga* eaten with
sushi

genmai brown rice
gochisōsama (deshita) said at the
end of a meal
gyōza fried meat dumplings

hakusai Chinese cabbage
hambāgu hamburger
(o)hashi chopsticks
hōrensō spinach

Ikki! a chant to encourage a
drinker to 'get it down in one'
ippon one bottle
itadakimasu 'bon appétit'
izakaya ordinary bar

kai shellfish
kamaboko fishcake
Kampai! Cheers!
karē raisu curry and rice
katsu karē pork cutlet with curry
sauce
kissaten coffee shop
kōcha Indian (ie Western) tea
kombu a kind of seaweed (not
usually eaten, used as flavour-
ing)
konyaku jelly-like tasteless sub-
stance, made from arrowroot
(an ingredient of *oden*)
korokke fried potato croquets
kyūri cucumber

maguro raw tuna, eaten as *sushi*

219

or *sashimi* (cooked tuna is simply *tsuna*)

mirin sweet rice wine, rather like sherry, used as seasoning

miso soy bean paste, used as base for *miso shiru* (soup)

mizu wari the usual way to drink whisky – with ice and lots of water

nattō fermented soy beans, strong in taste and smell

nihon two bottles

niku meat

niku jyaga meat and potato herring stew

nishin trout

nomi mono drink

nomi-ya an ordinary bar

nori crisp dried seaweed

ocha Japanese green tea

oden stew of fishcake, bamboo roots, *konnyaku*, etc

(o)kanjō bill

okonomi-yaki do-it-yourself pancake

omu raisu omelette filled with rice and pieces of chicken

onigiri rice triangle, filled with, eg, fish, and wrapped in *nori*

oshibori moist towel to clean your hands

osu vinegar

oyakodon bowl of rice topped with egg and chicken

pan bread

pilafu fried rice

rāmen Chinese noodles

robata yaki grilled food

ryōri food

saba mackerel

sakana fish

sake rice wine, usually drunk warm from tiny cups

sandoitchi sandwich

sashimi raw fish

satō sugar

satsumaino sweet potato

sembei savoury rice crackers

shabu shabu do-it-yourself meal, made by dipping raw ingredients into a stock to cook

shirano small fish, eaten whole

shio salt

shōchū clear vodka-like spirit

shōjin ryori traditional vegetarian food, usually served in Buddhist temples (it is light and delicate)

shōga ginger

snack expensive hostess bar

shōyu soy sauce

soba buckwheat noodles

sushi raw fish with cold rice

sukiyaki strips of beef which you fry at your table

supagetti spaghetti

tabemono food

tai bream

takenoko bamboo shoots

teishoku set meal

tempura batter-fried fish or vegetables

tōfu beancurd

tonkatsu pork cutlet

tori chicken

tsukemono vegetables pickled in a similar manner to sauerkraut

udon noodles

umeshu plum wine

unagi eel, usually served grilled with a sweetish sauce over rice

wakame a kind of seaweed, usually served in soup

waribashi disposable chopsticks –

the most common kind
warikan splitting the bill
wasabi a kind of horseradish
(eaten with *sushi* and *sashimi*)

yaki grilled or barbecued (*yaki-tori* are small chicken kebabs);
yaki imo are grilled sweet
potatoes)

Appendix 9 Festivals and holidays

Principal national holidays

1 January	New Year
15 January	Adults' Day (Coming of Age Day)
11 February	National Foundation Day
21 March	Vernal Equinox Day
29 April	Greenery Day
3 May	Constitution Memorial Day
4 May	National Holiday
5 May	Children's Day
15 September	Respect for the Aged Day
23 September	Autumnal Equinox Day
10 October	Sports Day
3 November	Culture Day
23 November	Labour Thanksgiving Day
23 December	Emperor's Birthday

Other national occasions

3 February	*Setsubun*, Bean-Throwing Day (throwing beans to drive out devils)
3 March	*Hinamatsuri*, Doll Festival (little girls put out sets of dolls)
Spring	*Hanami* (cherry blossom viewing: for a few weeks everyone goes out ostensibly to view the beautiful cherry blossoms, but also to get very drunk)
7 July	*Tanabata* (children tie poems to bamboo branches)
16 August	*Obon* (like Halloween, all the ghosts come out: lanterns are lit, there is *bon-odori* dancing, and religious rites are held in memory of the dead)
15 November	*Shichi-go-san* (literally '7–5–3': children of these ages are dressed up and taken to shrines)

Large local festivals

5 February	Hokkaido – Snow Festival
May (2nd weekend)	Tokyo – *Sanja Matsuri*, 100 *mikoshi* (portable shrines) and *sanjabayashi* (festival of music)
17 July	Kyoto – *Gion Matsuri* (parade of floats)
July (last Saturday)	Tokyo – *Hanabi* (fireworks) display on the Sumida River at Asakusa
6 August	Hiroshima – Peace Ceremony
16 August	Kyoto – *Daimonji* (bonfire)
16 September	Kamakura – *Yabusame* (horseback archery) display
22 October	Kyoto – *Jidai Matsuri* (procession of 2000 people in historical costumes)
2 December	Saitama – *Chichibu Yo Matsuri* (procession of floats, *kabuki* and *hanabi*)

Index

(T) means that this is connected with teaching this topic

accommodation, 37
  apartment, 40
  urgent, 38
  youth hostels, 44
  ryokan, 44
  minshuku, 44
  temples, 45
  pensions, 45
addresses, 37
advising (T), 183
aikidō, 71
airport, transport from, 36
Alien Registration Card, 26
apartment, 40
apologising, 95
arrival, 36
  immigration, 36
  accommodation, 36
  transport from the airport, 36
arriving without a job, 12
articles (a, an, the) (T), 172

ban, 38
banks, 66
baths, home, 41
  public, 65
batsu, 98
before you go, 32
beliefs, 86
blbliography, 211
blocking your time, 12
blood types, 88
bonsai, 75
bookshops, 34, 64
bunraku, 71
burakumim, 89
burikko, 93
business people (T), 194
businessmen, 93

case histories, 201
cha no yu, 75

chikan, 101
children (T), 196
chiri gami, 43
chōme, 38
chopsticks, 46
cinema, 70
class management (T), 127
classroom Japanese, 213
climate, 86
closed pairs (T), 121
coming home, 201
communication (T), 130
companies (T), 19
comparatives (T), 172
conditional sentences (T), 174
confectionery, 53
contacting schools, 14
conversation salons, 16
copying, 84, 96
correcting (T), 140
crowds, organization and noise, 100
cultural activities (traditional), 74
cultural exchange societies, 79
culture, communicating, 134
cuteness, 94

daimyō, 83
danchi, 40
daruma, 88
dialogue building (T), 124
discos, 69
drilling (T), 113
drink, glossary, 219
drinking, 53
  cheap, 54
  medium-price, 54
  expensive, 55
  customs, 55
  options, 56

eating, 45
  etiquette, 46

restaurants, 47
  cheaply, 48
  specialities, 52
  confectionery, 53
Education System, 105
efficiency, 100
eliciting (T), 112
English
  natural (T), 133
  list of schools, 204
  loan words, 208
enka, 76
environment, 100
eta, 89
etiquette, 46
expenses, 13

facilities, 65
  public telephones, 65
  baths, 65
  libraries, 65
  banks, 66
  health, 66
  launderettes, 67
festivals, 77, 222
finding work, 5, 14
flower arranging, 74
focus (T), 129
food *see* EATING
Food & Drink Glossary, 219
form, (T), 113
fudōsanya, 40
functions, (T), 179
  advising, 183
  greeting, 180
  introducing, 181
  inviting, 181
  offering, 182
  requesting, 182
  suggestions, 184
  permission, 184
futon, 41
future tenses (T), 171

gaijin houses, 38
gaman, 95
gambatte (Go For It!), 95
games (T), 148
genkan, 41
geography, 85
gestures, 96
go, 75
grammar (T), 163
  tenses, 164

articles, 172
comparatives, 172
questions, 173
conditionals, 174
modal auxiliary verbs, 176
reported speech, 178
glossary, 206
greeting (T), 180
groups, 91
groups, large (T), 130

hanko, 66
health, 66
help, 80
helping students talk, 119
High Schools, 105
history, 82
holidays, public, 77, 222
hospitals, 66

ikebana, 74
Immigration, 21
  offices, 25
  Alien Registration Card, 26
information gaps (T), 131
interviews, 6, 15
introducing (T), 181
introducing new language (T), 112
inviting (T), 181
jan ken pon, 97

Japan, 81
  country, 82
  history, 82
  geography, 85
  climate, 86
  politics, religion and beliefs, 86
Japan Rail Pass, 32
Japanese
  classroom, 213
  glossary of terms, 215
  character, 90
  education system, 105
  people, 89
  signs and gestures, 96
  typical lives, 98
  embassies, 11
  problems (T), 152
Japanese Association of Language
  Teachers (JALT), 20
JET programme, 8
job ads, 14
judo, 71
juku, 78

kabuki, 70
kaisūken, 58
karaoke, 76
karate, 71
kashiwade, 98
kendō, 71
kissaten, 50
kōban, 37
Kobe, 79
Kokumin Kenkō Hoken, 67
kotatsu, 42
koto, 69
Kyoto, 78
kyūdō, 71

language schools, 17, 204
language which students need, 107
laughing, 96
launderettes, 67
leisure, 68
lesson
    parts, 112
    first, 115
    planning, 188
libraries, 65
listening (T), 135
living costs, 29
    eating and drinking, 29
    taxes, 30
    discos, 30
    How far does the money go?, 30
    comparative table, 31
loan words, 208
local information – city by city, 78

mah jong, 77
maneki neko, 88
manga, 65
martial arts, 71
matsuri, 77, 222
meaning (T), 113
media, 68
meishi, 90
methods – standard, 117
    non-standard (T), 118
minshuku, 44
modal auxiliary verbs (T), 176
modelling (T), 113
money (expenses), 29
music, 68

natural English (T), 133
newspapers, 68

noh, 70
numbers (T), 161

offering (T), 182
ofuro, 41
omiai, 99
one-to-one (T), 130
onsen, 65
Osaka, 79
other methods (T), 118

pace (T), 129
pachinko, 76
parts of a lesson, 112
past tense, 167
past perfect tense, 170
permission (T), 184
personal contacts, 15
personalization (T), 132
places to teach, 16, 204
planning – lesson, 188
    syllabus, 193
politeness, levels of (T), 133
politics, 86
poor language learners, 107
practising (T), 114
prearranged job, 5
preparation, 32
present tense (T), 165
present perfect tense (T), 168
problems, Japanese (T), 152
pronunciation (T), 141
public holidays, 77, 222

questions (T), 173

radio, 68
re-entry permit, 24
reading (T), 138
relax, helping students to, 108
religion, 87
reluctance to speak, 108
reported speech (T), 178
requesting (T), 182
resident status, 22
restaurants, 47
revision (T), 150
rubbish collection, 43
ryokan, 44

sakura, 86

sarariman, 93
sayōnara sale, 42
schools, 17, 204
seating system (T), 127
sentō, 65
Shakai Hoken, 67
shakuhachi, 69
shamisen, 69
shinkansen, 57
Shintō, 87
shōgi, 75
shōgun, 83
shops, 63
signs, 96
skiing, 73
skills (T), 135
     reading, 138
     writing, 138
     listening, 135
sodai gomi, 43
songs (T), 149
special groups, 194
specific Japanese problems (T), 152
sport, 71
stratification, 90
suggestions (T), 184
sumō, 71
sushi, 52
     cheap, 49
     making, 64
syllabus (T), 193

talk, helping students to, 119
tatami, 40
taxes, 30
taxis, 60
tea ceremony, 75
teacher talk, 125
teaching, 16, 204
     privately, 19
     glossary of terms, 206
teikiken, 58

telephones – public, 65
     private, 43
television, 68
tenses, 164
textbook, using a (T), 192
theatre, 70
time, blocking, 12
tōyu, 42
training, 33
transport, 57
     trains, 57
     buses, 59
     taxis, 60
     bicycles, 60
     boat and ferry, 60
     driving, 61
     hitching, 62
     air, 63
travel preparations, 32
typical lives, 98

Universities and colleges, 18
used to (T), 160

video (T), 137
visas, 21
vocabulary (T), 138

Ward Office, 26
what to take, 35
where to teach, 16, 204
writing (T), 138

Yakuza, 94
yukata, 44

zazen, 75
zen, 75

TEACHING ENGLISH GUIDES

Teaching English in Italy *by Martin Penner*

A complete practical guide to TEFL in Italy. Contains substantial sections on 'Teaching jobs and how to find them' (including addresses of schools, qualifications, things to beware of when job hunting, finding a job before you go, finding a job on arrival) and 'Living in Italy' (including the cost of living, accommodation, entertainment, the Italians, learning the language). *Teaching English in Italy* pays particular attention to specific challenges posed by teaching English to Italians, including sections on pronunciation, grammar and business English.

Teaching English in Eastern and Central Europe
by Robert Lynes

Teaching English in the countries of the former Eastern Bloc has experienced enormous growth over the last few years. This complete practical guide concentrates on Hungary, the Czech Republic, and Poland. It also covers the Slovak Republic, Romania and Bulgaria. Practical details on how to get work are accompanied by information on the cost of living, accommodation, qualifications, etc. The language problems specific to each country are analysed, making this an ideal classroom manual as well as living guide.

Teaching English in Asia *by Jerry and Nuala O'Sullivan Publication: 1996.*

From the People's Republic of China to the Indonesian archipelago, the thirst for learning English shows no sign of diminishing. This book covers PR China, Hong Kong, the Indian subcontinent, Indonesia, Japan, South Korea, Malaysia, the Philippines, Singapore, Taiwan, Thailand, and Vietnam. Practical examples of how to get work in each country are given, together with day-to-day living information. The challenges posed in the classrooms of each country are explored, making this a valuable teaching guide as well as an indispensable manual on jobs, prices, etc.

Published in the UK by In Print Publishing Ltd, 9 Beaufort Terrace, Brighton BN2 2SU, UK. Tel: (01273) 682836. Fax: (01273) 620958.

Published in the USA by Passport Books, NTC Publishing Group, 4255 West Touhy Avenue, Lincolnwood (Chicago), IL 60646–1975, USA. Tel: 708 679 5500. Fax: 708 679 6375.